BOLD NEW WORLD

WILLIAM KNOKE

BOLD NEW WORLD

THE ESSENTIAL ROAD MAP TO THE TWENTY-FIRST CENTURY

KODANSHA INTERNATIONAL
NEW YORK • TOKYO • LONDON

Kodansha America, Inc.
114 Fifth Avenue, New York, New York 10011, U.S.A.

Kodansha International Ltd.
17-14 Otowa 1-chome, Bunkyo-ku, Tokyo 112, Japan

Published in 1996 by Kodansha America, Inc.

Library of Congress Cataloging-in-Publication Data

Knoke, William.
Bold new world : the essential road map to the twenty-first century
/ William Knoke.
p.   cm.
Includes index.
ISBN 1-56836-095-9 (hardcover)
1. Twenty-first century—Forecasts.   I. Title.
CB161.K63   1996   95-45174
303.49'09'04—dc20

Book design by Victoria Hartman

Printed in the United States of America

96 97 98 99   RRD/HAD   9 8 7 6 5 4 3 2 1

To Lou and Gerry, my past
To Evelyne, my present
To Pascal and Jérôme
and all the children, our future
For all of us

CONTENTS

PREFACE

IT FIRST CAME TO ME in a birch forest near St.-André-de-l'Eure, Normandy, France.

It was a hot summer day and time to pull over for a picnic lunch. Beneath a dense forest canopy out of the heat, an obscure dirt road led to nowhere, precisely where we wanted to be.

The kids were off collecting leaves. Leaning against a log, I watched the sunlight filter through the branches overhead.

I was perplexed. My mind fell to the research I was undertaking to see the future more clearly. The Soviet Union had fallen and the Gulf War had broken out, both sending shock waves to Wall Street; the economy reeled and the map of the world was being redrawn. A new world order was emerging. The world economy seemed to be in a recession, but this time it was somehow different from before.

My corporate clients didn't have the foggiest idea where the world was headed, nor did people wherever I lectured. At the Harvard Capital Group, we set out to solve the riddle by methodically researching the fundamental changes taking place in society. I sought not just the *trends* but the *dynamics,* not just *what* was going to happen, but more pertinently, *why* it was going to happen, and what the dynamics were among the elements involved. I had done this many times in scores of leading-edge industries and had developed the technique into an art.

Instead of looking at companies or industries, I turned to nations and society.

In time, I consolidated our findings into a report and submitted it to about twenty top executives, mostly company presidents, for feedback. They were ecstatic: the material was just what was needed to see the future, they said.

Yet I was troubled. We had distilled the twenty or so forces in our first draft to a dozen—the environment, migration, telecommunications, ethics, computers, war, money, and so on. The dynamics of *all* these factors were changing dramatically, and all at the same time. But left unanswered was why so many diverse "fundamentals" were changing at once. It could not be a coincidence; there must be a single cause. But what was it? What was the common thread in all the global changes? What did HIV have in common with the computer revolution? What did the shift to a service economy have to do with global warming? What did containerized shipping have to do with the rise of Islamic fundamentalism?

A bird swept down from the branch above and lit on the log next to my head. I thought of the fax I had drafted earlier on my laptop, which I had to send to my office from a pay phone in the next village. I took in the sun filtering through the tall birch trees one more time before getting up.

Then it hit me. Within five seconds—perhaps like Newton under his apple tree, or Buddha in northern India with his bodhi tree—the whole riddle unraveled. The birch forest! The vertical trees and interwoven branches suggested the three-dimensional, everyday reality of common experience. But I was contemplating sending a fax from nowhere to a place half a world away.

A universe that had been so nebulous minutes before suddenly came into sharp focus. *We no longer lived in a world of three dimensions, but four.* There was some sort of ether connecting everything to everywhere, making *near* and *far* one and the same. Our shift into the "Fourth Dimension" explained everything. It clearly explained the so-called information revolution, but went further in accounting for global trade, mass migration, global pollution, global terrorism, mass media, the rise of Islamic fundamentalism, splintering families, and degraded ethics, even major shifts in how wealth is created. Here it was, a universal force theory, the common thread linking society's most gripping problems.

———

Each chapter of *Bold New World* starts off with a fictional futuristic scenario written from the standpoint of a specific person. Here a corporate executive, there a housekeeper in Hong Kong. We are many people, and understanding is not possible without empathy for all.

I then give an analysis of specific current events that are bringing that future into being. In many cases, the future is easy to predict because it is already happening. This technique gives us a high degree of confidence that the book's predictions will actually happen.

As with my corporate clients, I conclude with a "so what?" What actions should one take as a result of the prediction? Predictions are only valuable if we can act today to benefit from the advanced knowledge.

The time frame of the book is over the next two or three decades. After that may be academically interesting but it is beyond the planning cycle of most people. Above all, I seek to be pragmatic and use common sense. In dealing with the future, for example, we need not invent some bubble home with elevators. I also avoid idle speculation about going to other planets because it would not affect our daily lives.

This book, like society, is a synthesis. It is based on a broad analysis of several thousand bibliographic references woven into a single fabric. With such a wide scope of material from a world as dynamic as ours, it is certain that some examples will have become dated by the time they reach the reader, or that better examples will have appeared. I excuse myself here by pointing out that the value of *Bold New World* lies in its broad assessment of where we are headed, and none of the conclusions is based on any single observation.

Similarly, in translating the scope of my analysis into a single volume, I took liberties to simplify and condense certain historical, scientific, and economic principles. Readers wanting more depth might review the bibliographic notes, or else consult other books focused on these narrower issues in greater depth. My purpose is not to be the end-all in all topics covered, but to stand back to see how the sweeping changes before us are actually part of a singular whole.

This, then, is the goal: to examine how our daily lives will be influenced, altered, and transformed by the onrushing future. We are moving into an age where near and far are one and the same; if ever we needed a road map to find our way, now is that moment.

Almayrac, France
August 1995

ACKNOWLEDGMENTS

ONE WAY TO BE SUCCESSFUL in the Age of Everything-Everywhere is to organize a team of people more intelligent and skillful than oneself and then take credit for the results.

Take Evelyne Combes. Quite simply, this book would not be what it is without her insightful collaboration. She forced me to question my assumptions, eliminate my redundancies, defend my reasons, and clarify my thoughts. It was not easy.

It is by the resolution of contrary viewpoints that good things arise. I am the American, she the French; I the chauvinist, she the feminist; I the capitalist, she the socialist; I with university degrees in business and economics, she in literature and language. We found ourselves discussing the oddest things at the oddest hours.

Although English is her second language, her mastery of it is surpassed by no one I know. She is the author of this book as much as I, and I am not sure any longer which words are hers and which are mine. These pages are largely the result of a tennis match long played and hard fought. I love her, page by page, inch by inch.

She is also my wife.

Al Zuckerman, president of Writers House, also played a big part. Going far beyond the role of a typical literary agent, he saw the potential in our earliest manuscript and worked with us to shift the thematic focus. He invented the structure of using fictional futuristic scenarios followed by analysis and recommendations.

I thank Philip Turner, my editor at Kodansha America, for recognizing the merits of the early manuscript and making erudite suggestions for improvement, and my publisher, Minato Asakawa, for providing the resources to make the project as successful as possible.

Pivotal was the herculean drive of Gillian Jolis and Claudia Guerra at Kodansha America and all the people at Farrar, Straus & Giroux, without whose effort this book would never have gotten into your hands.

I would also like to thank a zillion other people, some of whom have provided research at the Harvard Capital Group. Some gave early critiques and comments, others advice on the state of the world or support in areas where it was most needed. I can only list them alphabetically; to detail their contributions would fill another book: Paul Aron, Bob Barmeier, Jim Barmeier, Don Brooks, Greg Buckley, Joe Cammalleri, Clay Christensen, Gaston Dessornes, Ken Freeman, Dale Gray, Arlin Green, Jim Hackett, Thieo Hogen-Esch, Chet Huber, Gregg Ireland, David Ingram, Kelly Kowalchuk, Janis Lamb, Mike Lamb, Roy Lowrance, Woody McCally, Angelo Matthews, John Middleton, Bahman Mossavar-Rahmani, Bernard Nestasio, Robin Quinn, Paul Raeder, Kim Reynolds, Gary Rodkin, Bill Saltz, Charlie Schellhorn, Stephen Schlesinger, Tony Sun, Len Wanetik, Chris Westland, and David Winn.

Special acknowledgment also goes to those working on a television documentary based on *Bold New World,* and the many people coming forward with examples supporting the themes of the book.

These people all helped, but they are not the end of the story. In the Placeless Society, knowledge is not fixed and rigid, but dynamic and alive. *Bold New World* is only a contribution to the collective body of guesses about our future. There is more work to do, including much by you, as the lessons are applied, debated, fine-tuned, improved, and written yet again.

One can have the last word on the progress of human development only if one is the last human.

Part One

THE ROOTS

1

FROM WHERE WE CAME

SERGEANT JOE HARRISON slowly raised himself from the campfire, and carefully took a few steps away from it, toward the dawn's first hint of light. But the passage through the brush was unfamiliar. It was eerily quiet except for an occasional cracking of mossy branches underfoot. Occasionally a fly would buzz by and bounce off his sweaty face. The putrid air grew easier to breathe.

Then there was a movement somewhere to the side, in the darkness. He turned and it was gone. He leaped from the trail and chased the apparition, first through shallow puddles, then over grasping roots. Ahead, he saw a half naked body, its smashed brain and dried black blood alive with maggots. He spotted two more bodies, killed in some bizarre ritual.

Then it happened. Three barefoot men, clad only in loincloths, and bearing spears, charged at him. Joe attempted to aim his assault rifle just as three spears whirred toward him.

Suddenly everything went black. Sgt. Joe Harrison peeled out of his assimilation helmet to find himself safe in his bedroom; his little sister held the wall plug in her hand. The interruption made him feel both irritated and relieved. For Joey, age twelve, it was now time for lunch.

Judy Bluth, forty-six, didn't understand. Her body stiffened as she sat at her small kitchen table reviewing yet another job rejection. Only six years earlier, her future had looked bright. Corporate tycoons traveled from all over the East Coast to seek her approval on seven-digit bank loans. She'd been on the fast track with one promotion after another.

The banking debacles of the late 1980s and early 1990s were already forgotten history when she'd gotten out of college. Her parents had told her that banking was a solid industry—people always needed money.

Then the new century began with consolidations that sent shock waves throughout Manhattan. The industry was in flux. Financial centers became less important, as lenders could meet borrowers electronically without intermediaries, bypassing banks altogether. Banks themselves were seen as anachronistic throwbacks to the Paper Age of the twentieth century.

Banks that did not adapt quickly by streamlining their operations or offering new products were swallowed up; employees were thrown on the street. Her friends in other industries—manufacturing, distribution, retailing—were under equal stress. It seemed like the whole structure of the economy was changing, cutting out middlepersons, following new rules.

———

Don Constable, fifty-eight, put on a fresh pair of surgical gloves before picking up the sample. The fragment of green plastic board with small dollops of silver solder was unmistakably premillennium technology. On the corner was the all-too-familiar Arabic script lettering that he'd seen in Munich, London, New York, Tokyo, and now in Los Angeles.

After he sealed the fragment in a plastic bag to take back on the next direct flight to Zurich, he stood up and looked at the tangled concrete and steel around him. Another freeway interchange had collapsed during rush hour due to terrorist hands. The Los Angeles authorities thought that some two dozen cars were buried beneath the

Harbor Freeway rubble in this newest wave of global terrorism. He wondered if the World Government that employed him could track down the Allah Ahmad separatists that claimed responsibility for the blasts.

——

It was mid-July and the first time Buffy Brooks, seventeen, had been to Ft. Lauderdale. When she got to the beach, she quickly slipped into a satiny long-sleeved red bodysuit and carefully rubbed UV cream on her exposed face, hands, and feet. She glanced over at the group of seniors still sunbathing in their old ways, with exposed skin, and felt sorry for them. Didn't they study ozone depletion in school? Didn't they believe that UV radiation causes skin cancer?

Behind her, between the beach and the front row of condominium high-rises, was an eight-foot concrete sea wall that the city had built a few years earlier. The wall was needed to protect the property from a sea level that was much higher now than thirty years earlier. She remembered seeing pictures of Ft. Lauderdale taken in 1997, well before the greenhouse gases had melted the ice caps, and she wondered why the zoning commission had failed to anticipate these changes.

——

The above examples may seem like isolated snapshots of some far-off future. Yet as you read this book, you'll learn that they are all symptoms of the same root cause. And events very much like these will happen soon.

We all know that we live in a time of flux. Cities all over the planet are awash in waves of newly arrived immigrants; we read of nations cracking apart. Our corporate giants trip and fall; our economy and political organizations are effectively out of control. Educated engineers drive taxis. Everywhere pollution threatens our skies and water. Some say the strains of change are so great that society may well splinter during a transitional period of anarchy and chaos.

The economists and talk-show experts have made many attempts to explain and predict the future. One says we are at the birth of the Information Age; another describes it as the Postindustrial Era. Others fault the decline of morality, a lack of respect for authority, the degeneration of the family, or the underfunding of schools as the root problem. Yet another will argue that the cause is foreign powers or illegal immigration. But *none* of these factors encompasses the breadth of problems we face today.

Nor can they; they are only pieces of a larger puzzle. It is the thesis of this book that most of the gripping social problems we are bombarded with each day in our newspapers, jobs, families, and communities are all diverse manifestations of a single common factor: a shift into an "Age of Everything-Everywhere." The way we live, work, and govern ourselves is about to plunge into a fundamental shift, a major break from old trends. We are on the threshold of one of those rare moments in history—that have only happened three times before—when all the cards of power and wealth, of family and self, are being reshuffled and dealt anew. This book will show readers the new rules and explain how to adroitly play the game.

The implications are startling:
- Nations as we know them are becoming anachronisms.
- Terrorism will emerge with the upper hand.
- Labor unions are doomed.
- Religion will resurge around the world.
- World government is inevitable.
- Large corporations will fragment.
- Business strategies and economic theories need radical rethinking.
- The labor skills of today are already irrelevant for tomorrow.

A PLACE WITHOUT PLACE

WE KNOW OUR SOCIETY will change because the foundations of the world around us are shifting. Our society—which encompasses our governments and cities, our laws, customs, beliefs, religions, clubs, and schools—is based on some fundamental assumptions. If one of these assumptions collapses, the walls built on it crack too.

For example, many of us remember when the world price of crude petroleum quadrupled in 1973; gas lines stretched around the block, tempers flared, and on occasion guns were pulled and people died. Airlines and trucking companies went bankrupt and electric utilities were paralyzed. Speed limits were cut and harsh energy-conservation laws were passed. Commuters quit their jobs and found other work closer to home. The price of large cars and motor homes plummeted.

The problem, however, was not so much the high price of petroleum. It was that the structure of society was based on the premise of cheap gasoline. Suddenly that assumption was drastically turned around. The whole Western world faced crucial changes in the way people lived, but then, unexpectedly, the price returned to previous levels. The problem was soon all but forgotten.

As we enter the twenty-first century, a much more fundamental social foundation is rapidly slipping from beneath our feet. Unlike the price of crude, it will not slide back. This understructure is so integral to our daily lives that most of us regard it as a fundamental constant, like gravity or the rising sun. Until now, it has always been a constant force; *all* social structures have been based on it.

It is, quite simply, the primacy of *place*.

From the time *Australopithecus africanus* first went looking in the brush for berries to eat until today when our work brings money that can buy gourmet berries at well-stocked supermarkets, we have been living with this one indestructible constant—the importance of place, which is such an obvious constraint in social organization that we give it little thought in our everyday routines. It is the unspoken assumption behind our factories, offices, schools, temples and churches, clubs, families, and even our nations and our wars.

In factories, it is critical that raw materials be near the beginning of the assembly line before conveyor belts begin to turn. In our offices and schools, it would be foolish to suggest that it did not matter which room you sat in. Our parents and children come and go during the day, but it is the common *place* of eating and sleeping that often defines the family unit. Our countries usually define themselves in terms of borders, with all the land inside belonging to that nation. All traditional economic, political, and social structures are built with *place* being the primary determinant.

But what if location becomes irrelevant? Imagine a world where you could close your eyes and appear in Bombay or Paris as if you had been assisted by a Star Trek transporter. Picture the ability to make passionate love with someone while he or she is in another part of town or in another city. Think of being in two or three spots at once. Further visualize the ability to move objects around the world as instantly and effortlessly as Aladdin's genie. Such is a world without *place*. The Placeless Society is a world of everything and everybody being at once everywhere.

Such a world, of course, does not exist. Not yet. However, several mainstream technologies are rapidly evolving *right now* that may bring us pretty close. Only ten years ago, it would have been laughable to question the primacy of place. Now, at the dawn of the third millennium, it is irresponsible *not* to acknowledge the changes currently under way.

Advances in communications and transportation have already shrunk the world considerably. Immigrants now use jets instead of their feet to migrate, investments flow electronically, and fleets of supertankers move oceans of petroleum around the world in a virtual conveyor belt. The nightly news on TV brings the terror of far-off wars and famines into our cozy homes. Fax machines carry handwritten notes around the world; computer screens flicker as we tap into the knowledge of vast databases right at our fingertips. Pundits talk of satellite and fiber-optic links as being the "highways of the future," while design engineers throw around words like "virtual reality" and "cyberspace."

Taken one at a time, these incremental technologies seem innocent. They enhance our quality of life and entertain us. But collectively they have a much more powerful effect as vehicles that will carry us unwittingly to a changed world order. They are eroding the primacy of place, which in the end will lead to one of the greatest social upheavals the world has ever known.

To see why, let's start with a visit back to school. . . .

A DIMENSIONAL WORLD

THE CHILDREN FILE INTO the class. On the blackboard, the teacher has drawn a dot, a line, a square, and a cube. Pointing first to the line with her finger, she describes a one-dimensional world. "Here is a straight segment of railroad track," she says. "A train on this track can only move forward and back. It cannot travel left and right, or up and down."

The teacher then taps on the square. "This is a flat world," she tells them. She produces a single piece of cardboard and places a sow bug on it. The insect begins to crawl around. "This is a two-dimensional world," she explains. "One is free to move across either the length or the width of a square."

Finally, she motions toward the cube. "In this space, which could be a room, you can go up and down as well as moving across the length and width," she says. "This represents a three-dimensional world, like the world we live in." At that, she pulls a pigeon out from somewhere behind her desk and lets it flutter about the room and out the open window to a nearby treetop. The students watch the bird for a moment, which finally flies to another branch out of sight, and then they look back at the teacher.

One student raises her hand. "Why is there a dot on the blackboard? What does *that* mean?" she wants to know. "That represents the Zero Dimension," the teacher replies. "In the Zero Dimension, there is no freedom at all."

ZERO DIMENSION

FROM THE FIRST CLUES that early humans left behind of their existence some 2 million years ago to as recently as 5,000 years ago (only 250 generations back), our ancestors lived in a Zero Dimension world.

Early humankind "understood" a world of three dimensions. Trees had height and depth and width. The caves had walls and a roof.

Yet in a *social* sense, these Ice Age nomadic tribes were largely insular "dot cultures" with a minimum of social interaction. Although exceptional groups of up to fifty people occasionally lived closely together, typical hunting packs contained only two or three related families. The group was limited to the number of people that could be supported in any one area. If a group grew beyond that, it would splinter off in search of virgin hunting grounds elsewhere. In an entire lifetime, one would never see more than a few hundred individuals.

Like modern-day fishermen on a riverbank, early man had every incentive to spread out instead of concentrating in one area or communicating unnecessarily with other roaming hunters. Contact with other "dots" was just not helpful for survival. Each community was self-sufficient.

There is little doubt that this self-imposed isolation, more than anything else, severely limited humankind's advancement through its first 2 million years. When an idea was developed—such as a better way to sharpen flint stone or a new method to preserve reindeer meat—it only accidentally spread to other groups. To a great extent, each band needed to reinvent its own means of survival. Knowledge had little opportunity to accumulate and advance.

FIRST DIMENSION

AFTER 2 MILLION YEARS—around 15,000 BCE—the ice finally started to thaw out. The warmer climate made conditions ripe for farming and for domesticating animals. Here and there people began to grow wild grasses that provided edible seeds, and to exploit wild sheep and goats. No longer dependent on hunting migrating herds, larger groups of people settled in permanent villages. By 3000 BCE, the conversion was nearly complete; the nomads had become farmers.

What is most significant in this historic transition is that, as the Zero Dimension dot culture of people living in isolated packs gave way to permanent settlements, people began interacting on fixed trade paths with neighboring villages. These often followed river banks or natural mountain passes. The people who first traveled them were the early pioneers of the First Dimension.

In time, some routes developed more traffic and became major trade routes traversing entire continents. Camel caravans evolved linking oases across the Sahara like pearls on a string. Other routes evolved with donkeys, plying cargo between northern Africa, Egypt, and the Mediterranean basin. The "Amber Route" evolved in Europe to bring amber and tin from northern Europe to Greek traders in the Mediterranean. The "Silk Road" connected China to India and Europe. Villages—such as Baghdad, Antioch, Constantinople, Cairo, and scores of others—grew in unprecedented wealth and prestige because they straddled major trade routes.

More important, the dots of humanity had been connected, making it possible for *ideas* and *knowledge* to be traded. From India, the Arabs brought decimal numerals and the technique of vaccination. Turkey introduced the world to bronze and iron. From central Asia came horses; from Iran, the wheel. Egypt introduced paper and ink, arithmetic, geometry, linen, and glass. From Babylonia came astronomy, the zodiac, and the first libraries; from Sumaria, the first business contracts and the use of gold as a standard of value. China introduced silk, gunpowder, and the compass.

These ideas, and a thousand more concerning philosophy, business, the arts, and religion were able to mix and brew in a global cauldron. Each culture, each person, each dot added to the body of collective knowledge. The trade routes, more than anything else, lifted humanity from its primitive roots and set the foundations of civilization; humankind had made the leap to the First Dimension—the era of social interaction along fixed paths.

SECOND DIMENSION

AS THE SINGLE TRADE tracks grew and crisscrossed, in time a two-dimensional concept of the world evolved. Human beings left the First Dimension and moved on to where they could explore the length and width of their world. The village was not just a point on a road, but one that existed in a much broader context. The child who came to the village market saw the many vendors and their articles made from bronze and iron, cups cut from amber and sea shells, fine cloth and skins, and he developed a sense of intrigue about the outside world. In time, the idea of landmass developed; a concept of "society" emerged that included the people in villages in every direction.

The leaders of emerging trading centers saw the opportunity created by a two-dimensional world and began to use the roads to seize control of broad swaths of territory. Empires were born in Mesopotamia and Egypt, India and China, and later, others, in Persia, Greece, and Rome.

The new imperial leaders recognized the power of roads in consolidating power. The Incas masterminded a network encompassing an empire that extended from Chile to Peru and Ecuador; in the precipitous Andes, they etched 25-foot-wide roads into solid rock, complete with galleries, retaining walls, and suspension bridges to cross deep chasms. The ancient Chinese established a complex network of imperial roads radiating for thousands of miles throughout the empire, complete with bridges and ferrymen to cross wide rivers. The Romans, at their peak, engineered 53,000 miles of roads, usually in a straight line across marshes, rivers, forests, and mountains, defying all obstacles, and they built with such quality that they set standards used in creating roads even today. Wherever the roads were built, imperial soldiers could move quickly to maintain control anywhere in the two-dimensional empire.

With the networks of roads, two-dimensional maps of the world appeared. The Egyptians and Babylonians created detailed land surveys. By 450 BCE, the Greek historian Herodotus produced an uncannily accurate map of the world including the African coasts, the Red Sea, and extending far into western Asia. When Cortés met with the Aztecs, Montezuma presented him with a detailed map of the Mexican gulf coast area painted on cloth.

Yet despite an intellectual understanding of a world existing in two dimensions, and except in regional empires with complex road networks, remote areas were still reachable only by narrow roads, restricting travel to the First Dimension. The Phoenicians, Greeks, Romans, and Chinese had fleets of ships that could extend the imperial reach to the seas, but their scope was limited, and their paths often followed narrow routes within land's reach. The transition into the Second Dimension was not yet complete.

In the fifteenth century, all that changed. Maritime technology progressed. Carpenters built ships that were large and seaworthy, equipped with lateen sails and stern rudders that allowed them to sail close into the wind. Mathematicians made navigational tables, and craftsmen developed new instruments such as the distance log, more accurate astrolabes, and compasses. The stage was set for a new generation of sailors to cut the umbilical cord to the land.

The resulting Age of Discovery launched humankind fully into the Second Dimension. Within a span of only thirty-five years, European seamen had rounded Africa, discovered the Americas, and sailed around the world. The new capabilities allowed Europeans to extend their power around the entire planet. Within five centuries, by the dawn of the twentieth century, Europe had coalesced into twenty-five powerful nations holding a tight grip on 84 percent of the world's landmass. The Second Dimension revolution—the era when humanity began to interact freely over the Earth's surface—was complete.

THIRD DIMENSION

REALIZING THE POWER OF dimensional freedom, inventors as far back as Leonardo da Vinci fantasized about traveling beyond the horizontal to the vertical, and the Greek myth of Icarus addressed this tantalizing idea. In the eighteenth and nineteenth centuries, balloons and primitive gliders entered the skies.

Then, scarcely a thousand days into the twentieth century, man developed and built a flying machine powered by an engine. Only a dozen years later, the new breakthrough was being deployed in World War I, first for observation, then bombing. Soon men dueled with one another in aerial dogfights. By the end of World War II, a long-range bomber equipped with a lone nuclear bomb proved to be a more powerful weapon than a hundred battleships from the Second Dimension, or 100,000 ground troops from the First. Within a single generation, the realm of armed conflict had shifted fully into the Third Dimension.

It was no longer sufficient to guard borders or patrol nearby seas. In the Third Dimension, an enemy could attack your capital without ever setting foot on the border. As before, the new dimension had completely changed the balance of world power.

The new realities spawned a new political order. Two superpowers on opposite sides of the planet clashed in a deadly game to control the Third Dimension. In the end, each had amassed thousands of nuclear-tipped rockets, projected satellites into orbit, sent men to the moon, placed exploratory robots on the planets, and created proto-villages that floated in the Third Dimension, that is to say, in space. By 1980 one space rocket was launched every fourteen hours, and the superpowers had spent $3,000 per household on these missions, with a million people employed in a complex choreography of high-tech projects.

New realities were also developing in commercial aviation. Following World War II, the world was glutted with surplus planes, airports, and manufacturers. Air travel had proven its safety, and the new jet engine offered unlimited power at lower operating costs. By 1950 about 20 million passengers took to the air in the United States, compared to practically none ten years earlier. By 1990 the number of air travelers had grown to nearly 500 million a year. The Third Dimension had come of age.

COMMON ELEMENTS

THE FIRST DIMENSION LASTED roughly 5,000 years, beginning at the dawn of recorded civilization. The Second Dimension continued for 500 years, progressing with the conquest of the global seas. The Third Dimension has existed for only 50 years, advancing originally with the commercialization of aviation. The pace is accelerating, and as we approach a fresh millennium, humankind is about to make yet another leap into the fourth, and perhaps final, dimension.

To understand the scope of the coming transition, we can study the previous shifts into new dimensions. Each leap into a new dimension was accompanied by a complete shakeup in political organization. A major shift occurred during the First Dimension from the countless bands of nomadic cave dwellers toward highly organized collective governments in the growing villages and nascent city-states. The Second Dimension saw the rise of regional kingdoms followed by colonial empires spanning the globe. The Third Dimension gave rise to a superpower rivalry and a struggle to control the heavens. We will soon see why the Fourth Dimension, for good or bad, will herald global government.

The rules governing wealth will also shift.

Accumulating wealth is much like accumulating political or military power. Any new competitive edge, additional piece of information, or ability to maneuver can spell the difference between success and failure. Each new dimension gives birth to an additional degree of freedom and action, as well as the ability to reach fresh opportunities inaccessible to those who do not enter the realm of the new dimension. The new wealthy citizens of the First Dimension were the merchants and traders who capitalized on the new dimension—the vital trade route.

Similarly, when society progressed to the Second Dimension, those who accumulated unparalleled wealth were those who knew how to set up empires and control the seas (as did the Phoenicians and Greeks, later the Romans and Venetians, then the Spanish and the English).

The Third Dimension, the era of air transport, gave great new power to multinational corporations to move personnel, parts, and finished goods overnight. It made for easier competition against those who did not make this transition. Manufacturing could be established around the world to take advantage of differences in wages, materials, and skills. It allowed the creation of truly global organs of wealth that often outgrew the host nations in which they operated.

Who became wealthy? Those who *directly used* the new dimension, not those who *supplied* the direct users. It was not the keepers of donkeys or the carpenters of ships or the makers of aircraft that became the wealthiest. Rather, it was the *users* of the donkeys, ships, and aircraft who found the unopened treasures, the fresh opportunities. A powerful example is again found in petroleum, a vital resource to the Third Dimension. Certainly the vendors became wealthy during our era, but the *real* wealth was made by those who *consumed* the petroleum to create yet more wealth—the United States, Japan, and Europe.

The same principles will apply in the Fourth Dimension: the makers of the new tools will undoubtedly prosper—some extraordinarily—but, taken as a group, it is the *users* of the new tools who will accumulate the bulk of the unparalleled new wealth.

When the world jumps into a new dimension, not everybody jumps at once. Even today, many of the world's citizens are still living in the Second or First Dimension. Unfortunately, the latecomers seem forever cursed to relative poverty, because without the freedom to move in the next dimension, they will be forever subjugated by, and their economies will always be weaker than, those powers with more dimensional freedom.

Conversely, the biggest prizes await those who shift first into the next dimension. In the First Dimension, the early merchants who plied the trade routes were the *nouveaux riches*. Similarly, the cities that tapped into these major trade routes grew and flourished. In the Second Dimension, those who set up regional empires, and later the Spanish and English who claimed the New World first, got the spoils, which raised them to unheard-of world wealth. And in our current era, it is those global corporations that have gone to new markets first that have preempted the others. The implications for those who seek wealth in the emerging Fourth Dimension are clear: *get there first*.

But where is the Fourth Dimension? And how do I get there? More on how to find it in the next chapter.

2

THE GATEWAY
TO PLACELESSNESS

HER LARGE HAZEL EYES sparkled, and then locked into his. When she blinked, he blinked. Even their grins mirrored one another, as if dancing a waltz. He could feel her hand touch his, now sliding up one finger, now down the next. He caught her hand, and their fingers interlocked. It was so wonderful being with Gloria. She was his first love, and he wanted to hug her so much.

But he couldn't.

He was in his dormitory in Middlebury College, Vermont; she was in her boathouse in Banbury, Australia, half a world away. They had met electronically on a student Greenpeace project and had spent scores of intimate hours together on the network.

He wondered whether they should trade their datagloves in for a pair of datasuits, so that they could "touch" more than each other's hands. The current designs were much cheaper than the earlier models, and the social stigma of telesex was diminishing on campus.

Sylvia enjoyed shopping too much! As she glided down the aisle, a boldly colored package caught her eye; it looked like just the right gift for her nephew's birthday party.

After coming into the store, she had asked the sales attendant where she could find a biology science kit appropriate for an eight-year-old. She was immediately taken to a wide aisle half the length of the store with nothing but biology kits of every description marked "for age eight."

She picked up a kit and strolled over to the clerk. When asked how it worked, he pulled out a small monitor that showed a video demonstration. Satisfied, Sylvia placed it in her shopping bag and prepared herself for the part of shopping she liked most.

Raising her arm, she pointed toward the ceiling above the entrance door and, like Aladdin on his carpet, she began to float off the ground in that direction. Sylvia drifted through the ceiling to the floor above where she knew women's apparel would be. Within minutes, she quickly selected a peach cashmere turtleneck and tossed it in her bag. She knew the size was right because this store only stocked items that precisely conf_____ _____ ____ ____easurements.

____ ____ _____ ____ ____ bout this store was that Sylvia could visit it ____ ____ ____ _____ _____ her own bed at home. She wore 3-D ey____ ____ ____ ____ ____ saw and heard and touched was com-pu____ ____ ____ ____ ____ o, she knew the ordered items would arr____ ____ ____ ____ ____ hours. She looked forward to putting on ____ ____ ____ ____ _____ nephew and other guests arrived for lun____ ____ ____ ____ ____

Jon S____ ____ ____ etitors had just introduced a new line whos____ ____ ____ the core products of his company. This ____ ____ ____ vas only called fifteen minutes ear-lier. ____ ____ ____ th his senior vice president of mar-keting ____ ____ ____ embers file in by ones and twos. Across____ ____ ____ ors were discussing another com-pany o____ ____ ____ rs. Four others were gathered by the win____ ____ ____ _____ _____ ____. Finally, with twelve of the fourteen directors present, Steele called the meeting to order. One at a time, the officers laid out the problem as they understood it, everyone asking questions when appropriate. Within twenty minutes, a consensus was reached. The meeting adjourned.

Without wasting time, Steele darted over to the adjoining room where his operations managers were already assembled. This hand-picked team would transform the strategy of the board into specific operational tactics to use in the competitive world marketplace. They, in turn, would assemble the engineering staff to organize major product redesigns that would ripple within hours through his entire organization.

But Jon Steele was not in his office. He was traveling by himself 90,000 feet above the Pacific Ocean, streaking at 1,700 miles per hour—2.4 times the speed of sound—toward Los Angeles. The meeting participants were similarly scattered over five continents, with no more than three or four being even in the same country. Computer imagery merged multiple audio and video tracks from all over the world to create the illusion of a single meeting room, complete with a conference table and potted plants. It even provided for private chitchat during breaks. Six of the board members on the far side of the world were electronically reattired in full business dress to disguise their midnight bathrobes.

Even more remarkable, although English was the official language of the meetings, three of the participants chose to speak and listen in their native languages, with simultaneous translations provided by computers.

—

Are these examples far-fetched? Impossible? Hardly. By the year 2020, each of them could be as commonplace as faxes, home computers, and CNN are today. They unveil an emerging world where place no longer determines how we work, when we shop, or where we live. They illustrate the many technologies that will become everyday realities in the coming Placeless Society.

I define the Placeless Society as the awakening omnipresence that will allow everything—people, goods, resources, knowledge—to be available anywhere, often instantaneously, with little regard for distance or place. We already see it in many forms. CNN broadcasts bring an Ethiopian drought into lush living rooms. Multinational appliance companies subcontract manufacturing to wherever it is cheapest. Capital ebbs and flows freely around the girth of the globe defying government controls. Mass immigration into Western Europe and North America continues. Everywhere, people, money, goods, and knowledge flow so effortlessly from point to point that place becomes an irrelevant concept. The world is becoming placeless.

Although examples of placelessness are numerous and coming at us all at once from several directions, we will see that they largely distill down to two simultaneous revolutions—one in electronics and the other in transportation—that are sweeping every corner of the planet.

In electronics, we begin with one of the most stunning aspects of the two decades just ahead: the remarkable advances in the field of "telepresence."

When we finally take our first manned mission to Mars, telepresence is certain to be there in some form. Rather than risk sending a person through the treacherous Valles Marineris that runs 3,000 miles long and 3,000 feet deep, an astronaut will stay safely cocooned in the landing module and send a robotic cruising vehicle in his place.

From the comfort of a spacious home base, he or she will be connected to the robotic rover electronically. By wearing special headgear, the astronaut will *feel* as if she actually were in the vehicle. She will even run the controls. She will see in three dimensions, be able to look up and down, move her head around to see behind, hear the high-pitched whine of the battery-powered motors, perhaps feel the bumpy terrain. Only, she will not *physically* be there. Moreover, the ground controllers 50 million miles away on Earth will sit right beside her to hitch a ride. Some NASA planners even suggest that the astronaut need not even land on Mars; she could control the ground mission from a Martian orbit or stay on Earth!

Medical researchers, too, are discussing the implications of telepresence. Within a few decades, a specialist at New York University Medical Center will be able to perform a delicate surgical procedure on a patient in Pocatello, Idaho, without leaving the office. The doctor will hold the "scalpel" and feel its resistance against the actual patient. Through the monitor, he'll be able to watch the patient even though he is two time zones away.

Over the next fifteen years, telepresence will be used for everything from bomb disposal to aerial dogfights to inspection of aging nuclear reactors. It will bring dispersed students before outstanding teachers who are celebrated as the best in the world. Eventually, we may well see the Earth's Ping-Pong or racquetball champions challenge each other's skill as they remain in different cities. Most important, telepresence will become an inescapable reality in our homes and offices, forever changing the patterns of our everyday lives.

In many ways, it already has. . . .

THE NEW PHONES

THE TELEPHONE HAS ALREADY eroded the importance of place for routine meetings. We think nothing of telephoning a neighbor down the street or an office coworker in the next building. In our youthful love, we blow sweet nothings into a telephone mouthpiece as if it were the warm ear of the recipient. If three people want to talk, it makes no difference whether they are in the same building or scattered across London, Chicago, and Sydney. A conference call will put them in the same "room" within a few seconds.

Still, one limitation of the telephone is that we cannot *see* the other person. Highly paid executives travel thousands of miles, suffering airline meals and grimy taxi cabs, for a critical negotiation that may last but twenty minutes. The reason, too often, is that the telephone fails to convey the all-important body language—the worried eyes, the gritted teeth, the lost expressions—that can make or break critical face-to-face encounters. Such cues are often essential to exchanging ideas and to cutting through thorny obstacles.

To solve this, over half of today's Fortune 1000 corporations have set up videoconferencing rooms that link key facilities around the world. In these rooms, cameras zoom in on whoever is speaking,

questions and answers are fielded, documents are shared, and participants can discuss issues as if they were all in the same room.

As the price of electronics continues to halve every few years,
videoconferencing is no longer the privilege of the corporate elite
with a penthouse satellite dish. It is moving to smaller businesses,
even households. Low-cost videophones or PC-based desktop con-
ferencing systems are already starting to emerge. Some allow low-
grade images to be transmitted through everyday phone lines. As with
fax machines, the more people who have videophones, the more people there are to "see." And, of course, there will be more of us who
will want to purchase one. Today's *electronica exotica* will be tomorrow's minimum standard.

FREE CONNECTIONS

IT IS SAID THAT A picture is worth a thousand words, and the same is
true of videoconferencing. A high-quality video image can easily de-
vour the information capacity of a thousand voice lines.

To those of us who excuse ourselves for not calling Aunt Henrietta
in Ohio or our old school chum in Wyoming due to costs, the idea of
paying for a video connection seems a bit extravagant. Yet early in the
twenty-first century, there will be no difference between the cost of
local and long-distance calls, and the cost of both will plummet to
nearly nothing as technology advances. We will come to regard calls
to far-off places as no more expensive than making a photocopy or
flushing a toilet.

The distinction between "long-distance" and "local" is already
blurred. Today, a video connection between Los Angeles and New
York is often cheaper than connecting with the next county. Satellites
don't care if the call is relayed back to the same building or to the next
continent; once the switching system is built, distance just isn't an
issue.

And fiber-optics transmission makes long-distance calls practically
free. Fiber is extremely efficient. In the one second that it takes old-

fashioned copper wire to "transport" a few pages of typed text, a single strand of fiber the diameter of a human hair can carry the information of an entire *Encyclopedia Britannica*. While the cost of laying a transatlantic cable may be $400 million, the cable can handle so many calls that the phone company could charge customers as little as sixty cents an hour and get all their investment back in just one year. In 1993 alone, enough fiber was laid to wrap the equator 100 times. It is only a matter of time before competition brings long-distance rates down to almost nothing.

Competing technologies are also enhancing personal mobility with cordless, cellular, and satellite phones and beepers and pagers. We chat on the phone while zipping along the interstate, or tend our garden with a cordless phone poking out of a shirt pocket. As with long-distance services, competition, innovative technologies, and increasing usage are driving costs down.

With portable telephones, communications go to a person rather than a place. A single telephone number will soon accompany a person whether she is walking the factory floor or eating at a restaurant. As electronic devices continue to shrink in size, the once imaginary idea of a Dick Tracy wristwatch communicator is a likelihood just a few years away.

ELECTRONIC NEIGHBORHOODS

BEING ABLE TO CALL from a gridlocked interstate or while on an airplane is a great convenience. However, *receiving* unwanted calls, perhaps while taking a bath or during the main course at La Tour d'Argent, is another matter. The ease of reaching someone anywhere at any time may become intrusive.

The solution may lie in radically new versions of today's voicemail systems and answering machines. In a decade or two, if the party is not in, we will leave video messages with our voice and image. That person, in turn, will leave a full video response, revealing his or her body language, charts, pictures, and handwritten notes. Each successive reply, saved and replayed without the time gaps between calls, will simulate a live two-way conversation even though the two parties were never on the phone simultaneously. Not only is place irrelevant, time is compressed as well.

There is no reason such time-warp conversations cannot take place between three, five, or dozens of people, or even expand to an electronic "convention." Each authorized person would access the video messages left by others and share ideas. These capabilities represent a tremendous boon to office meetings, since each person could participate whenever time allowed.

Videomail will evolve the way electronic text-only mail already has. In conventional electronic mail, one can send a memo from one desktop computer to another—instantly and anywhere in the world. But in many environments, "groupware" has evolved allowing messages to be posted in semipublic electronic bulletin boards accessible to all. The systems have become indispensable in coordinating large, complex group projects such as in aerospace, defense, or large-scale engineering.

With a few taps on the keyboard, a user can cull correspondence by date, sender, recipient, or subject to quickly track down ideas or opinions to solve a problem. Such a capability allows home gardeners to find others interested in geraniums or empowers corporate executives to track down recent sales force comments on a competitive product.

Often the electronic conversations go back and forth on a topic between several correspondents like a conversation at a cocktail party. There are many digressions, side conversations, and interruptions. To help users keep track of who is responding to what, many electronic mail systems can display a special branching map that relates each message to other messages in the thread of the conversation. If an idea has five replies, they show up like five tree branches, growing out from a common point. If an idea has no replies, it becomes the end of a branch. With such a map, it doesn't take long to see which ideas generate the most offshoots and who the speakers are.

For organizations that have them, electronic mail has become a sort of nervous system for the company, connecting each individual into a common pulsing mind. In many organizations, once E-mail begins to take root, other desktop computer users scramble to get hooked online so as not to be left out of the loop. The effectiveness of electronic mail is causing networks to mushroom: four-fifths of office desktop computers are already networked to one another in some fashion.

The interlinkage of desktop computers is not limited to the corporate environment either. By mid-1995, consumer-oriented networks like CompuServe, Prodigy, America Online, Delphi, Genie, and an estimated 50,000 others with such diverse names as GayCom and Christian Net were already being used by more than four million American households and were doubling every three years. It was this growth that prompted Microsoft to join the bandwagon, providing access to the Microsoft Network as a basic feature of its popular Windows operating system, thus opening the door of computer networking to potentially tens of millions of additional users.

While these networks offer electronic shopping, home banking, online encyclopedias, news and journal articles, the most popular features are the electronic meeting rooms where millions of people come together to discuss any of an unlimited number of topics of personal interest ranging from dating to gardening, investments to Zen Buddhism, and terrorism to wine-tasting. Never before have so many people from every corner of the world been able to meet so often to discuss so much; in these electronic neighborhoods, millions of people already transcend place to find others who share their interests and to exchange ideas.

WHERE SCIENTISTS CHAT

THE POWER OF POOLING human knowledge is perhaps best demonstrated by the Internet. The Internet came to life through the efforts of the US Defense Department in the late 1960s; the goal was to link the giant computers at universities and research centers across the country, to make their vast databases of information accessible, to exchange computer programs, and to bring together processing power.

To coordinate this, users were provided with a way to send messages to one another from their terminals; this made the Internet the first electronic mail system in the world.

But unexpectedly, this new form of communication has mushroomed beyond anyone's wildest dreams. Today, subsidized in part by the US government, this nonprofit federation of dispersed computer systems has spread like ivy. The Internet, with its now-famous World Wide Web, has branched out to become the largest communication network in the world. As many as 30 million desktop users tap into the system each day from over 125 countries, and that number is projected to swell to 100 million users by the end of the decade!

Because the branches of the Internet originally grew from research laboratories and universities, scientists, academics, researchers, librarians, and policymakers may share the latest developments in their fields. It has become *the* worldwide nervous system for the advancement of human knowledge. For university researchers, the Internet has made meeting with their international counterparts as efficient as meetings with their colleagues on the same campus. Human knowledge is effectively compressed into a single room.

Its significance was brought home in 1989 when Stanley Pons of the University of Utah and Martin Fleischmann of England's University of Southampton made an exciting announcement—the development of cold fusion. Since their discovery would have allowed unlimited energy to be created from simple low-cost materials, it was imagined that the production of energy could be revolutionized and the world's dependency on fossil fuels lowered. Even the balance of world power might have shifted as the Middle East, with its vast oil reserves, would have lost its grip as the world's principle energy supplier. Undoubtedly, a lot was at stake.

Scientists from around the world immediately convened an ongoing placeless meeting in the Fourth Dimension. They learned details of the original experiment and raced to duplicate the results. Researchers were able to physically stay in their laboratories, yet share experimental results and techniques as they were developed. Some experts came up with complex mathematical models explaining how cold fusion worked or even claimed to have been able to duplicate the results. Others concentrated on refining the techniques or pointed to serious errors in Fleischmann and Pons's original work. Within a few days, the jury of global experts began to form a disappointing consensus that the original experiments were flawed. Within a few weeks, cold fusion was dead.

By meeting electronically, scientists were able to work simultaneously on a wide range of experiments, refining their techniques, comparing notes. A series of *physical* conventions would have slowed the process to months; by debating results in monthly journal publications, the discussions could have gone on for years. In the Fourth Dimension, however, everyone is compressed to a critical mass, accelerating the pace of debate and advancing the state of human knowledge in gargantuan strides.

KNOWLEDGE AMPLIFIERS

THE IMPACT OF CONCENTRATING knowledge in a critical mass is well illustrated by the compact world of Manhattan. This 22-square-mile islet sequestered off the edge of a continent would not be expected to be the center of anything. Yet the advertising agencies of Madison Avenue and the financial powers of Wall Street exert tremendous influence worldwide.

The secret of Manhattan's success is its critical mass of capabilities, with everything and everybody huddled together. The industries in which it is a world leader are those where personal interaction and face-to-face meetings yield a competitive edge—advertising, banking and finance, publishing, law, and fashion.

Fifteen-mile-long Silicon Valley exhibits these same characteristics. It has evolved into a worldwide Mecca of high-tech innovation responsible for a third of America's electronics components (Hewlett-Packard, Apple, Intel, Amdahl, Adobe, Atari, Tandem, Silicon Graphics, Sun Microsystems, Oracle, Seagate, National Semiconductor) and has also engendered hundreds of seedlings with names containing the coded syllables of high-tech: "auto-," "tex-," "bio-," and "-onics." Even Japan, Inc. has chosen to set up subsidiaries in Silicon Valley to benefit from its magic.

The "magic" is the Manhattan Effect coming into play—a critical mass of expertise exploding with world-class excellence. New ideas travel effortlessly door-to-door within an industrial park complex, as ideas cross-pollinate among employees and give birth to a frenzy of innovative development. Supporting sectors include nearby Stanford University, venture capitalists on Page Mill Drive, high-tech attorneys clustered in Palo Alto, and the special federal patent clearinghouse set up in Sunnyvale. This physical concentration of factors, not found anywhere else, has produced explosive new wealth because distances between industry participants were reduced to near zero.

It is ironic that physical concentration made Silicon Valley the success it is, yet many inventions of Silicon Valley now make physical concentration less vital. Since electronic communication allows information to be exchanged over wide distances, professionals no longer need to be physically gathered in Manhattan or Silicon Valley to be effective. In a placeless society, a computer company can write software in Orem, Utah, with little competitive handicap. In a world without place, an auto manufacturer can design cars in Spring Hill, Tennessee, and still have access to the same resources that are available in Detroit. In a truly placeless environment, all society is compressed into a virtual Manhattan and ideas flow without regard to distance.

Ubiquitous communication acts as a *knowledge amplifier*, making good ideas known to more people more quickly and accelerating the speed at which society can react to outside changes. Countries that come more fully into the Fourth Dimension will have better informed people, more innovative businesses, and more robust economies than nations that fail to make the journey. It is precisely this reality that is propelling industrialized nations on a race into the Fourth Dimension.

THE NATION RACE

THE ISLAND-NATION OF Singapore may be the first to totally immerse itself within the realm of placelessness. By 2005 Singapore expects to have every home, company, and government worker connected on a single fiber-optics information grid. Government records, customs bills, architectural blueprints, and even the precise location of each manhole cover will be reproduced electronically and available instantly. Every household will have terminals that combine the telephone, computer, television, video recorder, and camera.

Singapore, already one of the fastest growing economies in Asia, hopes to expand as a major world transshipment center within the next century. Its TradeNet computer network already saves shippers about $1 billion a year by reducing paperwork processing time. By bringing all sectors of the economy into the Fourth Dimension, even despite its human rights reputation, Singapore will be the place the rest of the world comes to if it wants tasks performed quickly, economically, and consistently. For the people of Singapore, it means a vibrant economy and jobs.

Other industrialized countries are not far behind. The Japanese plan to spend $400 billion to connect their schools, businesses, and homes with fiber optics cables by 2015. Not to be outdone, the European Union plans a unified high-speed European nervous system that would effectively pull all Western Europe into a single "Manhattan."

In France the groundbreaking Minitel network goes to over six million video terminals—better than one for every four households—which make half a billion connections a year. It is second only to the Internet in scope. Minitel's 20,000 different services are considered by many to be a second French Revolution, altering the way an entire country does business. Instead of housewives going to the butcher or baker, many order what they need on the Minitel and receive delivery within a few hours or minutes. Business executives use the Minitel to track stock prices, to order train and plane tickets. Truckers learn what needs to be shipped so they can round up cargo for return trips.

Farmers check weather and get up-to-date crop information. Students apply to schools or get missed assignments. And people can pick out a date, reserve tickets to a show, or review a local restaurant's menu without even getting out of bed.

As for the United States, politicians and industry titans are already comparing the transcontinental railroad of the nineteenth century and the interstate highways of the twentieth with the electronic "superhighways" of the twenty-first century. They believe that this will become an infrastructure indispensable to competing in a modern society. Just as the first transcontinental railroad in the United States was begun from opposing coasts with a fervent race toward the middle, the national information network will also evolve from multiple directions, both public and private.

On the private side, scores of telephone companies and television cable companies are swiftly moving to upgrade their *local* service areas with high-speed fiber-optic cables. They are also intent on offering services that will blur the distinction between today's telephone companies and cable operators. Each will provide video dial tone, allowing for movies on demand, high-quality home videoconferencing, and virtual reality home shopping.

As these local networks mature, they, in turn, begin to fuse into a national electronic superhighway. This is where the public side comes in. Governments everywhere are already relaxing their regulations to encourage competitive advancement. But more important, there will be a need for uniform technical standards to ensure that the ultimate national network is seamless. The owner of a videophone in Virginia will want to be able to communicate with one plugged in anywhere else in the world. The federally subsidized Internet may also form part of the network's backbone, especially the nation's burgeoning electronic mail.

In the race for dominance among industrialized countries, the United States is likely to come out ahead, but the sprint across the finish line will be close. Although American leadership is eroding in computers, software, and data storage technologies, it has by far the most advanced computer infrastructure in place, out-pacing Japan and Europe in the penetration of telephone lines, home and office computers, cellular telephone service, cable television, VCRs, and databases into daily lives. In contrast, few Japanese homes have computers and few people in Japan have ever used electronic mail.

As the networks in each region mature, they naturally become interconnected, and (subject to security locks to protect private files) will begin to merge into a single system. The examples are already around us. We can link our home computer with the bank's mainframe to transfer funds, receive weather photographs from satellite computers, or pull magazine articles from electronic libraries. A battery-operated laptop on a sailboat off Maine can already be connected by cellular phone to pull prices off the company computers in Hong Kong. By the year 2000, we will order video entertainment or news clips from centralized video "warehouses"; we will purchase newspapers, music, and books for immediate electronic delivery to wherever we happen to be.

The interlinkages between dispersed computers effectively create a single world "hypercomputer" whose resources are neither "here" nor "there," but everywhere, without regard to location.

CRYSTALS AND PEBBLES

THE POWER OF THIS global hypercomputer is immeasurable because, as we will see, the individual computers comprising it will have extraordinary power. What corresponds to today's home desktop computer will, in thirty years, be a *million times* more powerful, as inexpensive as a toaster, yet small enough to fit in an ink pen. Until now, processing power has doubled while computer size has halved every eighteen months, a progression so consistent it is referred to as Moore's Law (named for one of the founders of Intel).

The first large-scale computer, ENIAC, was built in 1946 by the US Defense Department to calculate the trajectory of artillery shells for a just-ended World War II. It weighed 30 tons, connected 18,000 vacuum tubes, and consumed extraordinary amounts of electricity. The same power now, available in a two-dollar chip the size of a thumb-nail, is a standard part of a Nintendo game.

The integrated circuits of tomorrow will not be built on flat chips but in solid "compu-cubes." Disk drives and CD readers will give way to memory crystals that will compress book, audio, and video libraries in the space of a penny. Computers will be further empowered by the infinite spectrum of laser light, thus replacing "electronics" with "photonics." The technologies of miniaturization will compress complete systems into grains of sand; today's supercomputers will be reduced to mere pebbles in size.

Their prices are plummeting too; the computing power that cost $1,000,000,000 thirty years ago is $1 today. The $5,000 system of today matches the power of the $500,000 systems of only five years earlier. Vendors are forced to offer increased capabilities even as prices erode. Quite simply, the true computer revolution has yet to begin.

How will all this processing power be used?

Part of the answer lies in better intermeshing humans with machines. Instead of interfacing with computers through flickering monitors, clicking keyboards, and clacking mice, we will interact in the same way humans interact with one another—with the five senses. The result will be computers that adapt so completely to humans that their use will be broadened to every conceivable task, whether it is designing advertising, driving a car, washing clothes, or . . . having sex. Just as contact lenses or hearing aids have become an integral part of the individual, the electronic world is rapidly becoming an extension of humanity.

ALICE IN WONDERLAND

SIMULATED REALITY provides such an extension: high-speed computers will replicate sensory stimulations so detailed that the individual will be psychologically "transported" to another place, a wonderland that exists solely in the electronic realm.

Already called "virtual reality," or "cyberspace" by some, present-day trade shows reveal how disappointingly primitive these technologies still are. The computer-generated rooms, tables, and characters are cartoonish; animated characters are unnatural and unconvincing. But that is largely because today's computers, for all their sophistication, are too slow to keep up with the extraordinary processing requirements. With the prospect of supercomputers-in-a-chip, we will be able to generate every breeze-blown blade of grass, every pine needle in infinite detail, and to use sensual equipment to link computers with humans.

Scientists are designing 3-D "eyephones" that change the image as one moves one's head up, down, and even behind—creating the impression that one is *inside* an animated cartoon, rather than looking at it through a monitor window.

To allow the user to manipulate objects inside this artificial reality, others have developed "datagloves" that sense movement. Using information channeled through the gloves, the computer recreates a three-dimensional hand that moves precisely as one's real hand moves. Employing this technique, an article may be turned, picked up, even thrown out a window as the computer calculates the trajectory. Some datagloves are equipped with touch feedback; when a simulated object is touched, vibrations in the dataglove create the illusion of touch. Even more remarkable, if a user wants to move to a new location, he merely points his index finger to where he wants to go, and is sent gliding effortlessly through space like a witch on a broomstick, say, through the simulated fireplace and out the chimney.

As for hearing, there now exists 3-D sound through stereo headphones, which fool the brain into thinking that a sound is coming from *any* direction, *any* height, *any* distance. Unlike conventional stereo, which has only "left" and "right," the technology can simulate a dozen people talking in the room, each coming from a distinct direction. Even blindfolded, one could be made to perceive scores of squawking parakeets flying in circles around the room.

These breakthroughs in interfacing with computers are highly educational or entertaining. We can fly airplanes, operate army tanks, play tournament golf, and practice downhill skiing in virtual reality simulation chambers.

Those in the new field of "teledildonics" are in a frenzy to develop simulated sex with sights, sounds, and tactile feelings of the real thing. Companies are proposing safe sex between people anywhere in the world, even perfecting special "bodysuits" that will simulate the body convincingly. Within a dozen years, soldiers stationed abroad will be able to communicate with their sweethearts in ways that are more intimate than sending love letters or talking on the phone, and prostitutes will sell their wares by telepresence.

Those who crack sophomoric jokes at the virtual reality trade shows miss the importance of teledildonics. Although it may never become any more mainstream than back-room magazines, it is nonetheless noteworthy. Sexuality involves all five senses: sight, sound, touch, smell, and taste, in highly sensitive and interwoven ways. If the sexual experience can be credibly reproduced, powerful lessons will have been mastered toward everyday telepresence, and the vital interface between humans and computers will be more complete.

This tight human-computer liaison cannot be overstated. Wall Street traders, for example, are swamped with data that change every second—stock prices, interest, and exchange rates. A trader who discerns subtle patterns across industrial sectors in each country can make millions of dollars by acting ahead of others.

One system providing this capability is already in use by a $100 billion pension fund in New York. Fund managers accessing the system enter a simulated *Alice in Investmentland* world, which offers all the information a bond manager could ever want. Dry tables of financial data are converted into a fanciful 3-D city complete with avenues representing different industries, streets corresponding to individual countries, and city blocks piled with buildings sporting corporate logos. Rooftops and vacant lots are stacked with chips of different colors. Most are stationary, but some spin frantically. Each has a symbolic meaning. A fund manager can soar like a bird over the city and swoop down to get a closer look or an up-to-date backgrounder on anything that moves. Using this technique, he can grasp opportunities undetected by those lost in tables of ever-changing numbers.

The system works because the marriage between man and machine is tighter than is possible with a mere stack of uninspiring numbers; by using the senses of shape, color, motion, distance, and texture, it taps into the very roots of our primeval hunting instincts. A tiny movement in the bushes is more glaring than a shifting digit in a monotonous table of numbers.

The medical profession is also increasingly overwhelmed with data. A surgeon often has to match X-rays with CAT scans and ultrasound readouts and still monitor respiration and pulse rates, body temperature, and a dozen other pieces of essential ever-changing information. In a surgical procedure, a few seconds can make the difference between life and death.

Within a decade or so, certain procedures will be performed by wiring the surgeon to a simulated reality that electronically combines hundreds of data inputs. As the surgeon cuts the skin, she will be able to see, superimposed on the patient, a 3-D image of exactly where the tumor is. This will help her guide instruments through a tiny incision to cut out the hidden tumor as if she could see *through* the patient's skin and tissue. In just two decades, the idea of making a large abdominal incision so the surgeon can insert her fists to examine fully exposed internal organs will be considered barbaric, and no longer taught in medical schools.

Such simulated reality will be the standard computer interface for a wide range of routine tasks. Shoppers will happily roam gigantic product databases converted into "real" stores with shelves and attendants. Chemists designing organic molecules will no longer have to analyze printed data but will reach out and "feel" a simulated complex molecule, pluck off atoms like grapes, and watch how the resulting molecules behave. Architects and homebuilders will no longer have to presume that a blueprint will achieve the desired effect; they will be able to walk through and inspect a structure to evaluate possible problems and scrutinize design elements before ground is even broken. By simulating the five senses, the output of computers will no longer simply be reams of printed pages but "experiences" for us to feel first-hand.

SILICON BRAINS

THE COMING COMPUTER-human interface is not limited to sensory images; it will extend deeply into the intellect. Soon, we will speak to home desktop terminals and computerized telephone customer-service "personnel," and the computer will chat back in coherent sentences. Later, the computer side of the conversation will be as sophisticated as the human side.

Speech recognition is progressing rapidly, with some of the most advanced work being championed by the US Defense Department. To measure progress among private companies, the government sponsors an ongoing competition among the ones wishing to receive government funding. Benchmarks have been established for the development of a mock telephone airline reservation system that listens to complex inquiries, asks questions, and gives coherent spoken responses about fares, schedules, meals, and in-flight entertainment. Although existing systems are limited in what they can answer, within five years, commercialized systems may well begin to appear on the market.

Computers are even piercing the language barriers that have so divided humankind. Just outside Tokyo, NEC researchers have come up with a system that can simultaneously translate spoken languages, such as English into Japanese. In the early twenty-first century, our telephone networks will include in-line converters to simultaneously translate French into English, Chinese into German, and so on, in the same voice, sex, and tone as the speaker. These advances will render language barriers nonexistent for the first time in the history of civilization. Tourists equipped with pocket interpreters will be able to chat with anyone they meet in a foreign country, opening new travel options for many people. Business executives will more easily negotiate complex deals across cultural boundaries. And schoolchildren, electronically connected, will be able to share ideas with those who speak a different language in their local communities and around the globe.

Besides speech, computers are accumulating knowledge, reasoning, and even common sense. By 2020 computers will converse with us during many routine tasks. They will "understand" complex questions and draft logical, concise answers.

Such a computer already exists in Austin, Texas. For the past decade, a consortium led by computer scientist Doug Lenat has programmed common sense into a gigantic computer program called Cyc (so named because it is an en*CYC*lopedia with a *psyche*). By day, some thirty programmers spoon-feed Cyc with knowledge; at night, Cyc dreams, sorting out the new information and relating it to what it already knows. Like a child growing, every day Cyc is a little smarter.

Cyc has synthesized two million interconnected facts, and more. Already, its knowledge base is nearly equivalent to that of a five-year-old child, and it will digest simple reading material on its own. Eventually, they will feed it a steady diet of reading materials (daily papers, magazines, and new books) that a well-informed person would digest. It will peruse encyclopedias, newspapers, magazines, and—at a later date—Shakespeare, Plato, Dickens, Mohammed, Voltaire, and Molière. The goal is to be able to ask Cyc a question in spoken English on *anything*, and get a tailored, insightful response.

Because the fifty-six companies funding the Cyc consortium include the giants Microsoft, Apple, Digital, Eastman Kodak, Motorola, and AT&T, within a decade, some of Cyc's capabilities will likely be cloned in household desktop systems—eventually on a single chip. Cyc and his brothers and sisters will be referred to as "knowbots," and they will help users track down hard-to-find information, answer basic questions, and even undertake complex analyses in written reports.

It is not inconceivable that Cyc's offspring may even evolve to rival man's intellect. Scientists believe that if they can duplicate the architecture for a slice of the brain, they may well be on the path to create an entire mind. Early tests are still primitive, but in Japan, Ricoh engineers have built what they claim to be the first neurocomputer built completely from a web of "nerve chips." The result is a system that can "learn" to recognize patterns and to control processes without being programmed. In a simple demonstration, a neurocomputer manipulating a robot through a maze would first bump into walls until it learned how to coordinate a turn and finally be able to make it through the whole maze without mishap.

Roger Traub, a neurologist at IBM's Research Center, may have taken it one step further. He built an anatomically accurate simulation of a tiny slice of human brain tissue. When he then fed it sensory input to study its behavior, it began, to his amazement, to spontaneously generate theta waves—a characteristic of human brains that neurologists use to monitor human brain activity. While the slice of electronic brain tissue was too small to do any "thinking," the unexpected theta waves indicate that scientists may be on the right track in duplicating the architecture of the human brain.

Wall Street gurus at Merrill Lynch are approaching neural networks from yet another direction. Rather than trying to *anatomically* duplicate the brain, they've programmed conventional computers to mimic the brain and to learn, not by being programmed, but by *experiencing* events. Merrill Lynch's neural network does this by immersing itself in historic stock market data and teaching itself to recognize patterns of behavior in pricing. Such systems are often clumsy at first. However, the more information they digest, the more they develop an uncanny ability to anticipate future events.

Each of these developments is in its infancy, but it is not inconceivable that within a few decades, the various technologies will converge into the new field of "cyberneurology," allowing us to begin to build large-scale neurological networks. Some theorists believe that as a system grows in size and its elements become sufficiently complex, the result takes on a life of its own. Just as inanimate molecules interact in a complex system to create life in cells, it is possible that inanimate neurons interact to form consciousness.

And if so, a "thinking machine" based on such an architecture could have a concept of self, experience wonder, appreciate Mozart, dream and fantasize. If it had a physical embodiment in a robot, it could be forced to contemplate survival and mortality, as even a machine can get "injured" or "die" if it goes off a cliff. Conceivably, it could eventually eclipse the thinking ability of *Homo sapiens'* quart-size brain; in the areas of raw memory and speed, computers already have. This unprecedented intellect could well become humankind's ultimate nemesis, in which computer intelligence is to humans as human intelligence is to ants. Such an omniscient, omnipresent force had better be our friend.

While such imaginings are the stuff of science fiction all the way back to "Hal" in Arthur C. Clarke's *2001: A Space Odyssey,* the seeds are growing and the technology continues inexorably to advance. And though the time frames are unknown, the inescapable conclusion is that computers may have no upward limit on their potential, and the computer revolution will likely continue throughout the twenty-first century.

AIR, LAND, AND WATER

SO FAR, ALL THE examples have been one form or another of electronics, each piece contributing to the spreading web of the Placeless Society. Telepresence boosts person-to-person communication, high-speed networks enable dispersed computers to merge into one, and simulated reality and intelligent computers enhance the interface between us and machines. Hence, ideas, facts, and knowledge gathered in one place are available everyplace; location becomes irrelevant. This glitz of electronics has led many pundits to simplistically label the twenty-first century the "electronic age" or the "computer era."

But one cannot eat electrons, and it is doubtful that we could feel fully satisfied in some simulated reality. Any notion that the twenty-first century will reduce humanity to a group of goggled cyberpunks is misleading. For behind today's humming boxes and their flickering monitors is a silent revolution taking place all over the world that will have great impact on pulling us into the Age of Everything-

Everywhere: the astonishing breakthroughs in present-day transportation.

Within two to three decades, one will be able to have a power breakfast in San Francisco, arrive in Tokyo for a lunch meeting, and be back in Los Angeles with time left to shower and unwind before having dinner with friends. Transport by air, land, or sea will reach limits scarcely imagined a century earlier. Further, people and products will shift seamlessly from one mode of transportation to another in a network more powerful than the sum of its parts.

One major change is that airplanes will perform at higher and higher speeds. The Boeing 747 already carries more than 400 people in a single load at nearly three-quarters the speed of sound, and many airlines see a market for air travel that is yet faster. Emerging technologies, however, must overcome limitations encountered by the Mach 2 French-British Concorde. This rapid airplane, which currently cruises at around 1,500 miles per hour, guzzles too much fuel, carries too few passengers, is too expensive to operate, and makes so much noise that over two dozen countries have banned its use. A new generation of aircraft is on the drawing board that could economically ferry 300 people nonstop to any point on the globe at two to three times the speed of sound.

Recognizing the potential, nations and aircraft makers around the world are scrambling to develop the necessary know-how, even if it means teaming up with former rivals. American aircraft makers Boeing and McDonnell Douglas are working together on the airframe, competing against British Aerospace and France's Aerospatiale. Pratt & Whitney is teamed with its competitor General Electric to make the engine, while competing against Britain's Rolls-Royce and France's SNECMA. Japan's powerful MITI is overseeing development of high-stress ceramics, new alloys, and composites. Germany's Deutsche Aerospace is shooting even higher with its Saenger project, planning *ultra*sonic Mach 25 flights by the year 2030. The Saenger would travel so rapidly that, once up to speed, no point on the globe would be more than forty minutes away.

Because of the high development costs for leading-edge aircraft, it is not likely that each of these participants will build a supersonic transport; rather, the best technologies from all over the world will be melded together in one or two competing designs. Experts predict a commercial supersonic flight will be in routine operation within a matter of decades. Initial routes will probably be sketched over the vast Pacific where economies are growing fastest; it is also where the need to compress time and distance is the greatest.

As the speed of air travel increases, customers will expect quicker airport service. There is little point in flying from Los Angeles to Tokyo in four hours if ticketing, customs, immigration, baggage, and airport commuting brings the total to eight. Airlines will respond by providing a fully integrated high-speed package. They will pick up bags at homes or offices and deliver them to hotel rooms; boarding passes will be issued electronically before the trip, or tickets may even be issued and billed midflight. Immigration will be conducted by clearing names through global databases. Customs inspections will be done automatically with equipment that scans the bags as they enter the planes.

As flights become faster and more convenient, more and more people will take to the air. Already, from 1970 to 1990, international passenger loads quadrupled, and today the top ten American airlines annually sell nearly twice as many tickets as there are people in the United States! As air technology continues to develop and as electronic communications broadens individual awareness of the planet's reach, air travel will be an ever-burgeoning industry.

Air cargo transport will also grow as fleets of specialized air freighters replace conventional ships, trucks, and trains as the standard freight carriers. Specialized air freighters now ply the skies ferrying heavy cargo (machinery and even cars) that once only ships could carry. New-age products miniaturized and built with lighter-weight materials render air freight even more compelling. Today, shipping a crate of computers by air may cost only a few dollars more than by sea. In competitive industries, the ability to get new products from factory to global markets instantaneously may become a requirement just to stay in business. Fashions change overnight, and technical products that get to the marketplace first often win the greatest following.

The pace is also accelerating on land. A new class of supertrains now moves passengers and freight at nearly half the speed of sound. In a few years, tomatoes from Spain will arrive in Paris just a few hours after being picked, cars and trucks may streak from Detroit to Houston in four hours, and Manhattan may become just a thirty-minute commute from downtown Boston.

We already see the potential in France's extensive network of Train à Grande Vitesse, or TGV. It is the fastest land network in the world, linking key cities at 200 miles per hour. Japan's famous *skinkansen,* or "bullet train," has already sold some three billion tickets—nearly equivalent to one for each person on the Earth. Its pace will increase to 320 miles per hour over the next few years. Not to be left behind, authorities throughout the developed world—Germany, Italy, Spain, Sweden, South Korea, Taiwan, and the United States—are planning supertrains over the next two decades.

The reason for the interest is that, over certain routes, travel by supertrain is the fastest form of transportation—even faster than hypersonic aircraft. It has already transformed transportation in France, where supertrains are robbing business from the lucrative midrange airline routes, sometimes cutting air traffic in half. Unlike aircraft, supertrains can depart exactly when scheduled, go from city center to city center (avoiding airport commutes, delays, and congestion), and stop economically anywhere in between. They also pollute less and consume correspondingly less fuel than any form of modern transportation.

While the European Union and Japan have extensive rail networks, the United States seriously lags in its train infrastructure. Though their countries are smaller, the average German or Frenchman travels a dozen times the distance by train as the average American, and the average Japanese travels three times farther still.

But American transportation authorities are scrambling to catch up. One possible 16,000-mile rail network, not unlike the original interstate highway, would connect forty-two states. Its network of 300-

miles-per-hour trains could reduce coast-to-coast freight time to an astonishing twelve hours. Texas may be the first state to link its largest five cities—Fort Worth, Dallas, Houston, Austin, and San Antonio. The proposed high-speed railway network would provide a line running right under the Dallas–Fort Worth airport. Stopping right at the American and Delta Airline gates, the system would effectively connect air and land. Florida, with its planned supertrain linking Orlando airport to nearby Disneyworld, may be the world's first commercial testing ground for the emerging "maglev" technology. This approach would allow entire train cars to be actually suspended above the tracks by powerful magnets capable of hurling train cars at speeds exceeding 300 miles per hour.

Pennsylvania, Illinois, Ohio, New York, and California are also considering high-speed trains over major traffic corridors. Although the cost of building supertrains is high, the emerging supertrain technologies are among the fastest and most economical ways to whisk regional transport into the Placeless Society.

While supertrains are redefining ground transportation, and hypersonic flight is stretching the limits of the air, the highly specialized fleets of cargo ships are transforming the seas. The world's bulk-cargo needs have swelled, and processions of purpose-built ships parade across the seas, moving enormous quantities of industrial feedstock in days. Small crews pilot petroleum supertankers a fifth of a mile long, bringing enough fuel to electrify a town of half a million people for a year with just a single load. Fleets of megaships dispatch molten sulfur or wine, methane gas or iron-ore slurry.

THE SUM OF THE PARTS

AS EACH MEANS OF transportation hastens its pace, yet another force is minimizing distance: our heightened ability to quickly transfer people and goods *between* modes. At some locales, ships arrive in port and their cargo avoids the dockside warehouses. Giant containerized bins are lifted directly onto a caravan of waiting truck trailers or train cars. The trucks, in turn, immediately head out to make deliveries.

Tacoma, Washington, an example of a location with near-zero-time transfers, has evolved into one of the top shipping ports in the world. By connecting vessels instantly to two major railroads and more than 200 trucking lines, Tacoma has emerged unsurpassed in its ability to keep cargo moving toward its final destination in one seamless motion. It is no accident that German shippers, looking for a port to ship autos to western Canada, selected "far-away" Tacoma over the more "logical" Vancouver; they chose the port that could take them closest to placelessness, where the distance between ship and train car is measured in seconds.

Authorities at Charles de Gaulle Airport in Paris are tapping into the Placeless Society too; Paris hopes to be the first international airport offering blink-of-the-eye connections between cargo jets, supertrains, and trucks. Their goal is to become the number one gateway to Europe. According to plan, within minutes of a freight plane taxiing into position alongside specialized loading docks, cargo will be unloaded onto waiting supertrains. These trains will then fan out to London, Frankfurt, or Milan and arrive just two hours later. All Western Europe will have high-speed freight connections with the rest of the world.

Clearly, for such systems to work, tight timing is critical; the train has to be in position to start loading the moment the plane arrives. Perhaps among the best coordinators of multiple modes of transportation is Federal Express. FedEx handles a million packages a day, most of which travel via hand couriers, trucks, and jets to be resorted over 200 miles of conveyor belts in Memphis, Tennessee. The packages are then sent back through the same network to arrive at their destinations only hours later. The company's secret is not that its vehicles are faster, but that each element is tightly choreographed.

Packages move almost nonstop from pickup to delivery, and they can be tracked down throughout the process. From the moment a courier touches a package, its bar coded electronic presence is entered into a global information grid. A shipper can call in a package number at any time, and Federal Express will tell within seconds exactly where it is, whether it is likely to be delayed, and even change its destination address while it's already en route.

As FedEx-type precision spreads throughout the airlines, railroads, and trucking fleets, the whole becomes faster than any one part operating by itself. A high-speed pipeline will develop from factories to offices and homes around the world. The end result is that emerging transportation technologies warp the nature of distance as an obstacle that once determined human organization. The time it takes to travel from Los Angeles to Tokyo on a hypersonic aircraft becomes no more than what it takes to cross Los Angeles by car in rush hour. The expense of shipping overnight packages across the country is no more than shipping them across the street.

In the Age of Everything-Everywhere, distances still exist, but they no longer so powerfully determine how society will be organized.

INVESTOR BEWARE

MOST, BUT NOT ALL, of us in industrialized countries will enter the realm of placelessness over the next two decades; some trailblazing organizations and individuals already have. The question then becomes, how does one prepare for it? What can one do to get ready? It certainly affects how organizations are structured, how individuals behave, and how wealth is created. We begin with this advice as we approach the twenty-first century: *investor beware.*

Many of us will be lured to invest blindly in the very industries that are propelling us into the Age of Everything-Everywhere—telephone companies, cable television, cellular phones, fiber optics, satellites, computers, virtual reality and flight simulators, videophones, video games, database archives, and "hypertransportation."

Even the investment gurus on Wall Street and the strategy czars in corporate boardrooms will be hypnotized by the glamour of high technology. The fervor for cabling the world, for example, is such that, over the next fifteen years, more money will be invested in the telephone infrastructure than since phones were invented in 1876.

Expect merger and acquisition activity to continue to heat up among telephone, cable, and entertainment companies as they tout the future of interactive television. Satellite and cellular companies will vie to provide mobile connections to the global communications grid. Companies will lure money for new investments touted as the path to riches in the Information Age. Look for stock prices to be bid up to extraordinary levels—and new billionaires to emerge—as investors and business executives see an unlimited potential in the new products and services just ahead.

But while vast fortunes will certainly be made in these leading-edge fields, the success of a company may well be short-lived. Many of these companies, even the giants, find their competitive advantages ripped away by yet newer technologies. Already, mainframes have largely been replaced by desktop systems, and now there are "notebooks." Microwaves replaced long-distance copper wire; satellites have replaced microwaves. Now fiber optics seems to eclipse everything, but the evolution is not complete as recent advances in satellite technology may yet put it back on center stage. Cable television companies may provide local telephone service and newspaper delivery, and many existing cellular phone companies will collapse in the face of newer ways to connect mobile phones. Everything is in flux, prices are dropping, and little is permanent.

Because many of the new technologies represent revolutions involving different types of expertise, and because entrenched giants are slow to make obsolete their investments in existing products, it is often the new companies that win over the old. It was upstart MCI that dethroned AT&T as *the* telephone company, and innovative Apple and Microsoft that led to the eventual toppling of IBM.

Yet smaller high-tech companies are not immune either. Especially vulnerable are seemingly successful one-product companies that fail to develop yet newer capabilities for a changing world. This happened to Ashton-Tate in database management and may yet happen to WordPerfect in word processing, or Lotus in spreadsheets. Even Apple is limited in its product offerings, and a few missteps in judging the market could cause it to be eclipsed overnight by eager competitors. If history is any guide, even today's darlings, Microsoft and Intel, walk a narrow tightrope, with plenty of emerging technologies that may throw off their balance.

As always, the secret for investors is to know *which* companies to buy and *when* to sell. The technologies are often so complex, or potential competing products seemingly nonexistent, that many investors are drawn by illusory glamour rather than long-term strengths. Without intimate understanding of the particular technology and markets, such investments are pure lottery plays. The winning investors will be those who follow companies closely and head for the exit before it is too late.

WEALTH TO THE USERS

AS TECHNOLOGICAL ADVANCES drive costs down, the bulk of the long-term wealth of the revolution just ahead will flow not to the providers of placeless capabilities, but to the users.

As history has shown us, in the Age of Everything-Everywhere, the smart investment money will go not to the tool makers but to the companies that learn first how to use the new tools to transcend place. As many organizations navigate the transition to a new dimension, the most successful ones will be those that visualize the future in the extreme: free and unlimited computing power, "chargeless" telecommunications from anywhere to anywhere, low-cost transportation that is instantaneous. The successful helmsmen will begin to conceptually reengineer the organization, temporarily ignoring the existing structures rooted in a mere three-dimensional world. The leaders will see the power of creating an organizational Manhattan Effect where every employee and resource is compressed to a single point, to a critical mass, in the Fourth Dimension.

We already see the beginning signs: banks that can serve any customer from any branch; grocery chains that know the minute-by-minute sales of any cash register in any store; airlines that electronically link hundreds of thousands of retail travel offices into its flight schedules and tariffs. There are the freight companies that can pin-point the location of every shipment, vehicle, and employee; manufacturing companies that can connect dispersed facilities by air, allowing them to act as one organism. These and thousands of organizations like them will be the winners in the Fourth Dimension. Often, the organizational shifts will be mandatory just to stay in business.

While each industry, each organization, has its own special requirements, the sweeping result will be organizational structures and ways of operations with little resemblance to existing forms. As we will see, there will be less reason to have a manufacturing operation concentrated physically in one place when it can be physically scattered around the globe. An insurance claims agent can stay at home and "telecommute" to work. Work groups can be dynamic and spread among various locations—and still focus on immediate problems. Components and services can be subcontracted to others without loss of control. Customers can be tracked and targeted, products designed and transported to market more quickly, middlemen eliminated, and processes automated.

Change will not happen overnight. Costs of computers, telecommunications, and transportation are coming down, but are not yet insignificant. Also, the organic quality of human organization suggests that the best evolution is gradual, not radical. Human habits evolve more slowly than technologies. For these reasons, most organizations are testing the waters one step at a time. But the scope of change in a world without place is breathtaking, especially as an entire generation of children raised on television and Nintendo joysticks enters the workforce.

USING ROBOTS AND JETS

THE BENEFITS OF THE Age of Everything-Everywhere are not lost on those wishing to design new products or cut costs. Design teams, marketing groups, manufacturing personnel, and the shipping department can be in the same "room" when new products are conceived, allowing the entire company to act as a holistic, seamless unit to bring new products to completion in record time—with few surprises. Some companies even extend the interdepartmental coordination to include suppliers and key customers, with each connected electronically.

The intimate linkage between supplier and customer in a placeless world is already apparent in the manufacture of auto seats. Once a car leaves the automaker's paint booth—and not before—seat maker Douglas and Lomason is advised electronically of the seat style, upholstery, color, and trim that has to be delivered to their customer, sometimes within ninety minutes of the order. The seats are then quickly assembled and delivered "just in time" for installation. The coordination between the customer and supplier is so tight that the seats are even unloaded off the truck in the same sequence as the cars on the assembly line. As each seat arrives on the conveyor belt, it matches the next car in line.

Motorola's pager operations are similarly streamlined. Its production line in Boynton Beach, Florida, is totally automated with scores of robots choreographed in a complex waltz by interconnected omniscient computers. If a bottleneck occurs in one place, every robot in the production line is instantly "aware" of the problem and can adjust its operations. Even more impressive, a large number of models can be assembled, or radio frequencies installed, without losing pace. Place is compressed.

Within twenty minutes of a salesperson anywhere in the country entering the unique specifications for a Motorola rush order, it is relayed by computer from the company's headquarters in Schumburg, Illinois, to the main computer in the Florida plant. Within two hours, a completed unit is built, boxed, and ready for shipment. The company is coordinated to act as a single organism.

The interconnectedness of geographically dispersed operations means that physical products have to flow from one place to another as effortlessly as electrons. If any one of General Motors' worldwide assembly plants runs out of a critical part, the operations are often forced to shut down. To keep them running smoothly, GM pays about $100 million a year to Emery Worldwide to air shuttle parts—overnight or even the same day—between operations in the United States, Canada, and Mexico. GM sometimes even charters an entire cargo jet. Because GM and Emery are connected electronically, GM is able to track parts anywhere in Emery's transportation system, effectively making Emery part of GM's assembly line. For companies like GM, the world becomes a single manufacturing plant.

THE EFFECTIVE EMPLOYEE

WHILE THE PROMISE OF placelessness will attract ever more organizations to plunge headlong into these sweeping changes, it is a mistake to change too radically. Organizations should be seen as complex alliances of *people,* aided by tools to accomplish particular tasks. While the mechanical aspects—the computers, the transportation systems—can often be changed overnight, the human element displays much more inertia. If individuals fail to grasp the usefulness of the new tools, the tools lose their potency. The success of any organization will fundamentally depend on its people.

Individuals, like organizations, can be leaders or followers. The new capabilities allow the front-runners to be in several places at once. Curious about technical capabilities and quick to use them to solve everyday work problems, these pioneers will get the sought-after promotions and contracts, and they will accomplish more with less effort.

We already see these trailblazers everywhere around us. She is the sales distributor who uses a cellular telephone in her car to coordinate with customers and the home office on the way to appointments. He is the CEO with a computer in his office that allows him to review sales data instantly without calling a staff meeting. She is the product engineer who uses voicemail for low-priority calls to avoid interruptions of her concentration, but who checks her mail several times daily to give complete and timely responses. He is the manufacturing strategist who receives constant updates of shipping costs and exchange and labor rates to evaluate where to best produce subassemblies. They are the sales managers who have set their computers to track competitive product announcements daily.

For the individual, the most important single factor in adapting to the Placeless Society is the ability to embrace change and new paradigms and technologies, and to use the new realities as levers to ease their work. Those who cling to old methods, or believe that somehow *their* situation is different, will be surpassed by those who know how to deploy the new tools.

For many, the voyage into the Fourth Dimension will start by becoming computer literate—to be familiar with a computer keyboard and mouse, to be able to dance through one or more computer applications in all their complexities. Although we have seen that computer interfaces will become increasingly user friendly, it is computer-literate persons who will be the least intimidated about experimenting with yet newer capabilities, and they will be able to push their limits to solve real workplace problems.

When their company has already entered the Fourth Dimension, the successful individuals will attempt to learn every facet of the company's electronic mail system. There may be relevant information on the electronic bulletin boards, or financial and product plans that can help them "tap into" the company—oftentimes the same information that is available to the president! In one company, when a young new employee posted a particularly well-crafted memo on the electronic-mail system, senior executives immediately saw her talent and broadened her responsibilities.

The trailblazers will also find out how to use their company's video-conferencing facilities when they exist. In some companies, the original costs of setting up the conference rooms and communication links have already been paid off. That means it can cost close to nothing to put a given meeting together.

If one's organization has not yet adapted to the new realities, it does not prevent the individual from jumping ahead. People who work in the field, especially in sales and service, may be able to persuade their companies to pay for cellular telephones. Others may be able to set up home offices with fax machines and computers linked to the rest of the corporation, and they may convince their employers of the benefits of telecommuting. Still others will tap into outside electronic networks (like CompuServe or the Internet) to gain access to vast storehouses of public information sources and individuals with common professional interests.

Those with the greatest clout in pulling an organization into the Placeless Society, of course, are the managers and executives. Effective leaders will be constantly sifting for ideas that can bring people and resources together. These managers will systematically interview new employees to learn what placeless capabilities other companies have, particularly if the former employer is in the same industry. They will review trade journals to be current on competitors' developments. They will attend electronic and industry trade shows and invite vendors to unveil new technologies and services that move materials, people, and information quickly. Most important, they will be ready to make a decision as soon as the ever-decreasing costs are less than the ever-increasing capabilities.

━━

We are all confronted with the same avalanche of innovation resulting from the electronic revolution. Simultaneously, advances in transportation have created a high-speed conveyor belt propelling people and freight around the world at ever-accelerating speeds. The convergence of these two vast bodies of technologies—communications and transportation—makes the Age of Everything-Everywhere possible.

We are a society that spent its childhood in a highly parochial world determined by place. We enter our awkward adolescence in the twenty-first century as the old structures become cumbersome. *Near* is no longer closer than *far*, distance is less relevant, and our social institutions (families, schools, offices, factories, cities, even countries) are slowly breaking loose from their moorings rooted in the primacy of place.

As society changes, just how will it be organized? What inevitable shifts will overcome our national and city governments? How will industry restructure to survive? What will be the keys to unlock the doors to power and wealth?

As we answer these questions, we will first unveil how wealth will be created in the new society just emerging.

Part Two

THE VANISHING
FOUNDATIONS

3

FOOTLOOSE HUMANITY

IT WAS MARÍA AQUINO VILLANUEVA's day off, and she popped out of bed at first light to prepare a picnic basket with roasted chicken and *pansit bihon.* She weaved and bumped through the crowded streets clutching her refreshments, until she arrived in the cool shade of the colonial-style courthouse. Her friends had already laid out the straw mats, and she was eager to share gossip about the prior week. People were gathering on the steps by the concrete fountains, chatting with friends or relatives. Vendors were hawking copies of the *Manila Times* and *Balita* with its local gossip. Except for a few Chinese with ice cream carts, no "foreigners" were within sight. Everything—the people, the food, the language—was from the Philippines.

Except that Statue Square is in downtown Hong Kong.

For the 70,000 Filipina domestic workers in Hong Kong, Sunday is maids' day off. With little space at their employers' homes to invite guests, and not enough money for restaurants or shopping, the maids assemble at the park from sunup to sundown, once a week, to relax and talk with friends.

These women play a part in migration patterns and evolving family structures. María's husband is a driver in Saudi Arabia. Her three children live with her parents and sister in the Philippines, and another sister is staying in an apartment in Brooklyn. The family fabric is held together by faded photographs and a global patchwork of letters, occasional telephone calls, faxes, and bank transfers.

More than anything else, the far-flung migration pattern of María's family may be typical of much of humanity in the early twenty-first century.

———

Nguyen Hao, age seventeen, didn't quite understand that he was supposed to go to the nurse's office. He sat in the Southern California classroom remembering all too well his secret departure out of Cambodia—the rickety boat, the pirates, the thirst—but not that he had a medical appointment today at his new school.

He looked up and was startled as the teacher and all the kids were looking right at him, waiting for him to answer. His friend—the only person at La Quinta High School who could speak his Khmer dialect—explained that he had to get up and go with the woman waiting at the door.

As Nguyen and the woman crossed the playground in silence, they passed a group speaking in Spanish, one in Korean, then others in Arabic, Japanese, Farsi. Like these students, he came from somewhere else, and they all had a story: Yoshiro's father transferred from Japan to an Orange County subsidiary; Jorge's family could not survive in Guatemala; Karim left Iran to escape Islamic fundamentalism.

In less than two decades, a once homogeneous all-white school had been deluged by a swell of twenty-seven languages. The administrators at La Quinta were as lost as Nguyen was.

———

Jean-Pierre Richelieu was livid. He was late for an appointment, and up ahead they were at it again. At 1:00 on a Thursday afternoon, they were blocking the road, facing Mecca on their prayer mats of woven reeds or fabric. Some were in traditional robes, others in casual clothes or business suits. But all were kneeling as if with one mind, with foreheads nearly touching the ground while the *muezzin* cried out Koranic incantations.

Jean-Pierre knew it would be another half hour before the traffic could move on again. It wasn't like this when he was a boy, he thought to himself. To pass the time, he flicked on the radio and chanced upon another of Jean-Marie Le Pen's pronationalist speeches. For once, he was beginning to understand that a change was swiftly overtaking France, indeed all Europe.

———

To see the future of our own hometowns, we need only look where changes are already happening. We see migration patterns in Hong Kong, Los Angeles, and Marseilles echoed in the suburbs of Sidney, Tel Aviv, Nairobi, Munich, Liverpool, and Vancouver. Each example has its unique fingerprint, yet is from the same hand of the Placeless Society.

Citizens from once remote areas are pouring into the rich countries, landing at international airports, or using an armada of makeshift boats and ships. Others arrive legally in neighboring countries, then slip over borders at night. Never before have we had such sustained migration on such a global scale, one that will define cities, even countries, in the Placeless Society of the early twenty-first century.

A XENOPHOBIC SIEGE

WITH ITS MASSIVE INFLUX of Latinos and Asians atop a population already Black, White, Brown, and Yellow, Los Angeles emerges as a rainbow soup, a prototype of what is in store across the rest of America. Demographers predict that soon California will no longer have an ethnic majority, Texas and New York will follow by 2020, and the entire nation will have become "Losangelized" by the mid-twenty-first century.

Western Europe is also under "siege." The tidy stereotypes of Frenchmen with their *baguettes,* or German villages with their central Lutheran churches, are giving way to a new Europe awash with refugees from afar.

In the Placeless Society, Islam has finally achieved what the holy caliphs sought for over a millennium: nearly 10 million Muslims in Western Europe. With 2,000 mosques (compared to 10 in 1965), France has more Muslims than Protestants. To be a "Western European" is a changing concept as more and more neighborhoods fill with Algerians, Moroccans, Tunisians, Sri Lankans, Indians, Cambodians, Serbs, Croats, Bosnians, Turks, or Pakistanis.

A million foreigners, all migrant workers, have already pierced Japan's xenophobic veil. Thai bar girls, Filipina housekeepers, Bangladeshi construction workers and Malaysian restaurant workers often do the work that the Japanese don't like.

"Asia's England," Australia, also faces a drastic change of identity. After the first British shipload of convicts in 1788, it only accepted White, English-speaking immigrants until 1973. Today nearly half the immigrants are Asian, and new arrivals are coming in at such a rapid rate that Australia has the highest population growth of the industrialized world. A third of its residents were born elsewhere.

National lines are blurred in Africa as boundaries imposed by colonial powers left unnatural borders cutting across age-old tribes. Fueled by regional wars and population pressures, Africa is a hotbed of transnational migration. Thirty-five million Africans, *a tenth of the continent's population,* live at least some portion of their lives outside their "home" country. Each day, hundreds of thousands of Africans cross borders without formality. In Gabon and the Ivory Coast, half the population is foreign born.

In nearly every nation and city of the world, the percentage of people born somewhere else has grown. Many of us, feeling lost or resentful in a home culture increasingly "invaded" by these newcomers, use foreigners as handy scapegoats for social and domestic ills. The backlash against immigration has spread from California and Florida to Illinois, from Europe to Russia, Japan, and Australia. Politicians grumble about welfare fraud, displaced jobs, social services. In France, some evoke the large families of Africans with multiple wives. In California, immigrants are blamed for the budget deficit and in Russia, for the AIDS epidemic. Meanwhile, German skinheads burn Turks alive in their apartments, and some governments in Asia, Africa, and Eastern Europe encourage waves of "ethnic cleansing."

Yet, whether for good or bad, the advance of an everyone-everywhere culture is too strong to halt. Our society is now the most mobile in the history of humanity.

PUSH AND PULL

THE FUNDAMENTAL UNDERPINNING to global migration is, of course, a perceived disparity between one region and another. Citizens in one nation who encounter population pressures, poverty, or war at home, decide to seek higher wages and "paradise" abroad.

This is nothing new; human beings have been wanderers for two million years. Europe itself has a mixed heritage of Goths, Vandals, Huns, Gauls, Franks, Teutons, Romans, and others. The Japanese are the product of complex migration patterns from Korea, East Asia, the South Pacific, and even Siberia. Americans came first from the Asian tundra, then later from Europe and Africa. A common thread in our stories is that many of our families came from somewhere else.

What has changed is the *pace* of global migration: what once took centuries and several generations now takes hours thanks to modern transportation. The old barriers of mountain ridges, rivers, and even oceans have all but disappeared. Migrants no longer meander haphazardly across countries, but span *hemispheres* in one jump, as denizens of the poor South flock like migratory birds to the rich employment grounds of the North. Modern transportation has provided the means, and communications have offered the knowledge.

The mounting population and environmental pressures show no signs of abating. From 1980 to 1995, the number of global refugees doubled to 16 million people. Whether it is Afghan rebels, suppressed Iraqi Kurds, disgruntled Palestinians, displaced Cambodians, land-poor El Salvadorans, or war-torn ex-Yugoslavians, no sooner has one conflict recessed than two more erupt. Now Somalia, Rwanda, Sudan;

then Mozambique, Liberia, Armenia, Turkestan, Georgia; again Angola, Sri Lanka, Guatemala. . . . Each fresh conflict pours hundreds of thousands of new refugees onto the world stage.

While each war has its historic origins, the common denominator is destitute poverty coupled with extraordinary population growth. In most warring regions, the population will *double* within one generation; half the war-torn countries have per-capita incomes less than $29 per month. The seven largest countries with the dual strains of fertility and poverty—Pakistan, Bangladesh, Nigeria, the Philippines, Indonesia, India, and China—constitute *half the population of the world*.

Moreover, the erosion of topsoil, the depletion of forests and fisheries, and the dearth of water will push hundreds of millions out of their homelands over the coming twenty years.

As population growth and environmental degradation fuel the push, income differentials provide the pull of migration into industrialized nations. Fledgling immigrants to America can earn in an hour what their cousins in Mexico make in a day. The jump in wages for an African who moves to Western Europe can be even greater. Nigerian workers who come to Switzerland earn in a *single day* what would take *over a month* back home. Many immigrants return home on holidays like Third World Marco Polos, telling tales of unbound riches confirmed by movies, television programs, and glossy photo magazines available to the world's poor. So they see, and so they come.

POROUS BORDERS
AND TRAVEL AGENTS

EACH COUNTRY HAS ERECTED barriers to check the flood of immigrants, but none has worked. The scope of the problem was illustrated when the Albanian economy collapsed in 1991. Thousands of Albanians simply commandeered the freighter *Vlora* in Durrës to make the 130-mile trek across the Adriatic Sea to Bari, Italy. When the Italian government attempted to round them up, 12,000 escaped a makeshift prison and fled into the streets. Some 20,000 Albanians managed to slip into Italy and seemingly disappear into thin air.

Though politicians worldwide labeled the *Vlora* episode an "Italian" problem, it is much more. If Italy, the world's sixth largest economy, could not stop the rusting *Vlora* from docking in broad daylight, how can Europe stem the teeming population of Africa? There are simply too many people, too many departure points, and too many points of entry.

The United States's 2,000-mile border with Mexico has proved most porous, as many Latinos cross the Rio Grande or the desert at night and then hit a US highway. Others pass by daylight with fraudulent documents, or ride across packed in hidden compartments beneath cars. A million a year are apprehended, but for each person caught, two others slip through undetected.

Despite thousands of agents, squadrons of patrol planes and helicopters, high-tech night-vision binoculars, and detention centers, the US government has failed to control the border. The aliens who get caught keep reappearing after being deported. As in Europe, illegals can move about the country almost unimpeded once they cross the border.

The idea of fining US employers who hire undocumented aliens miserably failed. In 1991 one print shop alone in Los Angeles supplied up to a million fake documents, birth certificates, Social Security cards, and work permits through distributors located across the United States, as well as in Mexico and as far away as India and Pakistan.

As the rich countries keep erecting walls at their borders, global "travel agents" guide undocumented travelers around the obstacles. The *coyotes* in Mexico, the *yakuza* in Japan, the *buscones* in the Dominican Republic all bypass immigration barriers. For a thousand dollars, an "agent" will walk the "client" across the US border, drive him to Los Angeles, and even arrange a flight to New York, Seattle, or Hawaii, where immigration controls are lax. Chinese crime syndicates earn hundreds of millions of dollars a year by bringing Asians to the United States for $30,000 a person on average. The *yakuza*, Japan's mafia, recruits Filipinas to work as singers, dancers, musicians, or prostitutes in Tokyo's fashionable nightclubs. In Poland the grassy square in the middle of Slubice is known locally as "the Bermuda Triangle": travelers meet their "tour guides" there to disappear into the West. In the Placeless Society, borders are porous and a multibillion dollar underground industry finds the holes.

STREET SWEEPERS AND VALEDICTORIANS

BUT EVEN IF WE *could* plug the holes, *should* we? Curiously, the dawn of the Placeless Society coincides with a singular demographic shift characterizing all the rich countries: we've stopped having babies. As a result, our populations (excluding immigration) are shrinking, our labor forces are dwindling, and the number of our nonproductive retirees is swelling. Japan has the largest proportion of aged persons in the world, and over half of its workforce will disappear by 2015. Europe, the United States, and the rest of the industrialized world do not lag far behind.

With so many economically inactive groups, who will doctor our elderly and run our retirement homes, design our buildings and sweep our streets, pilot our jets and repair our cars? Who will support the swelling ranks of pensioned retirees? In the rich countries, instead of population growth, population *aging* will be the demographic nemesis of the early twenty-first century.

While xenophobic resentments will no doubt arouse more anti-immigration barriers, the senior citizens who demand quality care, the employers who need workers, and the governments seeking productive citizens to tax will want the gates open. Far from stopping it, the winning nations will know how to *benefit* from controlled immigration.

Many economic studies in the United States conclude that there are enormous benefits to having immigrants: contrary to popular belief, they produce more than they consume, pay more taxes than they take in social benefits, and are less prone to crime. It is the energetic, entrepreneurial, hard-working, forward-looking, even courageous person who seeks to immigrate; the others stay home.

In the United States, a quarter of arriving immigrants are professional or technical workers, compared to only 15 percent for the American population. Their countries of birth may invest precious funds in education and health care only to find those investments lost in a global brain drain. Europe and North America are swarming with computer programmers and biological scientists from India, Asia, and Latin America who came to Western universities never to return to their homelands. Nearly half the Soviet émigrés to Israel are well educated in medicine, engineering, and science.

American science depends on immigrants: although the foreign born comprise only 6 percent of the US population, they constitute over *half* the graduates in computer science, engineering, and math. American electronic and computer firms have hired armies of technical specialists who were born abroad; they represent half the workers of California's Silicon Valley or Massachusetts's Route 128. The 15,000 Asians employed by Silicon Valley alone have been crucial to the success of US technology. From blue collar to white collar, the world's labor pool is more mobile than ever before, and the pace will keep on quickening. Labor has become placeless.

THE NEW DETACHED LABOR

THE FORCES THAT HAVE made labor mobile have also irreversibly altered its nature. Traditionally, the worker and the work had to be in the same place. Not so today: America sells cotton to India, which spins it into yarn. It is then woven into fabric in Japan, sewn into shirts in Hong Kong, and sold back to America. The workers don't have to be in America to fashion the raw cotton into the finished shirt.

The *effect* of the labor is what is moved, by sea, air, and even satellite.

When US customers of Quarterdeck Office Systems call a toll-free number for technical service, they may be connected to Ireland, where average salaries are a third to half of those in the United States. Not so long ago, long-distance costs would have required a local worker for technical services, but increasingly, place is irrelevant.

The data-entry business illustrates how "detachable" labor can be. Cartons of data handwritten on forms or contained in microfilm files leave America and Europe by jet, headed for companies like Satec or Equidata in the Philippines. There, for a dollar an hour, thousands of college-trained women keypunch the information at 10,000 characters per hour. The data is immediately sent back electronically.

California-based Sun Microsystems uses Russian scientists to adapt its advanced SPARC architecture to supercomputers, while Hewlett-Packard hires programmers in China. US Datametrics runs its operations in India, Germany's Volkswagen is in Brazil, and Japan's Nissan is in Malaysia. It no longer matters where workers do their jobs. As long as there is a telecommunication link, an international airport, or a deep-water seaport, the fruits of labor can be dispatched anywhere while the laborer remains in place.

This new global reality is pitting worker against worker in the marketplace, depressing wages in "expensive" countries and enhancing them in "cheap" ones. It explains, in part, why in the mid-1990s wages and employment are not rebounding in industrialized countries as they used to after business downturns. It accounts for the miracle growth in the low-cost nations of Asia and Latin America, and simultaneously, for the loss of white-collar jobs elsewhere. In the Age of Everything-Everywhere, *where* you live is declining as an issue, as long as your skills are in competitive demand *globally*.

WHERE ARE THE WORKERS?

NOW THAT LABOR HAS become an interchangeable, omnipresent, and fluid commodity, it is not needed as much. This may prove to be the biggest irony of the Placeless Society.

This phenomenon is evidenced in the desert outside Bakersfield, California, where society has taken another step in its march toward zero-labor agriculture. A gigantic, self-propelled "Bolthouse Harvester" rambles along speedily, enabling only three workers to pick seventy-five tons of carrots an hour. Nonexistent ten years ago, two dozen harvesters supply over half the US carrot market today, revolutionizing the industry and throwing thousands of laborers out of work.

Today fewer than three US workers out of a hundred are needed for agriculture, and developments now under way are likely to reduce that number. In 1850, just before the Civil War, about sixty-five out of a hundred US workers were growing food. The agricultural industries have become so efficient that governments in Europe, North America, and Japan often buy up surplus production (or engage in other subsidies) just to keep farm workers employed.

The success of the past hundred years in agriculture foreshadows what we will soon experience in manufacturing, thanks, of course, to the extraordinary advances made in manufacturing technology. By 2025 a mere 5 percent of the world's workers could produce all the manufacturing needs—cars, stereos, dishes, beds, toys, clothes—of the total population.

One early step in our industrial progress was to displace human muscle power. The ox displaced the "plowman," later the diesel engine replaced the ox, but a human was always necessary to guide the course. In Ford's early automotive assembly line of 1913, every screw, bolt, and rivet in a car had to be put in place by some thoughtful soul. In the following decades, streamlining manufacturing did little to remove the necessity of human hands to run the machinery.

The spread of low-cost computers in the 1970s and 1980s changed all that. Computers were highly adapted to control the mechanical muscle power harnessed in the machines. They could accept sensory input to "feel" or "see" the parts, navigate them through complex steps, and take the appropriate actions to handle special problems such as rejecting a defective component, slowing down when a conveyor belt got overloaded, or turning over an upside-down part.

When touring a brewery or cheese factory, a textile mill or auto plant, the most notable feature for today's visitor is the scarcity of people. Except for the overseer at a computer console, or the "maintenance personnel," manufacturing plants run with hardly anyone on the shop floor. As if by magic, raw materials arrive in bulk by train car at one end, and out the other can pop pallets of finished goods labeled, boxed, and ready to ship—all the while never touched by human hands.

The factory itself has become one organism. Each conveyor belt, stamping machine, and painting booth "knows" what the others are doing, each waltzing to microsecond choreography.

At GM's Pontiac East pickup-plant, for example, the whole process is driven by computers from customer order to final delivery. Covering 50 football fields, 25 miles of conveyor belts, and hundreds of robots, the plant transforms raw sheet metal, along with 2,200 odd parts, into drivable trucks in just twenty-two hours. Every minute, a new truck emerges out through the exit door.

Each truck is custom designed for paint, trim, rims, bumpers, radios, and so on, from several thousand possible permutations. The computer coordinates the build sequence; automatically welds, screws, bolts, and snaps components; paints the interior, chassis, and doors the right combination of colors; and prints the window price sticker and dealer-routing ticket. Humans do only what the engineers can't yet automate.

INFORMATION WORKERS AT RISK

IT IS NOT JUST THE blue-collar workers who are being displaced, but also the information workers—engineers who design the equipment, accountants who track the profits, and programmers who run all the numerically controlled robots. Ironically, they are displaced as computers grow in power.

For instance, sophisticated CAD (computer-aided design) programs take skeleton drawings and transform them into component pieces right down to detailed drawings of brackets, assembly points, and material specifications. CAD programs are also linked to CAM (computer-aided manufacturing) programs, which take basic blueprints and use them to orchestrate the manufacturing robots. In turn, the manufacturing plant is linked to automated accounting systems that order parts (often directly into the supplier's computer), track costs, issue invoices, and cut salary checks.

A customer will soon be able to design his or her own customized car. He or she will select the body shape, any color of paint, trim, and options, and the vehicle will be delivered to the customer's home within twenty-four hours—with very little human labor involved.

A warning: those who see a future for programmers should reconsider. Today's programmers are fast at work designing software that writes software. The programming built into today's integrated circuits is so complex that only computers can design them. Within a few decades, a programmer will merely tell the computer what's needed, and the computer—not the programmer—will figure out how to do it.

Information workers such as telephone personnel, data-entry typists, and even doctors are among the endangered species. Telephone operators are already being replaced by voice-recognition systems, and data-entry is giving way to optical character reading. Even the work of medical doctors is often so routine that expert systems may well do a better job at diagnosing rare diseases, prescribing the newest drugs, and keeping track of case histories, hereditary disorders, allergies, and avoiding dangerous drug interactions.

The pace of this technological displacement of workers is heightened in the Age of Everything-Everywhere. New ideas spread like wildfire from one division to the next within the same global megacorporation. Clever employee recruitment and espionage carry ideas over corporate boundaries, and mutual vendors and consultants cross-pollinate labor-saving techniques across industries. Each step drives global competitors into a frenzy to outdo the others in cutting costs. Every worker's job is at risk.

THE COMING DISUNION

SINCE THE INDUSTRIAL REVOLUTION, two economic thinkers have nearly polarized the world into two different camps. One followed Adam Smith with his *Wealth of Nations*, which espoused the virtues of pitting individuals against one another in the free market; the other agreed with Karl Marx and the ideas he expressed in *Das Kapital* about centralized economies. Curiously, both camps recognized one main principle: all wealth was to be derived from the judicious marriage of the three "factors of production"—labor, capital, and raw materials. They disagreed, however, on the share that labor should receive for its toil.

Labor, the first of the three pillars, is now crumbling. Marxism has already proved itself erroneous, but we are just beginning to understand that, soon, the tools of "Smithism" will also be obsolete. The declining importance of labor will fundamentally shift the role of unions as their power and influence continue to weaken in most industries. Still, labor unions may thrive in certain segments of the economy. To see why, we start with history. . . .

Labor unions originated in the wake of the Industrial Revolution in reaction to the gross abuses and inequities of early industrialization. Following the Great Depression, unions were encouraged in the United States as a way to increase wages and consumerism. Union rolls swelled from 3 million in 1930 to 14 million by 1945—enlisting more than one out of three US workers.

Yet, since World War II, the ranks of the unions have not kept pace with the expanding labor force. In the United States, the proportion of union workers had fallen by 1995 to less than half its midcentury glory, and the union roster keeps shrinking. Other industrialized countries have experienced similar declines. Improved government labor standards, increased numbers of part-time workers, and the rise of service over manufacturing may account for the shrinking union rolls.

But even without those factors, unions would be in decline. Formerly, unions gained power largely by organizing whole industries rather than single plants. Wage increases or work rules would apply uniformly to *all* companies in the industry, and costs could be passed on to customers without losing sales to a competitor. But in the age of global labor, unions' efforts at organizing industries are frustrated.

Today a machine part can be made abroad by any of a thousand vendors as easily as it can be made locally. Union shops lose business to more competitive nonunion upstarts, and technology has reduced plant sizes and eased relocation. Furthermore, the decentralization of manufacturing to hundreds of subcontractors in scores of countries makes it hard for unions to identify targets and organize. In the Placeless Society, the few workers needed are set against one another in an infinite global labor pool. The unions have simply lost their grip over industry.

Unions have their place in the twenty-first century, but their forms and roles will be very different. Those most at risk are in industries where labor is easily shifted around the world: automobiles, electronics, appliances, software, data entry, and programming. Unions will thrive in industries where the work must be done locally: transportation, waste disposal, janitorial services, restaurants, hotels, schools, automotive repair, retail and wholesale distribution, and government administration.

AND MY CAREER?

ALL SOCIETY IS AFFECTED by the displacement of labor as we can now manufacture more with proportionately less labor. Since the end of World War II, every business recession has left the nation with a higher level of "natural unemployment" than the previous cycle. Each time we have experienced more automation, mechanization, and now computerization, than before. Robots are displacing humans.

In many industries worldwide, real wages have declined. The governments of France, Britain, Germany, and Canada are now considering what was unthinkable only ten years ago—a four-day work week to give more people a turn at the few jobs left. And for the first time, recessions are affecting not just blue-collar jobs, but middle management and executive white-collar positions as well. Just when lifelong executives are reaching for the next rung in their career ladder, they find it missing. These are not recessionary-cycle changes, but systemic long-term ones striking the very core of our economy.

Many have simplified the future by reducing our future employment to mere slogans: "Manufacturing jobs will dry up." "The future belongs to the information worker!" But this misses the point. Information jobs such as telephone operator, receptionist, secretary, stenographer, bookkeeper, and clerk will all disappear because they can be automated. On the other hand, even though manufacturing labor is being displaced by technology, those specializing in process flow, design, and synthetic materials will be in great demand precisely because they *cannot* (yet) be automated. But the threshold of automation and intelligent systems is advancing so rapidly that professions like general doctors, family lawyers, grade-school teachers *may*, in time, be practically automated. It is not enough to say that the future is in "information."

The only certainty is that the world beyond the turn of the century will be unrecognizable to those living today. Technology is again freeing us from routine and repetitive tasks, especially in manufacturing, but not only there. In twenty years the classified job listings will sport titles like "cyborg technician," "fusion engineer," "genetic biochemist," "software talent agent." In the future, labor, not altogether obsolete, will shift to areas difficult to automate.

To keep ahead of advancing technology, people entering the job market will, on average, change *careers* (not just jobs) three to four times during a lifetime. The trick will be to get into each particular specialization early enough to get the longest possible ride on each wave. Individuals will no longer undergo early-life education and then work, but will need lifelong education mingled with work.

The growth jobs will be those that are difficult to automate, where a human touch is needed, or where technology is a tool for the worker rather than a replacement.

The biggest areas of growth center on three types of people. The first group will *use and develop technology* instead of being displaced by it. It comprises the software developers and computer graphic artists who bring functional glitz to a product; the mechanical engineers, industrial designers, and material specialists who give new products their function, shape, and form; and the operations research people who fine-tune automated processes.

The second growth group will *respond to fundamental demographic shifts* in industrialized countries. Dual-worker households will need chefs to feed them. The swelling number of late-marrying couples will turn to fertility doctors to conceive. A rising tide of weekend athletes and our increasingly aging population will enlist armies of physical therapists and health care workers.

The third growth group will *help society's organizations adapt* to new and seemingly absurd operating rules—management consultants, human resource specialists, international lawyers and bankruptcy lawyers, environmental engineers, and, alas, government administrators.

The world will not be *unem*ployed but rather *rede*ployed, and there will be jobs for those offering needed talents and possessing extraordinary skill. Through automation, the few will do the work for the many. While certain skills will be in great demand, labor of the manual or repetitive kind will no longer be a constraint on creating wealth. It is just too easy to automate, and a growing number of global hands are competing for a dwindling list of manual tasks. The global economy makes this fact universal now; raw labor is no longer a limiting factor in the creation of wealth.

Next we turn to capital.

4

SYMBOLIC CAPITAL

CHARLES DEBOIS WAS JUST drying off from a shower when his E-mail colleague in Bangkok buzzed that Pagan Lumber in northern Thailand would receive permission within forty-five minutes to clear hardwood from the remote northern jungles. Charles put on his bathrobe and sat down at his desk computer to purchase "future options" on Pagan covering 300,000 shares. A few minutes later, the transaction was done.

Over coffee and danish, he scanned a database of patent applications in Argentina, which led him to a doctor in Argentina who was about to announce the discovery of a certain plant from the pampas whose genetic material was ideal for creating more drought-resistant cereal crops. Charles immediately set to work to sell half his position in Pagan and buy positions in arid farmland in Texas, Ethiopia, and Bolivia. By noon, he had sold everything and bought heavily into Filipino pesos and Korean won. His computer told him that his portfolio had already gone up 3 percent for the day, and he hadn't even had lunch yet.

——

The board meeting had just adjourned for lunch and Michelle Geldheim sprinted off to her office to arrange financing for the $100 million plant expansion in Kentucky. After analyzing the numbers for twenty minutes, Michelle set things in motion.

She first logged into the public money network and made direct contact with a Swedish pension fund looking to invest $60 million in a ten-year high-yield bond. She then tapped into the company computer to spin off their Idaho injection-molding facility for $40 million to a related company in Malaysia that had solicited ready-made North American capacity. Because detailed information about both transactions was so readily available, they were both completed within a half hour.

As she walked back into the boardroom and waited for the board members to reassemble, she thought back a few decades to the late 1990s. The same transactions would have taken months to arrange and would have involved extraordinary middleman fees to banks and stockbrokers. Electronic data systems now made the same complex transactions possible in less than an hour, with practically no transaction fees.

———

Don Stasis, the production manager, was in his office making related arrangements on the global capital markets.

In building the new plant, the board was concerned about the potential rising costs of purchased materials—new plastic resins, certain integrated-circuit components, and recyclable packing materials—even before it got into operation. If that happened, it could spell disaster for the venture.

Don knew the solution was in the global capital market. He estimated the amounts of materials they would be purchasing during the next three years. By tapping into a futures market, he was able to guarantee future prices over the next three years of everything from electricity to steel and labor. Now, whatever happened in the world economy, as long as his plant shipped products, his production costs were locked in.

———

Welcome to the Age of Digital Capital. Over the next twenty years, we will witness an unprecedented revolution in the world's capital markets. The world's stock exchanges, currency trading, financial centers, banks and investment houses, insurance companies and pension funds will all become so electronically intertwined that they will effectively merge into a single organism without a center. Yet they will be engaged in a torrent of free-flowing global capital of such magnitude that the very nature of capital will never be the same.

Capital will flow so effortlessly across national borders that the world will effectively have one currency. The global integration of banks will ensure that interest rates between countries will be no different from those in neighboring cities today. The various world stock markets will merge into a web of automated trading, enabling a home investor in Detroit, Michigan, to research, buy, and sell stock in a little-known garment manufacturer somewhere far off in central China as easily as home-town General Motors. Further, the public reporting of companies will have a universal format making comparisons easier. The world's capital will be one.

Originally, *capital* was defined as any physical item used to produce things—hoes and hammers, horses and carriages, textile mills and inventory. Classical economists have long taught that capital, labor, and raw materials form the tripod upon which all wealth is built. Over time, the term *capital* has expanded to include any form of wealth or asset—money, stocks, real estate investments—that could be used to accumulate more wealth.

Today, the shift away from the *physical thing* to the *investment* in the physical thing has become so complete that we've lost our connection to the underlying object. Capital is no longer a physical thing but ethereal numbers that show up on an accountant's balance sheet or as electronic blips on a computer screen. Ownership in real estate can be converted into liquid cash, then into an airplane or boat with just a few signatures. Ownership of a piece of Exxon can be converted into a piece of IBM in microseconds.

Digital capital has strange properties. Electronic transfers allow today's capital to be moved from place to place so fast that it flies around the world several times in a day. The money float allows checks to be sent to creditors, with funds wired into the account just before the check clears—effectively allowing the same capital to be several places at once. Credit cards and international letters of credit even allow parties to get paid before the money is sent.

Governments are almost powerless over the flow of capital. When wishing to go undetected, it passes instantly and silently through the fabric of society. Capital is what electronic symbols define it to be, high tech and *transnational,* with a power beyond anyone's imagination.

CAPITAL, CAPITAL EVERYWHERE

IN AN ERA OF EVER-INCREASING physical global trade, the flow of currency through the world's exchange markets is growing faster still. More currency moves in one day than the amount of world trade in two months. Each day, $600 billion is changed from one type of currency to another—well over $100,000 per year, per family worldwide (compared to global income per capita of under $4,000). More than a trillion dollars a week flow through money-exchange houses in London, New York, and Tokyo, of which only a tiny fraction is related to the shipment of any physical product.

Cross-border stock transactions are multiplying as American, European, and Japanese investors frantically invest in each other's countries twenty times more than in the early 1980s. By 1990 foreigners controlled one in ten American manufacturing workers. And by 1993 American investments abroad had risen to $130 billion a year—over $1,340 per US household, and ten times the $13 billion invested abroad only five years earlier. The scale of global investments is exploding.

The shift to international investments is also reflected in the holdings of the world's biggest accumulators of capital: the pension funds, insurance companies, and mutual funds. From 1981 to 1991, British pension funds more than doubled their foreign holdings, American funds quadrupled, and Japanese ones increased sixteenfold.

Global capital is changing hands at a frenetic rate, partly because there is too much of it. During the Industrial Age, every automobile, shirt, and toy produced has had its attendant profits reinvested in ever-more improved technologies generating yet more wealth. Every drop of gasoline consumed has had profits rippling back to its supplier and into the global economy to create yet more riches. Every paycheck deposited in banks has been recycled to make still more capital. Countless individuals, corporations, pension funds, and insurance companies in Europe, Asia, and the Americas have accumulated unprecedented *trillions* of dollars—each dollar looking for the highest return. There has never been as much capital looking for investments as now.

And investment opportunities abound. Exotic lands like East Asia, Latin America, and elsewhere are offering double or triple the growth rates of Europe and North America. This has invited capital flows into once-shunned stock markets at unprecedented levels.

As their economies blossom, Thailand, Hong Kong, Malaysia, the Philippines, and Turkey have stock markets that now enjoy triple-digit percentage increases. International mutual funds set up in industrialized countries to seek out the top investments are often two to eight times more profitable than local markets. In the 1980s, $10,000 reinvested each year in the best worldwide markets would have returned $1.4 million by the end of the decade, compared to only $35,000 if invested in the United States.

Since Second World° countries produce 40 percent of the world's GNP but have only 7 percent of the world's stock values, more capital will be traveling abroad until an equilibrium is reached. We have only seen the tip of the global-capital iceberg.

°In the late 1950s, the term *Third World* came into our vocabulary to differentiate the poorest countries from rich capitalist nations and heavy industrialized communist states. Since the fall of world communism, only two groups remain. The term *Second World* in this book refers to the parts of the world's population that are economically underdeveloped, with little prospect for improvement. *First World* refers to the economically richer and technologically proficient people of the world. We enter the twenty-first century with a two-part world, a reality whose impact we will return to later.

FRICTIONLESS PIPELINES

AS GLOBAL CAPITAL GROWS, global banks—the pipelines through which capital flows—wield enormous power. Many have become so large as to outstrip the national treasuries of many countries. Each of the top five global banks alone has more assets than the government reserves (including gold) of the United States, Japan, and Germany combined. These financial giants are redefining banking and greatly facilitating our shift into a global free-flow of capital.

With 2,200 overseas offices in eighty-nine countries, Citicorp is the most far-flung bank in the world. With 20 million customer accounts, it also has the greatest number of clients, scattered throughout Europe, Asia, North America, and the expanding economies of the Second World.

Only a decade ago, its customers in Hong Kong or Australia could only get local services; going from one branch office to another was almost like changing banks. Then Citi spent a billion dollars on state-of-the-art computer and telecommunications equipment and melded thousands of branch offices in scores of countries into a single bank. Citicorp had gone global.

Today any terminal in the bank can scour a hundred countries for the best interest and exchange rates and the best combination of currencies, taking local tax codes into account. Corporations can collect bills from customers abroad because the receivable can be sold to Citi, which has the global clout and local muscle to make buyers pay up. Ten years earlier, the technology to operate on such a scale simply did not exist.

Citi's new global services are for corporations and individual clients as well. Its best customers receive multicurrency accounts enabling them to write or cash checks in any currency. Its 2 million credit cards are valid all over the world, no matter where the holder lives or how he or she is billed. Citi's 2,000 ATM machines worldwide are tied into a single network, allowing a tourist in Buenos Aires to tap into account balances in New York or Paris. Home banking terminals have leveraged Citi's services even further: they bring the services of a mega-bank into every home or office equipped with a phone line.

Competitive pressures are forcing banks to follow Citi's lead and integrate branch offices into a single whole. Banks are also exchanging data with one another through credit card or ATM transactions, check clearinghouses, and wire transfers. They will soon share the same global regulations. In the end, while the logos on the bank doors will vary, they will all have effectively merged into a single organism.

REDEFINING WALL STREET

THE SAME FORCES ARE also transforming the world's stock exchanges and financial centers. Until recently, the various national stock exchanges had evolved surprisingly little since the first gathering of Dutch merchants in front of the Van der Buerse home in the thirteenth century. Five centuries later, two dozen stockbrokers met under a buttonwood tree on lower Wall Street in much the same fashion. Over time, that meeting place became the world's largest marketplace for securities, the New York Stock Exchange (NYSE).

Today, the tree is gone but the trade is conducted in ways similar to the Van der Buerse's, with buyers and sellers running, crowding together, raising hands, frantically yelling to get their order entered in the books. These procedures are followed in Paris, Brussels, Copenhagen, Stockholm, Zürich, Tokyo, and elsewhere.

Over the next twenty years, a radical transformation will occur in how sellers find buyers in the Placeless Society. As centers are no longer needed, stock markets as we have known them will become extinct. The reasons, of course, are computers, telecommunications, overnight couriers—and the sun. In a global economy, the sun never sets. As investors hold an increasing proportion of their portfolios in foreign companies, they are no longer willing to wait until foreign stock exchanges open in order to buy or sell. Because of different time zones, a seller in Bonn would have to wait until midafternoon before the NYSE even opened for business.

The future belongs to Fourth Dimension clearinghouses like the NASDAQ, which, unlike a physical stock exchange in one location, are networks of brokerages connected electronically. Their operations are simultaneously accessible by anyone in the world. Although the NASDAQ is much younger than the NYSE, it already enjoys the same share volume.

Yet other avenues of trading are already developing. Nadoff, Instinet, Posit, Transvik, and other systems execute trades on an automated basis. And the big brokerage firms like Merrill Lynch match buyers with sellers in-house, linking up to other networks as needed. These automated systems will necessarily become interlinked and competitive, bringing transaction costs to near zero. Thus the world's stock markets will have merged into a twenty-four-hour auction with automated middlemen. Liquidity, geographic scope, and transaction volumes will never have been greater.

The automation of global capital flows will make financial "centers" obsolete. Almost everyone in the global web has access to the same information and can effect the same transactions. Hence the concentrated power of London, New York, and Tokyo may be reduced to mere processing nodes in a ubiquitous network.

London, the world's premier financial center, has more international banks and orchestrates more international financial transactions than any other city. Yet the decentralization caused by digital capital is rapidly eroding its preeminence; power is diffusing to offices and computer terminals everywhere. The world no longer needs a financial "center."

Nor does the world need banks as we have known them. Banks once supplied the crucial missing link between providers of capital (depositors) and borrowers. In the Age of Everything-Everywhere, a borrower no longer needs the bank to find the cash. With computerization, large corporations go directly to cash-rich insurance companies and pension funds when they need to borrow cash, eliminating the need for middlemen. Large institutional investors set up computerized networks, look for ways to swap shares among themselves, and bypass the stockbrokers altogether.

Eager to keep their jobs, investment bankers are crafting new types of products to sell: "designer" securities, an emerging form of investment certificate. By bundling various stocks, bonds, and options, the new gurus are creating a hybrid of synthetic securities that track the Dow Jones Industrials, the dollar-yen exchange rate, interest rates, future popcorn prices, and so on. This new species of digital capital is so totally symbolic and abstract in nature—with so little relation to the physical world—that they are called *derivatives*.

Derivatives may be abstract, but their power is very real.

In September 1992, a Hungarian-born speculator, George Soros, demonstrated the power of derivatives to the whole world. Soros and the rest of the financial community knew that the values of one European currency against another were locked in by government treaties. In order to prop up their currencies, some countries like Britain and Italy had to buy on the open market to keep currency values up. Soros and his friends knew that the central banks of Britain and Italy were about to go bust. Once they did, there would be a dramatic realignment of currency exchange rates.

Using computers, Soros the Clever designed derivatives that would enable him to tie up billions of dollars of currency with just a few million dollars invested. His actions put so much pressure on the currency markets that the central banks had to give up any efforts to prevent a currency crash. The result: $1.5 *billion* in profits for Soros in just a few hours, and European central banks left in tatters.

Without derivatives, it would have been almost impossible for an individual to play currency poker on such a large scale.

In the twenty-first century, derivatives will become so commonplace that companies and individuals will routinely use them to "lock in" prices for commodities as diverse as real estate, labor and waste disposal, gasoline and hotels. They will become so sophisticated that computers will symbolically mix, match, and recombine various financial "instruments" to such an extent that the value of the symbolic capital created will match (or offset) the future value of almost anything in the world.

Derivatives serve as a striking example of our detachment from *physical* capital in favor of *symbolic* capital. Derivatives have no underlying physical nature, but are merely complex combinations of symbols. Each symbol represents some price, obligation, or promise to pay: here the promise to buy soybeans at price x, there an agreement to sell Japanese yen at not more than y, again an agreement to lend money at some set future rate z. These symbols, and a hundred variables like them, are added, substituted, and multiplied by high-speed computers in complex algorithms to create yet other symbols, perhaps as the input in someone else's derivatives. The result is a dizzying array of investments that have little basis in the physical world.

This shift would have been impossible before the 1980s, when the technology wasn't yet in place. The computer revolution has utterly transformed the nature of capital and the role of investment houses: in 1992, almost half of Goldman, Sachs's $1 billion trading profits came from derivatives.

NATIONS OUT OF CONTROL

BUT FAR MORE HAS changed than the nature of capital or the institutions that manage it. At stake is the very role of the nation-state. This is an era in which capital has become so fluid and omnipresent that it can no longer be controlled by individual countries. When capital represented physical things (tractors or inventory), it could be stopped at the border. But when capital is conveyed in electrical impulses, borders become meaningless. For a capitalist in the Age of Everything-Everywhere, nation-states no longer exist.

John Maynard Keynes argued in 1936 that a government could fine-tune its economy by modulating its levels of taxing and spending. Later the monetarists further argued that governments could control their economies by regulating the interest rate and money supply. For the last thirty years, Keynesianism and monetarism were the two levers used by industrialized economies to control their expansion.

Fiscal and monetary policies worked somewhat in the 1960s and 1970s when national economies were still closed systems. In the

Placeless Society, they no longer work, and both Keynesianism and monetarism are obsolete. The enemy, of course, is digital capital.

Today when the American government wants to change interest rates to regulate its economy, it first goes, with hat in hand, to the Group of Seven (G7) to get them to do the same. If the United States lowers interest rates unilaterally, the cheap money is snapped up in the United States and lent abroad, where it can earn a greater return. It no longer stays put.

With digital capital, a nation operating in the world is like a city run in a national setting. A city cannot effectively stimulate its local economy by deficit spending or by lending cheap money to downtown national banks. Yet that is exactly what nations still attempt to do. The finance ministers and central bankers do not realize that the Placeless Society offers too many leaks. Digital capital has taken the wind out of governments' fiscal and monetary policies.

The fluidity of digital capital is also a problem for poor countries. Economists estimate that half the cash lent to them in the 1980s left quickly by telex or suitcase as their citizens transferred billions of dollars to other countries bidding higher returns. Digital capital, like a rope, must be pulled, never pushed; it can be attracted, but never shoved into place. Regional development economists now realize that getting foreign aid is not sufficient; they must first make their national policies conducive to attracting and holding the investment. Global capital has no flag. Infinitely liquid, it flows to the highest bidder with laser speed.

BUSINESS WITH NO MONEY DOWN

WHILE THE PLACELESS SOCIETY enables capital to move at unprecedented speed and in prodigious amounts, it also brings with it a new irony: less capital is needed. From the start of the Industrial Revolution through the middle of the twentieth century, it was largely the sparse supply of capital that limited the number of would-be entrepreneurs. A manufacturing plant, whether a textile mill in 1850 or an automobile plant in 1950, required great investment in land, building, and equipment before the first unit of output could be assembled. That wealth was required to make wealth created a permanent class structure in society that, more than anything else, was the genesis of the Marxist rebellion that later swept half the world.

Entrepreneurs without capital can bypass that situation today: they can build businesses with just ideas. They no longer have to own the tools of production to have access to them. The major airlines don't *own* the planes they fly anymore; they lease them using day-to-day cash receipts for payment. The Sears delivery vans cruising the streets of Chicago belong to Ryder Truck Rental, which leases them with maintenance, insurance, and uniformed drivers. In the United States, a third of all new capital equipment is acquired through leasing.

Many high-growth companies in the Silicon Valley have accessed top-of-the-line production equipment through a complex maze of joint ventures and subcontracts: the circuit boards are made in Singapore, the cases in Taiwan, and the final pieces assembled in Mexico. Even the R&D, marketing, distribution, legal, and accounting are often subcontracted. Thus, multimillion-dollar enterprises are operated by just a few employees armed with telephones and fax machines, a file cabinet full of contracts, and very little capital investment.

Even when companies choose to own machinery, technology enables them to produce more with less-expensive equipment. We all know that low-cost photocopiers have replaced expensive lithographic presses, and that the cost of fax machines, computers, and cellular telephones is plummeting. The modern mini-steel mills produce at a fraction of the cost of their capital-intensive predecessors. The newer automobile plants built by the Japanese in the United States reach a profit at a much lower level of production than their older-technology competitors. The cost of nearly every industrial machine goes down each year vis-à-vis its performance.

Manufacturing plants also are able to coordinate with customers, suppliers, and themselves with such precision that less capital is tied up in inventory. Raw materials arrive "just in time" from suppliers before being cut, drilled, poured, polished, boxed, and sent immediately to customers, who pay electronically. By managing accounts payable and receivable, some manufacturers even collect from customers before their own bills are due to suppliers. In the Placeless Society, capital is no longer a prerequisite to begin, operate, and expand a profitable, thriving business.

WHERE DO I INVEST?

WHAT DOES THE ADVENT of placeless capital mean for the individual investor?

A few decades ago, investors were largely restricted to investments in their home countries. Information was scarce, investments were hard to find, currencies fluctuated too much, and transaction costs were prohibitively high. Global investing was too risky.

Today, however, the smart investor discovers that the world has completely flip-flopped: it is *less* risky to invest globally than nationally. Communication and transaction costs have plummeted, and currency fluctuations can be "hedged." Most important, the global investor has more investment options than his or her national counterpart, which translates into lower risk. Then, since the business cycles of the various economies of the world are not yet synchronized, the global investor enjoys business-cycle diversification not found within a single country.

Besides lower potential risks, investors from rich economies have an "insider's" advantage. They know the explosive growth of fast-food franchises and photocopy stores. They understand how consumer electronics are used, how metro systems are needed to eliminate traffic congestion, and how cable television transforms lives. To invest in developing economies is like going back ten years and enjoying perfect foresight about which horses are likely to win.

Still, global investors cannot act blindly; they need to tackle foreign accounting and tax laws as well as local political and economic shifts. Many stock markets are not yet fully in the Fourth Dimension; stocks are illiquid and buyers not always forthcoming. Transfers through the physical exchange of paper certificates may take weeks, or longer. So, although Mexico, Thailand, Singapore, Malaysia, Portugal, China, and others may be on tremendous growth curves, modern investors need to adapt to their less-than-modern business infrastructures.

Many investors in the United States have discovered a simple way to invest internationally, in everything—from Mitsubishi and Deutsche Bank to Teléfonos de Mexico—through any of 1,400 world-class companies traded on US exchanges as American Depository Receipts (ADRs). The ADR certificates represent ownership of a pool of shares of foreign-based corporations that are held in bank vaults. The bank, in turn, takes care of dividend distributions, foreign-currency conversions, foreign taxes, and paperwork. The trading of ADRs has now topped $200 billion a year; with fifteen new companies listed each month, the volume has been doubling every two years for the past decade.

Global investors may also buy into a mutual fund that offers a cocktail of several stocks lumped together. Operated for a small fee by professional fund managers, mutual funds absorb the still-present idiosyncrasies of global investing. They benefit from the extraordinary investment opportunity available in areas of rapid growth, and, like ADRs, translate remote-country investment opportunities into all the advantages of digital capital transacted in a flash.

International mutual funds come in several flavors to suit the investor's tastes: there are country funds like the "German fund" or the "Chilean fund"; regional funds, which group related countries together, as in the "European fund," the "Asian fund," or the "Latin America" fund; and "global funds," which target the best of the planet.

The Placeless Society has utterly transformed the nature of capital, reducing it to symbols detached from any physical object. Without a home, without a flag, it pulses through the veins of a newly omnipresent world.

In this new world, capital has never been more plentiful. Yet, especially in manufacturing, never has so little investment been needed to produce so much. Our predecessors would not recognize the face of capital today.

Labor has changed in a similar way. People move freely, hopping by a hemisphere at a time; so does the fruit of their labor, by ship, jet, or satellite, oblivious of national boundaries. And the work itself has become a world traveler as it soars from place to place in search of cheaper labor markets.

Next, we turn to the third pillar of classical wealth: raw materials.

5

UBIQUITOUS RESOURCES

THE AFTERNOON SKY was clear and bright, and the air, crisp. Warm inside the car, Todd Lynx smiled at his girlfriend. He was ready to show Tanya what he could do. This was Nanoose Bay's last traffic signal traveling north, and ahead was the wide-open shoreline drive up Highway 19.

He checked the rearview mirror one more time to make sure no one was watching. The glare from the yellow light told him he was next. At green, he snapped his foot to the pedal, which punched him and Tanya back into their vinyl bucket seats. In 3.2 seconds, he was at 60 miles per hour; within 6.8 seconds, he had reached 120 and was still accelerating. The side windows became a blur; only the road in front of them was discernible.

Inside the car was silence, almost as if the car were thrust forward by some invisible force. Todd calmly whispered "drive automatic" to let the on-board computer anticipate the curves so he could chat more freely with Tanya. Within 45 seconds, the console buzzed that he'd been spotted by the police. The system shut itself down.

Todd's car had almost no metal in it. Fashioned from clay into high-temperature ceramics, the engine needed no radiator or lubricant. It burned fuel at such a high temperature that it got 100 miles per gallon with scarcely any pollution. The electrical cabling, alternator, and motors were made from superconducting ceramics. The components in the on-board computer were silicon fashioned from beach sand. The frame, body, and tires were composite polymers fashioned from corn husks, raw sewage, and carbon fibers. Thanks to these materials, the car was fast, light, gasoline efficient, and crash resistant. Such a specimen didn't exist fifteen years earlier.

In a few years, copper, steel, tin, lead—eventually even oil—will likely be eclipsed by technologies making them as obsolete as horseshoes, rubber plants, and sailing ships are today. Some metal prices may drop so low that exporting countries in the Second World will have nothing left to sell to other nations.

Entering the Fourth Dimension, we are on the edge of a revolution that will redefine what constitutes "raw materials."

KANSAS CRUDE AND MAINE CANE

DRAMATIC CHANGES HAVE already occurred in raw materials, because proximity to the supplies of these materials is no longer the advantage it once was.

When the US automotive industry was born in the early twentieth century, automobile engines, frames, and bodies were made almost 100 percent of steel. Steel, in turn, was made from various ferro-alloy metals and coal, which were found in abundance around the Great Lakes. Detroit, strategically situated like a modern-day Constantinople, became the natural center of the industry. Making cars elsewhere without the rich Detroit telephone book of suppliers would bring a "natural" disadvantage. Besides, transportation constraints locked everything firmly in place.

But modern transportation technology is gradually changing that. GM's Saturn plant in Spring Hill, Tennessee, Toyota in Georgetown and Lexington, Kentucky, and a joint venture with GM in Fremont, California, attest to the fact that proximity to raw materials is irrelevant to manufacturing in the Placeless Society.

Our sophisticated transportation system—container trucks that can piggyback on barges and trains, nonstop interstate highways, squadrons of air-cargo freighters, and low-cost, door-to-door overnight delivery services—have all acted to break factories free from their traditional servitude to place.

In the United States, lumber is no more expensive in the deserts of Texas than in the forests of the Pacific Northwest. Oil costs the same in Kansas, Texas, or Alaska, and cane sugar is no cheaper in Hawaii than in Maine. Transportation costs are now so low that place no longer determines where raw materials are dear.

The omnipresence of raw materials internationally is most striking in Japan, a crowded place void of mineral or oil wealth, yet one of the top manufacturing countries in the world. Raw materials in Japan cost almost the same as in the countries that supply them. A mere dollar will transport a barrel of petroleum from Saudi Arabia to Tokyo, and lumber and sulfur are shipped from Vancouver to Tokyo for just a penny a pound.

GOLDEN DIRT

IN THE 1960s AND 1970S, the experts thought we would soon exhaust the Earth's resources and our own future, as both population and consumption of material goods kept rising.

On the exhaustion of minerals, the gurus could not have been more mistaken: raw materials today are more plentiful than ever before. From 1950 to 1990, taking inflation into account, the global commodity prices of energy dropped by 46 percent; minerals, 48 percent; lumber, 41 percent; and food, 74 percent. And during this same period, the known reserves of oil, gas, coal, and other minerals increased. What happened is technology.

In reality, the earth is rich in resources; the problem is getting them out. For instance, a cubic mile of backyard dirt contains enough aluminum to make a solid cube over 2,300 feet on each edge, and nearly half again as much pure magnesium. As for "rare" strategic metals, with the dirt left over one could fashion six Great Pyramids of Giza of pure titanium, and have enough pure cobalt left over to exceed the weight of 100,000 midsized automobiles. Every cubic mile of sea water contains over 18 pounds of gold, and four cubic feet of silver.

These metals, however, are useless unless they can be economically extracted from the dirt or sea water in which they are found. Each year, technology provides new keys that allow us to unlock useful material from the pile of dirt upon which we live. An "ore" is only that which can be commercially exploited; in this sense, even as we consume resources, our body of useful ores continues to expand. What was useless mud before acquires new value.

In 1800, for example, the primary lamp oil came from whale oil; then in 1855 Benjamin Silliman distilled oil rock into kerosene, which provided a much brighter flame at a lower cost than whale oil. Because of his discovery, the black gunk that once had to be removed from farmland at great expense became a usable resource. Over time, we have dug ever-deeper oil wells and made tremendous strides in using seismographic echoes, gravity meters, and satellite data to track down elusive reserves. Each step has enlarged our reserves and lowered costs, despite our increasing consumption.

Another excellent example is gold. Until the 1950s, gold ore had to contain over half an ounce of gold per ton to make mining worthwhile. Today we mine ore at less than one-twentieth that concentration, considerably expanding our known reserves and the world's output. We are even learning how to process pure gold from pyrite, the legendary "fool's gold" that for centuries prospectors would toss aside. Scientists have discovered a bacteria that eats the sulfur and iron like so many termites, leaving behind a residue of concentrated gold dust.

Sulfur-eating bacteria may also be useful in converting acid-rain-producing high-sulfur coal into pure carbon cubes. In time, "biometallurgists" may develop designer bacteria to create rare metals from raw dirt, just as we use bacteria today to make cheese, beer, and yogurt from raw agricultural inputs.

DIAMONDS FROM PEANUT BUTTER

AS WE CONQUER NATURE'S bounty and extract the materials under our feet with greater ease, we need them less and less. Our most useful materials like iron, cement, and paper, or more recent ones like aluminum, ammonium, chlorine, and ethylene, have had their consumption per capita in the United States—*and* as a percentage of the GNP—level off or decrease. The same trends apply to all industrialized countries, primarily because manufactured goods are smaller and more compact.

In 1950 an average automobile used 30 pounds of copper; today it is less than 10 and dropping. A single 500-pound communications satellite does the same work as 300 million pounds of transoceanic telephone cables. By 1990 manufacturers of Coke cans had figured out a way to get 7,000 more cans out of each ton of metal than they could ten years earlier.

Moreover, a fundamental shift is taking place, away from raw materials found in nature to man-made ones. Humankind started with wood, stone, and iron as basic building blocks, but soon improved on nature by making blends. We mixed copper and tin to create a bronze harder than iron, and we mixed iron and carbon for still harder results. Each time, the end product was superior to any of the raw ingredients used alone.

The 1920s began the Plastics Age, which increased our independence from natural materials. Today the breadth of colors and strengths and the simplicity of injection manufacturing have turned plastics into the material of choice for toys, computers, refrigerators, cars, and countless other products. Synthetic materials have long ago surpassed their once-cheap image. Today they mean products that have higher durability, strength, and aesthetic appeal than ever imagined possible.

The revolution in material science is progressing so fast that raw materials will no longer be a constraint on manufacturing. We are leaving the "material" ages—the Stone Age, the Iron Age, the Bronze

Age, the Plastics Age—to enter an era we might best call the Dematerialized Age, one of high-value physical products manufactured out of almost nothing.

The world we are entering is filled with advanced ceramics so resilient that "pottery" coffee mugs could be slung against a stone wall and not so much as chip. Home appliances will be made from composites and laminates of microscopic fibers stronger than steel, making the appliances virtually indestructible. More amazing still, these exotic materials will be assembled from exotic blends of clay or burned carbon—even spent corn husks or municipal sewage. Scientists have even managed to make diamonds from peanut butter.

Over the past few decades, the list of new materials has become so extensive that we lose track of its significance. A new vocabulary of "raw materials" is born. Builders make windows of Plexiglas, insulators of Bakelite, and paint with latex and acrylics. We cook with Teflon pans on Formica countertops and clothe ourselves in Dacron, Lycra, Ultrasuede, and Gore-Tex. Our cars are assembled from fiberglass bodies, Naugahyde upholstery, Thiokol gaskets, and soon, Lexan windshields. Our children listen to Mylar tapes and play with Plasticine modeling clay. Our sporting equipment and bulletproof vests are made of Spectra and Kevlar. Yet over the next few decades, this list is likely to expand a thousandfold.

By using supercomputers, scientists are now able to play with atoms, the building blocks of all materials. By altering the interatomic distances here, and adding a silicon or carbon atom there, "materialogists" are already creating new substances by rational design, rather than serendipity or expensive trial and error. Yet others are working on "biofabrication" techniques where the fundamental DNA codes in living tissue are altered to cause them to mass-produce highly complex materials from standard protein building blocks. Such notions were absolutely unthinkable just two decades ago.

HOT JETS AND FLOATING TRAINS

THE ABUNDANCE OF NEW "raw materials" in the next twenty years will completely revolutionize manufacturing and construction by making products more functional at less cost.

For example, a California group has proposed utilizing some state-of-the-art construction materials for a 450-foot bridge spanning San Diego's Interstate 5. These composite materials would be reinforced with carbon, plastic, and glass fibers. According to computer simulations, the bridge would weigh one-tenth as much as one made with concrete and steel and be more durable, easier to build, and more resistant to earthquakes. Others envision a 10-mile suspension bridge spanning the deep chasm that divides Africa from Western Europe, made with carbon fiber and epoxy, hexacelsian glass, and silicon carbide.

Researchers in Texas took molecules of standard natural gas and rearranged them into a thin coating of pure *diamond*. This could lead to scratch-free eyeglasses, low-friction coating for ball bearings, and never-dull razors. Other scientists have developed a translucent glass called aerogel that is only four times heavier than air yet can support its own weight hundreds of times over.

Aircraft manufacturers may yet obtain their El Dorado "unobtanium"—a mythical material with lilliputian weight, gargantuan strength, and an unreachable melting point. Japanese, European, and American scientists are working on a new generation of ceramics able to withstand up to 4,000 degrees Fahrenheit, a temperature that turns nearly all other materials into liquid. These ceramics will be used for the turbine blades of the new generation of jet engines. Such hyper-hot engines will be feather-weight, burn fuel more cleanly, and turn everyday hypersonic jet travel into reality. Aircraft designers will use composites and plastics to make the fuselage and wings so that, twenty years from now, the commercial jet will scarcely contain any metal at all.

Glass fibers, plastics, and ceramics are rendering copper wire obsolete. Fiber-optic cables made from these materials are replacing un-counted tons of copper telephone cabling beneath the streets of Man-hattan and in office buildings everywhere.

Even more revolutionary is the prospect of room-temperature superconducting ceramic materials—an idea thought impossible just five years ago—that may replace metal wires in high-voltage power transmission lines, electric motors, and computers. Unlike metals, su-perconductors conduct electricity with no resistance and no waste heat, thus making motors and transformers superefficient, microcir-cuits faster, and power distribution cheaper. By avoiding unnecessary electrical resistance, we will be able to make magnets so powerful that entire trains could be magnetically levitated, riding at 350 miles per hour and actually floating above the tracks.

THINGAMABOBS AND DOOHICKEYS

IF, IN THE LAST CENTURY, a world economist could have asked Alad-din's lamp for three wishes for humanity, the requests would certainly have been for the removal of the constraints on labor, capital, and raw materials—for their elimination opens the door to an unlimited sup-ply of material objects.

As we enter the Age of Everything-Everywhere, these wishes have been granted; an era of near-zero-cost manufacturing seems within our grasp.

We have seen that we can transport raw materials and track down minerals more easily. We can pluck individual atoms from minerals and reassemble them in any of a billion new configurations, each with a different, unique property. As a result, our new industrial society will be able to build its future with an abundance of raw materials.

The three factors of wealth—labor, capital, raw materials—are no longer important constraints in determining where or how wealth is created. These wealth-building components are needed less and less, and when used, they are available to everyone everywhere.

But as in many enchanted fables, a wish granted is a Faustian bargain received. Picture robotically controlled manufacturing plants that churn out a nonstop flow of plastic toys and paper cups, polluting cars and toxic herbicides, tin foil, cans, and plastic wrappers. Imagine the ability to level mountains and build row after row of low-cost deluxe estates in their place. Envision the unemployed masses drowning in a rising sea of *things*, of gadgets, devices, thingamabobs, and doohickeys.

Economic constraints are like nesting Russian *matryoshka* dolls: behind each barrier to wealth is another one, hidden from view until the first is cracked open. In the next chapter, we will unveil the two emerging constraints on wealth in the Placeless Society.

Part Three

THE NEW CHALLENGES

6

THE POLLUTION
ROADBLOCK

SAMMY GORONGE WAS EXCITED about his new job. He liked his title, vice president of purchasing, and the small manufacturing plant that assembled designer telephone systems felt like just the right place for him.

For his first assignment he was to track down a better price for the microphone assemblies. On his second day at work he received a call from a new supplier offering a price that could not be beat anywhere through the conventional databases. The product seemed to meet, or exceed, design specifications and could easily be dropped into the current models.

The new vice president approved the purchase, and within twelve hours, three truckloads arrived. Sammy examined some of the assemblies that were brought to his office. He okayed the shipment and payment was wired to the vendor.

The next day Sammy strolled by the receiving area, stopped for a closer look, and then panicked. He noticed that the parts had been delivered in Polyextrene shipping crates. This material had been banned the prior year by global agreement because it couldn't be recycled or remanufactured, and it didn't biodegrade.

Sammy never thought of checking the *packing* material before ac-

cepting the shipment. Now the vendor had already disconnected its
E-mail address and could not be tracked down. Tipped off that government environmental regulators were scheduled to show up at his
plant within two hours, Sammy wondered how to dispose of the materials promptly.

She was following a golden-red eucalyptus leaf spinning to the ground
outside the window when the doctor tapped her on the shoulder.
With one look into his eyes, she knew what he was going to say. The
mole on her daughter's shoulder was malignant melanoma.

He explained how it had metastasized, spinning cancerous cells
through her blood and lymphatic vessels. Doctors knew how to treat it
in the early stages, usually by removal with laser scalpels, but once it
reached this phase, there was little they could do. He gave her daughter one chance in ten of seeing her next birthday. She would have
turned twenty-three.

After the doctor left, Joan gazed out again at the trees outside. As
the sun above was filtering through, she wondered how sunbathing on
Bondi Beach, near Sydney, could kill her daughter and so many of her
friends. She knew that ozone depletion had something to do with it
and that the ozone problem had been caused by man-made chemicals
called CFCs. She also knew that CFCs were not banned throughout the
world; they were still produced in Second World outposts in Tibet,
Angola, and Libya and used to build lower-cost refrigerators for the
black market. Her daughter was being killed by unseen profiteers
many miles away.

Again and again, the same issues reappear in our newspapers: ozone
depletion, nuclear disposal problems, toxins in the water table, ship-
wrecked oil tankers, gridlocked cities, municipal air pollution, over-
stuffed landfills, acid rain, topsoil depletion, endangered species. . . .
Society *does* react to these problems, but seems unable to cope with
their sheer magnitude. Despite progress on several fronts, we are

backsliding on many others. Over the next twenty years, environmental constraints will prevent us from raising our standard of living. Our limitations will not come from an inability to *produce* more things, but from difficulties in *disposing* of them.

All over the world, our refuse has been expelled into the skies, our effluent channeled into the rivers, our sewage routed into the seas, and our toxins dumped into the soil, because the effects seemed out of sight and no tollkeeper cared. Our appetite for Nature's free gifts has been tremendous. Meanwhile our population keeps growing and our global wealth rising.

A CAR IN EVERY GARAGE

A THOUSAND YEARS AGO, the human population of the *world,* at 340 million, was less than today's Western Europe. By 1900 it had grown to 1.6 billion, little more than today's China. Today, spaceship Earth is host to nearly 6 billion people, and bloating at an additional quarter of a million people per day. Villages and towns are forever expanding, and metropolitan areas bursting.

In the past, the world population was kept in balance by an even ratio of fertility and mortality. In a typical village, the rapid pace of births each year was matched by an equal number of deaths. During most of history, adults were lucky if they lived beyond thirty years. Infectious and parasitic diseases killed a third to a half of children before they turned one.

A critical factor in our rapid growth today is that more of Earth's children are surviving. From the standpoint of medieval mystics, *we have conquered death.* We have developed magic potions in the forms of low-cost vaccines and medications, and all but eliminated the Black Death, polio, and smallpox. We have learned proper sanitation and hygiene and, despite pockets of humanity that are still malnourished, have made great strides in lowering food costs and distributing it worldwide—to levels never imagined only a few decades ago.

As the economies of different regions of the world are advancing, we also find that women are having fewer children—perhaps because they are becoming aware of other options for family and job, perhaps also because in rich cash economies, it is easier to save money than to have children who will care for you in old age. Everywhere, the effect of economic development has been met with a tempering in population growth. Most demographers believe that the world population may stabilize by the end of the twenty-first century at 10 to 12 *billion* souls—roughly twice that of today. And each one will be expecting his or her share of the world's riches.

As material *things* become easier to manufacture and move around the world, consumption rises. The average American of 1996 owns twice as many cars, drives nearly three times as far, and uses more than twenty times as much plastic as his or her counterpart in 1950. Today, two-thirds of American homes have air conditioning, microwaves, and videocassette recorders; nearly all have color televisions. Each Japanese is four times as likely to own a car, and eats nearly twice as much meat as forty years ago.

The Age of Consumption is not confined to rich countries. The fall of world communism has greatly accelerated the pace of global consumption as 350 million East Europeans are demanding Western-style goods and services. In the 1980s over a third of Chinese households acquired a color television, use of washing machines quadrupled, and the number of refrigerators grew twentyfold. In India and Latin America, an exploding middle class is being exposed to credit cards, compact disks, automobiles, and frozen dinners.

Manufactured goods proliferate, our global wealth rises, and our numbers swell while we buy, wear out, discard, and replace at a frenetic pace. In the last fifty years, we have produced, consumed, and disposed of more things than in all the rest of history combined.

SWIMMING IN SEWAGE

AS THE STREAM OF waste surges, we must seek creative solutions to the problem of disposal. Today's refuse sites are overflowing with soggy telephone books, plastic bottles, soiled diapers, Styrofoam cups, half-full cans of paint, cigarette butts, and spent batteries. The typical European or Japanese household produces about a ton of garbage a year, the average American family twice that, and the numbers keep growing each year.

Biology tells us that animals excrete bodily waste that is toxic to their organisms, and when the concentration of waste gets too high, the animals die. Society's garbage and pollution is its excrement, and no healthy community can thrive in its midst.*

While the quantity of refuse keeps growing, the number of landfills is fast dwindling. Around the globe, municipalities are running out of places where their trucks can dump trash. Sprawling megacities simply have no land left for garbage, and rural areas are mobilizing to block new dumpsites. In Germany, 50,000 landfill sites have been declared threats to the groundwater; in the United States, half the landfills have been shut down in the past decade.

The soil under our feet does not act as an infinite sponge absorbing unlimited quantities of society's waste, but rather as a river that carries toxins far away. Radioactive groundwater from Washington state's Hanford Nuclear Reservation flowed to the Columbia River and contaminated over 300 miles of beaches on its deadly voyage to the sea. Groundwater in Arizona contains high levels of toxic organic compounds from Mexico. Fishermen from Finland, Sweden, and Denmark are affected by heavy metals and other toxins from landfills

---

*The classic definition of *pollution* is limited to the discharge of harmful substances into the environment. In this book, we extend the definition to any action disrupting the natural environment. Pollution, therefore, includes felling forests, endangering species, and damming rivers. As we will see, environmental degradation will be such a pervasive issue over the next few decades that we now need a single word to embrace its full scope.

and sewage plants as far away as St. Petersburg and Warsaw.

The deleterious effects of consumerism also assaults the air we breathe. Since 1950, our global fleet of vehicles has increased tenfold, and will double yet again over the next two to three decades. Scattered across the world, waste incinerators and industrial processes spew deadly toxins like beryllium, benzene, cadmium, and mercury into the sky.

Air pollution has become an inescapable fact of life from Tokyo to Los Angeles to Bombay. We may soon see trendy "designer" protective masks on people's faces on high smog days. In Mexico City, the life-threatening smog once prompted entrepreneurs to consider installing coin-operated oxygen stations to help pedestrians make it to the next block. In megacities around the globe, eyes and throats burn, and fancy skyscrapers disappear deep in the gray-brown haze.

RADIOACTIVE MILK

NEVER BEFORE HAVE humans defiled their water, air, and soil at such a rapid pace, or concocted such exotic and destructive chemicals. As global capital and technology help to accelerate per-capita consumption in the Second World, pollution will rise to a screaming crescendo. Already, *pollution has become placeless,* affecting everyone on the planet. We can no longer hide waste in isolated spots without its hideous effects leaking out into the water and air. Our garbage has become too toxic and its quantities too great. We've entered the Age of Global Pollution.

Just look at Chernobyl. The nuclear reactor that exploded in 1986 spewed fifty tons of radioactive debris into the air and rendered vast tracks of land uninhabitable for decades, perhaps centuries. The Soviet government tried to keep the disaster a secret, but didn't succeed.

Within forty-eight hours of the explosion, nuclear-detection alarms were screaming in nuclear plants across Sweden. Soon the radioactive death cloud had silently fallen on vegetable farms and schoolchildren throughout Scandinavia, Poland, the former Czechoslovakia, and Germany, where background radiation shot up a hundredfold or more. Thousands of tons of radioactive dried milk and beef products were sent to unwitting buyers in Egypt, Brazil, and elsewhere in the Second World. It is estimated that over the next few decades, more than 25,000 people, including a thousand in the United States, will perish from leukemia and other cancers. Chernobyl holds the sad privilege of belonging to the Placeless Society.

But it does not stand alone. Pesticides—a by-product of our "efficiency" in food production—are affecting our food supply. Every year the earth swallows 2.5 million tons of pesticides, roughly one pound for every person on the planet. In the United States, their use since 1945 has increased tenfold overall, and a thousandfold in corn fields. As costs come down and the world population swells, this trend will continue.

Where do all the pesticides go? They do not just "disappear." As with toxins from landfills, much is washed into rivers, lakes, and oceans—weakening species in its path. Another portion is washed into our soil, causing contamination in one out of ten US public drinking water wells. More than a third of the US food supply today tests positive for pesticides—and that only includes the few for which we know how to test.

The most toxic ones have been banned in several countries, but they are used so pervasively that they end up on our plates anyway. Look at chlordane and heptachlor, two carcinogenic pesticides that move freely to many points on the earth. After they were banned in the United States, the Memphis-based manufacturer, Velsicol Chemical Corporation, continued to export them. The two chemicals turn up, like global travelers, in imported fish from Norway, red chilies from Thailand, squash from Mexico, rice from Pakistan, and mushrooms from France. Like a migratory bird flying back to its "home" nest, these chemicals have come full circle.

THE NEW AIR

IN 1974 RESEARCHERS realized that chlorofluorocarbons (CFCs)—a man-made chemical widely used in refrigerators, aerosol cans, and circuit-board fabrication—could have a destructive impact on the upper atmosphere. Their theory was that CFCs destroy ozone, thereby letting more ultraviolet light reach the earth. Increased UV rays, in turn, cause sunburns, skin cancer, cataracts, crop damage, and may affect the world's forests, plankton, and weather patterns. Throughout much of the 1970s and 1980s, the world manufactured over 5 million pounds of this chemical each day, much of which will continue to ooze into the atmosphere for decades to come.

The problem is advancing more quickly than anyone imagined: the gaping ozone "hole" over Antarctica is expanding each year, and wide gashes have appeared over northern Europe and Canada. In Australia, the ozone depletion has created a national campaign to keep people indoors during the day and have them wear long-sleeved shirts and pants at the beach. Two-thirds of Australians are likely to develop at least one form of skin cancer. Australia may be the harbinger of the future for the rest of the world's population.

Related to ozone depletion is the "greenhouse" effect. Just as glass in a garden greenhouse traps heat from the sun, certain gases in the atmosphere act like a blanket to hold heat on the earth; carbon dioxide helps retain heat better than other gases.

In this century, we have been burning fossil fuels at an escalating rate, causing the level of greenhouse gases to rise by 50 percent. The amount of these gases is likely to double by 2050 as the population grows and the Second World develops.

So global temperature will increase. While we don't fully understand the precise effect of temperature on weather patterns, we know that even the tiniest fluctuations cause dramatic changes in world climate. This scenario would be apocalyptic for much of the world—but not because of the temperature change itself (the world climate has been wildly cyclical over the past billion years). It is the *pace* of the change that would deliver the wallop. This time, the temperature shift could be ten to fifty times faster than anything the world has seen before.

We may get heat waves, droughts, flooding, hurricanes, and storms of unprecedented force. The droughts that have plagued parts of Africa and the Americas over the past decade may be just a hint of more to come. Breadbaskets such as the Ukraine or the American Midwest could become parched desert outposts, endangered species would be pushed over the edge into extinction, century-old forests would wither.

As the polar ice melts, the sea level may rise 5 to 7 feet over the next several decades. It could climb 20 feet if the west Antarctic sheet gives way—forever drowning coastal cities like New Orleans, Bangkok, Venice, and subjecting hundreds more to seasonal flooding. In Bangladesh and Egypt, tens of millions of people would be uprooted, and island-nations like the Maldives, or resorts like the Florida Keys, would cease to exist.

LIMITS TO POWER

IT IS THE Pollution Barrier, too, that limits our energy resources. Ours is a problem of disposal, not production.

Over the past century, the real cost of energy has declined, despite the tripling of world population and a virtual explosion in economic output. The quantity of fossil fuels buried beneath the earth is far greater than anyone could have anticipated. We have developed sophisticated technologies for locating fossil fuels, for drilling and pumping. While we occasionally lament the shortage of cheap liquid petroleum, we forget that they represent only a drop in the bucket compared to incredibly vast coal (and gas) reserves in America, China, Russia, the Ukraine, and elsewhere that alone could conceivably power the world's growth for centuries to come. Emerging technologies are finding ways to convert coal into gas or liquid forms that are more convenient for commercial applications, or even converting it directly into electricity in exotic fuel-cell soups.

We also create energy from nuclear power, which already supplies three-fourths of France's electricity, and more power in the United States than gas, hydroelectric, and all other renewable sources combined. We are making breakthroughs in fast breeder reactors that, by creating more fuel than they consume, can actually be used to energize yet other reactors. Fusion energy, which by 2050 may be using even sea water for fuel on a commercial basis, could provide us with unlimited energy at perhaps one-third of current prices.

The problem is not the *supply* of energy. It is the pollution that energy production entails. To unlock energy from its home in nature requires a destruction of that home, potentially altering the environment drastically. This may prove unacceptable on the massive global scale required in the century just ahead. The new reality is that success in creating energy translates to a disaster for the environment. This is the energy crisis of the twenty-first century.

"Environmentally friendly" sources of energy are often touted as the end-all solution, but they are certainly not friendly to the environment. Hydroelectricity requires the blockage of mighty rivers, wind generation covers hilltops with unsightly turbines, and solar panels mar landscapes and may lace far-off deserts with cobwebs of power transmission cables or explosive hydrogen pipelines. Agricultural sources, such as growing crops for ethanol, may result in an acceleration of the clearing of ancient tropical forests that is already so prevalent in much of the equatorial world.

As the Asian economies develop, China's vast coal reserves will likely energize the region's power grid. Already, China's industrial areas are choking with smoke, and plans are to burn the coal at an ever-quicker pace. If other countries follow China's path—and worldwide coal reserves are vast indeed—the result may well be an unprecedented level of environmental destruction.

Nuclear power could have been humankind's cornucopia of unlimited power, except that nobody knows what to do with the radioactive waste. The pollution issue has virtually halted nuclear plant construction in most countries and put to rest any plans to develop fast breeder reactors on a wide scale. It has made Three Mile Island and Chernobyl the enduring curses of the nuclear power industry.

Fusion power that mimics the sun by fusing hydrogen into helium may *eventually* be the answer. This technology, however, is expensive, and commercial breakthroughs are not expected before the middle of the next century. Even then, fusion on a massive scale is impossible without radioactive by-products. And it could open a new chapter in world pollution: How do we dispose of the extraordinary waste heat created by duplicating a hundred suns on the earth? It could well be that thermal pollution will become the Achilles' heel of the late twenty-first century.

MERCHANTS OF DEATH

FACED WITH POLLUTION and obvious environmental degradation, governments are trying to stem the problem. Yet some powerful counterforces will thwart society's efforts to redress the situation.

Pollution, however devastating for society, is often too "convenient" for the offending individual or corporation. When a car speeds down a street belching smoke, the polluter escapes the full effect of his own pollution, leaving pedestrians in his wake to suffer the effects. When an oil refinery releases emissions that are over the legal limit, its management may believe paying fines is easier and cheaper than overhauling the plant.

Moreover, many pollutants "disappear" readily after they've been released, making it very hard to detect them. CFCs and carbon dioxide are invisible gases that dissipate instantly, leaving no trace that they were ever present. The uncounted tons of garbage that communities burn each day seem to vanish as if by magic. Nuclear canisters cast off ships into the deep sea become nonexistent, although, in time, their ugly effects can seep to the surface.

Even when full detection is possible, society chooses to pollute because it is the cheaper alternative. Some fear that enforcing restrictions means closing down factories, losing jobs, or pricing products uncompetitively. For the Second World, it is just too expensive *not* to pollute when vast regions barely have enough food and only minimal shelter.

Most governments fail to act because of powerful interest groups. Why would Exxon want to restrict the worldwide use of fossil fuels? Why would EDF (Electricité de France) curtail the use of nuclear power in France? Or General Motors, the use of cars? Or Monsanto, plastics and pesticides?

These groups and a thousand more—the merchants of global pollution—are forever its apologists. Armed with a battery of high-budget studies to buttress their claims, they assure us that no problem exists. It took decades to "prove" the link between cigarette smoking and cancer; with pollution and environmental degradation, the demonstration of cause and effect may take longer still. Meanwhile, in the parliament buildings of the world, yet new reports are issued. Our legislators listen and our children cough.

Despite all the predictions of global warming, ozone depletion, water contamination, endangered species, et cetera, we don't *know* the future with any precision. We are overwhelmed by scientific "truths" that extend beyond our current grasp. As a society, we will likely spend the next several decades fighting fires already out of control instead of preventing them in the first place. And the resulting clean-up bills will be compounded significantly.

RISING ECO-LIMITS

AS WE STRADDLE a new millennium, citizens of rich countries find themselves carried forward by the momentum of centuries of cumulative technology—one that has largely delivered its promise of unlimited material objects. But the future will force us to shift away from the creation of "goods," toward the prevention, or elimination, of "bads." We must treat air, water, and soil as limited supplies that are no longer free, and therefore accept these as new constraints on our ability to create wealth.

Because it is often profitable for the individual or corporation to pollute, unregulated, unrestrained free-market capitalism actually *rewards* the polluters. At the same time, the success of capitalism in delivering unprecedented material wealth will ensure its ideological acceptance in most cultures through the middle of the twenty-first century. How can we reconcile capitalism with the necessity of curtailing pollution?

Capitalism can survive, but not without a rising tide of eco-regulations that limit individual and corporate freedoms in favor of communal well-being. This is not new. Historically, governments have always found a role when social interests conflict with individual ones. Governments conscript soldiers in time of war and lock drunkards in jail in time of peace. In each case, individual rights are displaced in favor of broader social goals.

With environmental laws and enforcement mushrooming, the manpower devoted to environmental oversight is rising. Worldwide, the government's role has already swollen in taxing, monitoring, policing, fining, terminating, or incarcerating polluting entities, even assessing billion-dollar eco-fines, such as in the Exxon *Valdez* disaster.

The reach of pollution-liability laws is broadening to pin responsibility on the manufacturers of a pollutant—whether it's a pesticide or a soft-drink can—even when the producers do not *directly* pollute. In some cases, responsibility extends to employees, banks, transport companies—all of the entities that have anything to do with a toxic spill. As a result, banks are becoming skittish about making loans to certain customers; industry is increasingly cautious about the firms they hire to dispose of toxic wastes; and municipal landfills are selective about what waste they will accept. Trash cans and bins will come with locks, and landfills with armed guards, as the costs and liabilities of disposal mount.

A new class of punitive eco-taxes will be imposed to prevent pollution: a hefty carbon tax on coal and gasoline, a horsepower tax to favor fuel-efficient cars, a toxin tax on pesticides. In some areas, this has already taken the form of deposits on cans and bottles, fees exacted to encourage recycling. The cost of pollution will escalate the price of everything, from toys made from nonrecyclable plastic, to inefficient incandescent light bulbs that put more energy into heat than light.

Sweden already taxes pesticides, fertilizers, and batteries containing cadmium or mercury. Italy taxes plastic bags, Finland and Norway charge high fees on nonrecyclable containers, and Japan and Germany apply higher landing fees to noisy aircraft. Western Europe and Japan have such hefty taxes on motor fuel that they more than double or triple its cost. In the United States, regulations have made it twenty times more expensive to dispose of machine oil laced with toxic heavy metals than the purchase price of the raw ingredients.

In other instances, governments will ban certain goods and activities altogether, like leaded fuel in most parts of the United States. In Rome, Athens, and Mexico City, people may drive their cars only on certain days, based on a lottery of license numbers. A long list of endangered animals (bobcat, cheetah, eastern cougar, Asian elephant, gorilla, marine otter, giant panda, gray whale, red wolf, California condor, peregrine falcon, Imperial parrot, American alligator and crocodile, leatherback sea turtle, Gila trout, red salmon, and scores of others) are protected from business commerce. CFCs, noxious paints, varnishes, and heavy metals are increasingly banned.

In some regions, polluting businesses simply cannot operate at *any* price. Factories are relocating—even to other countries—on the basis of local pollution laws. In already impoverished India, 212 factories have been shut down to protect the Taj Mahal from pollution-related erosion. Nuclear reactors and power plants cannot get licensed; new landfills cannot get approved. And when services can be performed, their cost is skyrocketing. It is no longer enough for business to offer goods and services; it needs to do so without polluting.

LIFE WITHOUT POLLUTION?

INDUSTRY WILL REACT to the new realities by viewing pollution as an output of each step in the production process, from the procurement of raw materials, to fabrication and packaging, delivery, use, and disposal. We may have been prolific polluters in the past because engineers, businesses, and government didn't treat the preservation of the environment as a constraint. By giving engineers new constraints, we can hope that they will design novel products and processes free of pollution. But they must begin to do this soon.

Germany, which has the highest landfill costs in the world, is also the most advanced in precycling: a product has to be recyclable as a design constraint. Germany's "green dot" program requires vendors to take back packaging materials or arrange to recycle them. So manufacturers package products with recyclable material, use less of it, and make it durable enough to use over and over. In time, the Germans envision recycling *all* manufactured products from refrigerators and computers to clothing and automobiles.

Cars will no longer be just fast and stylish, but also fuel efficient and precycled. Engineers will consider assembly and *dis*assembly costs, making possible the sorting of a car into its raw components of metals, plastics, rubbers, and composites. All components will be reused in newer models.

Governments may begin to grant "enviro-credits" that give the holder the right to emit certain pollutants into the environment. If a company modernizes its equipment to eliminate pollution, the enviro-credits may be sold on the open market to the highest bidder. Or companies may be able to earn additional credit by making major investments in replanting tropical rain forests, preserving wetlands, or even manufacturing oxygen from carbon dioxide. Thus, for the first time in history, the preservation of the environment will have an explicit economic value and cost.

The results already include many successes. In London, the choking pea-soup fogs have lifted; oxygen levels in rivers once given up as dead—like Italy's Tiber and Spain's Guadalquivir—are rising. In the rich countries, lead and sulfur dioxide emissions have dropped.

Yet, like running up the down escalator, the tide of global industrialization is causing the world to slip back. Throughout Asia and Latin America, the air in key cities worsens each year with acrid fumes and choking smoke. Rivers in Poland are too dirty even for industrial use, and farmland is too filled with toxic chemicals for safe farming. Around the globe, rivers support fewer fish, and ancient forests are being leveled. Taken as a whole, the world is slowly slipping further and further behind, and global demand for fresh solutions will only heighten.

Corporations that recognize the changing rules of wealth just ahead will have a leg up on their competitors. They will learn to use the new environmental constraints as a competitive tool, some by finding clever ways of circumventing antipollution laws, but most by monopolizing novel materials, processes, and products that are friendly to our environment. Companies are already developing niche businesses in recycled paper, biodegradable plastics, and reusable flashlight batteries. As the prices of these enviro-friendly products fall, latent consumer demand and government regulations will lead to an explosion in new business opportunities.

As we find ways to turn dirty coal into clean methane and to recycle heavy metals found in industrial oils, we'll give birth to new industries. Geneticists will patent new strains of rice and wheat that convert carbon dioxide into oxygen at an accelerated rate, or plants that filter noxious fumes from the air. The changing rules of wealth will create opportunities for the nimble.

Yet, as our corporations learn to jump over the new constraints imposed by the Pollution Barrier, up ahead a second hurdle is coming into focus. It may prove to be even more formidable to surmount.

We'll call it the Service Barrier.

7

SERVICE, PLEASE

HEIDI SCHNELL LOOKED at her watch, then down at the street below where her car was parked. It was precisely 2:15 and the service truck arrived just on time.

Within seconds, a woman technician in a white jumpsuit opened the locked hood. An automated hydraulic hand reached inside, grasped her motor package, held it in midair, and gently set it in the back of the service truck. The arm then selected a new engine and placed it in Heidi's car. The hood cranked down on its own, the technician got back in her truck, and she was gone.

Heidi's car would be at peak performance for another 60,000 miles.

Paul Casanuevo was reading a file from his work associate when he remembered in horror that he had forgotten to get the new room ready for his first child. The baby was due within two days.

He called the local home-decoration center, and twenty minutes later a design consultant was studying the unused bedroom down the corridor from Paul's home office. Paul looked through her catalogue and decided he wanted KinderRoom #62, except for the customized wallpaper copied from the frontispiece of a children's book that belonged to his grandfather.

As he watched, the designer electronically conveyed a copy of the

117

frontispiece to a wallpaper supplier, while a crew arrived to start painting and carpeting. Within an hour, the wallpaper was delivered; within two hours, it was installed; and within three hours the room was decorated, down to a fully stocked chest of drawers, complete with blankets, diapers, and toys.

Welcome to the Service Age of the twenty-first century.

Over the next two decades, our economy will be based on flexible service. Consumers will expect their whims to be satisfied, whether they want a customized automobile with six wheels, a vacation riding an elephant on the beach, or a wedding dress made from black and orange fabric.

Manufacturers and suppliers, for their part, will no longer regard themselves as the purveyors of things, but as the satisfiers of personal needs for which the production of a *thing* is only incidental. Indeed, the quality of *service* will rise to the forefront in determining which companies and individuals earn wealth in the twenty-first century.

VACUUMED AND READY TO GO

GENERIC BRANDS ARE everywhere on supermarket shelves, from canned soup to washing detergent to aluminum foil and drugs. Computer manufacturers find it much harder to compete because each uses the same commodity components that end up in every garage-shop assembler. Buyers of cameras, sound systems, and video equipment are inundated with diverse manufacturers touting near-identical features in each year's product offerings. Even car makers seem to mimic one another's developments, from fuel injection to talking dashboards to disc brakes.

In the Placeless Society, ideas and technologies flow at such a rapid pace that manufacturers can no longer differentiate themselves on product features alone. Each manufacturer has access to the same machine tools, global labor pool, business school graduates and engi-

neers, computer technology, and patent licenses. In such an environment, how can the manufacturers of the future compete?

The manufacturing companies that survive will increasingly view
themselves as service companies. It is no longer enough to provide a
thing: when physical objects become so easy to stamp out, their value
to each of us declines unless the object is conceived so cleverly that it
renders superior service. For service, we will pay.

We are now learning that all economic activity can be viewed as a
service. Some manufacturers understand this and respond by embed-
ding the service into the product itself. Computer programs have
built-in personal tutors, and complex machines come with how-to-use
videotapes. In the future, we will see cars that wash themselves inside
and out, and vacuum their carpets. Books will listen to the children
reading them, and correct their pronunciation. Cameras will electronically download pictures at night, and glossy prints will arrive the next
day by mail.

But even with these design upgrades, it is impossible to provide
everything that is needed in a physical package. With cars, no matter
how clever the design, we still need to buy gas or electricity to make
them run. Clothes need cleaning, food needs cooking, televisions
need programming. We are continually forced to pamper our *things*,
when all we want is the end-service of "to go," "to dress," "to eat,"
and "to be entertained."

The successful manufacturers of tomorrow will understand that
things alone don't fully satisfy the needs of the customer. They will
look at what they are offering the customer as a holistic package of
goods and services, providing the appropriate mix of things, information, training, customer service, and personal attention to fully answer
the consumers' *real* needs.

It is no accident that Toyota's Lexus enjoys the highest repeat purchase rate of any luxury car in the world. Toyota, synonymous with
effective manufacturing, has now shifted its expertise into streamlining service. Instead of a luxury *car*, you buy a luxurious transportation
experience.

Even manufacturing something as low-tech as *enchilada con*

frijoles qualifies for entering the Service Age. PepsiCo's Taco Bell has grown to revenues of $4 billion by shifting out of food manufacturing to food delivery. The chain has established over 15,000 omnipresent points of access where hungry people are likely to be found—school cafeterias, college campuses, airports, and street corners.

To get out of the food manufacturing business, Taco Bell has shifted its heavy-duty food preparation—like dicing cheese, crushing beans, and washing lettuce—to outside contractors. These changes have turned kitchen space into customer space, and kitchen personnel now focus on customer service.

THE RISE OF THE "SERVICE-PROD"

THE THRIVING COMPANIES of the twenty-first century will throw away the blueprints that describe what they provide, and look at the customers' needs. Whether it is renting a car, repairing a bathroom sink, or buying food, we'll give our business to the ones meeting our specific needs in the most effortless, pleasant, and economical way.

Our needs are rarely satisfied by a pure service or pure thing alone. Over the next two decades, the distinction between "service" and "product" will become blurred—everything will be a "service-prod": some combination of information, instruction, service, and access to a physical thing or things.° This is already the case whenever a doctor prescribes pills, a waiter delivers a dinner, or a teacher educates a child—and will soon characterize every facet of our economy.

The quintessential marriage of products with service is found in retail operations. To gain vision into the future, let us look at what many regard as America's best-operated retail organization: Home Depot. By packing 35,000 different products into an arena-sized emporium, by attracting top-quality store personnel with lucrative benefit packages, and by providing a no-frills bare-concrete-floor environment,

---

°I will often use the terms *service* or *product* as substitutes for the term *service-prod*. But the reader should understand that they are merely two forms of the same essence.

Home Depot offers a high-quality service at can't-be-beat prices.

By stocking shelves at night after closure, store personnel are free to circulate and help customers, and take the time necessary to answer questions. By offering free clinics on plumbing, tiling, and home repairs, the store has converted once helpless homeowners into hammer-swinging contractors who keep coming back to the store. Home Depot also arranges full installation right down to a computer-aided interior decorator. As a result, the company enjoys extremely high repeat sales and is among the most profitable and fastest growing retailers in the country.

Another example of the coming Service Age is provided by Hertz with its ubiquitous rental cars. To be a member of Hertz's $50-a-year Club Gold program is to travel into the twenty-first century. By calling a toll-free number, you can make a truly personal car appear at any major airport in the world. On arrival, a Hertz courtesy bus picks you up and takes you directly to your car. The driver radios ahead to others who start the engine and set the air conditioner or heater. Above the car, your surname is glowing in bright lights. On departure, you simply show your driver's license at the exit gate—no counter lines, no signatures, no credit card stubs, no lengthy insurance forms. Even if one had a private car already parked in the airport parking lot, the service could not be better.

In these examples, *placelessness* is the key to providing service. In a breakdown, Lexus provides road service anywhere, any time. Hertz provides personal cars at any airport that can be reserved from any phone. Taco Bell serves food wherever hungry people can be found. Home Depot conveys knowledge to its do-it-yourself customers, and installs cabinets for the others. "Service" entails providing things, knowledge, and ideas ubiquitously, regardless of *where* they are needed.

DEATH TO THE CHECKOUT LINE

AT RISK IN ALL of this are the middlemen. Given our easy telecommunication, low-cost point-to-point transportation, and unlimited computer power, intermediaries of all stripes will come under increasing pressure to justify their existence. Why pay for them when placelessness puts manufacturers directly at each person's door? Legions of wholesalers, regional warehouses, and retail stores all over the world are at risk.

Retail stores flourished when they were the only places to compare prices and products against one another. To bolster sales, retailers often boast advertised specials and lure customers into buying additional merchandise, or convert them to more expensive items, or else offer limited-time sales to limit their ability to comparison shop.

But the monopoly of the retail store is rapidly collapsing. While twentieth century shoppers still clamber into their cars and fight for a place in noisy checkout lines, a new breed of shoppers is seeking greater convenience by turning to catalogues, toll-free ordering numbers, mail, television shopping, consumer product guides, computers and fax machines. Without ever leaving home, the new consumer has the products delivered to the door—and usually at a lower price.

With revenues fast approaching $1 billion, and over 3 million loyal customers, CUC International is breaking ground for a new type of store for the twenty-first century. Using CUC's catalogue, users tap their orders into their home computer for, say, a Whirlpool washer. CUC then orders the washer directly from Whirlpool with instructions to "drop ship" it to the front door. There is no need for a store, salespeople, inventory, insurance, or checkout lines, and the transaction cost approaches zero.

Lands' End is doing the same thing in apparel. With a catalogue going to 14 million individuals, this megaretailer maintains 1,500 employees taking telephone orders around the clock, every day of the year. Lands' End has also set up ordering capabilities through computer networks like Prodigy and CompuServe, complete with color photographs of merchandise—essentially providing window shopping from the home. Given the ease of shopping, often coupled with a no-hassle return policy, no wonder the number of US consumers purchasing by catalogue has doubled over the past decade, while department and apparel specialty stores keep losing ground.

THE NEW INTIMACY

THE CLOSER TO THE customer a company will get, the more successful it will be. In the Service Age, vendors will seek to get into our homes, our bedrooms, even our minds. The AC Nielsen Company has already extended the tentacles of Fourth Dimension surveillance into living rooms and bedrooms to see who is watching even televised advertisements. Nielsen has installed tens of thousands of households with electronic "people meters" that monitor whether the television is on, whether people watch cartoons or news, if they zap channels, and when they look away or leave the room during advertisements. The data is then sold to advertisers.

Citicorp even knows what items are hidden away in millions of kitchen cabinets, bathrooms, and linen closets. It has over 2 million households wired in selected supermarkets, where every purchase is tracked to each household. The information is then relayed electronically to companies like PepsiCo, Ralston Purina, and Pillsbury so that they know who is buying what and when.

In the Fourth Dimension, use of the telephone is no longer anonymous. When we dial a toll-free telephone number, computers are busy tracing the call not just to the city prefix, but down to the phone from which the call is placed. Customer service representatives are trained to be discreet about what they know, and that's quite a lot: even before they answer the phone, high-speed computers have already sifted through billions of records to display name, address, past account activity. . . .

Even lifestyle. Some scan automobile registrations to see how often individuals purchase new cars and which ones they buy. Credit card records tell who borrows money and where they shop. Magazine subscriptions show whether one is interested in guns and pornography, or home gardens and music. Increasingly, computers are cross-comparing information from multiple sources. Databases show whether one is likely to donate, pay or default, reorder or not, how much money one makes, and how much one's house is worth.

In the Placeless Society, we leave permanent electronic fingerprints everywhere, and few of us are strangers. The salesman will know all about us before we even "enter" the store. Even after a product or service is purchased, the smart companies will continue to track their customers and satisfy their needs.

Perhaps the quintessential company providing top quality postpurchase customer support is WordPerfect Corporation, which developed one of the most successful application programs in the history of the computer. With corporate offices close to no major metropolitan center, in Orem, Utah, WordPerfect's customer service telephone system can handle up to 1,300 calls at any one time. Technicians are immediately at customers' desks, anywhere in the world, taking them through difficult problems. The result has earned WordPerfect one of the highest ratings of all word processing packages; but it has also given technicians insight into every conceivable product glitch, and ideas for future product designs and improvements. WordPerfect could not have become a dominant player in word processing without such intimate contact with its customers. The competitive battles of the twenty-first century will be those of service.

TORT ATTORNEYS AND MOVIE STARS

FUNDAMENTAL TO SERVICE are people. The shift into the Service Age will redefine the role of the worker, and the skills necessary to compete in the job market. We have seen that much of the shift into the Service Age is due to the technologies that have brought us low-cost manufacturing. But the same technologies that have blessed us with bounty have also displaced us. Just where will the "excess" people work?

Humankind's ability to invent new jobs seems unbounded, even when technology displaces old tasks. We know that displaced workers will enter the service economy because there is nothing else left to do. The fall of the manufacturing economy will give rise to new industries, new "necessities."

With only a handful of people needed to grow the food, a giant "leisure" class is busy preparing and serving food: we have chefs and chef schools, restaurants, supermarkets, frozen foods, TV dinners, health foods, microwaves, caterers, home- or office-delivered pizzas, all unthinkable years ago but necessities today, employing a large part of the workforce. Manufacturing will shift into service just as agriculture already has.

Over the past century, American manufacturing and agricultural jobs have shrunk in importance each year. The percentage of the workforce in manufacturing has fallen by half, causing an unprecedented shift of workers into service jobs. Today, 80 percent of the US labor force is in service, and over the next few decades almost all new jobs will likely be in service. Similar trends are occurring in Japan, Germany, France, Canada, the United Kingdom, and nearly every industrialized country.

In every case, workers are no longer making things, but contributing by helping solve specific human needs. For the aged, we have a phalanx of nurses, physical therapists, and cardiac surgeons. For the two-earner households, we have battalions of child-care providers, cleaning crews, and even professional shoppers. For design work we have legions of architects, engineers, and programmers. Investment advisers, aerobics instructors, tort attorneys, insurance adjusters, interior decorators, even movie stars—these and a thousand more like them no longer make a living by growing or by making, but by *doing*. We have risen above an economy driven by *things* to an economy driven more and more by *actions*.

Even the job descriptions in "thing-oriented" industries—mining, manufacturing, and agriculture—are increasingly those of service jobs. These industries are becoming highly specialized. Agriculture is chock-full of packaging specialists, pest experts, and artificial inseminators. Manufacturing plants are run by programmers, engineers, and maintenance technicians.

To thrive in the Service Age, we will all have to learn new skills: the service worker generally must interact with other people, be empathetic and articulate. The ever-changing technologies and techniques will require an ability to solve novel problems, use new resources, and work with a minimum of supervision. Employees who grew up under the rigid command-and-control hierarchies of the Third Dimension will have to adapt to in the free-flow of the Fourth.

The shift to the Service Age will also require employers to value employees more. In traditional manufacturing or agricultural jobs, workers were often mere cogs on a wheel, easy to monitor and easily replaced. As we move into the Service Age, business organization will no longer *use* people, but it will actively *be* people.

Good employees will be essential to win customers and keep them, to expand business, and to build work teams to solve new problems creatively. The successful service companies today are the ones that pay their employees well, accommodate their personal needs, and provide frequent training.

Over the next few decades, the service companies that attempt to maintain an anachronistic manufacturing mentality of grinding a few cents more from each time-card-punching employee, will end up with unsatisfied customers and will be swallowed by competitors. Unlike in the Industrial Age, every employee of the Placeless Society is a salesman; even back-room employees will have contact with the customer.

BOND . . . JAMES BOND

IT IS OBVIOUS THAT underpinning any service—whether designing a clever product or providing information to a customer—is knowledge and information. We've often heard that we are entering the Information Age or even the Electronic Age, but those titles miss the point: we are entering the Service Age. The *thing*—the fancy computer with the multicolor screen and low-cost telephone connection—is far less important than *what the thing is for: service*. Just as the plow was a tool of the Agricultural Age, or the factory the tool of the Industrial Age, computers, electronics—even knowledge—are tools of the Service Age.

Service can be provided through many routes, but it always depends on special knowledge. It can be delivered personally and directly, like piano lessons or automotive repairs. Or it can be built into a product: clothes that do not soil or require ironing, computers that talk and teach, photocopiers with disposable components. Knowledge is an essential part of what is being offered, and, in general, whoever has superior knowledge will provide superior service.

It is the battle to provide superior service that explains why corporations all over the world spend trillions of dollars each year on marketing research, product design, and packaging. It explains why governments in all industrialized countries subsidize R&D and universities.

While over two-thirds of the Fortune 500 companies have some form of corporate intelligence divisions, most are half-cocked efforts. What army would attempt a maneuver without knowledge of enemy troops, equipment, and positions—and extensive efforts to keep its own secret? But this is exactly what too many corporations are doing today, ignorant of how to access information, or how to prevent it from flowing out.

The undetectable mobility of knowledge makes it cheaper to steal than to develop. A company may spend millions of dollars in a new design for fuel injection for a sports car, only to have the blueprints sold by a disgruntled employee.

Even when a company is successful in blocking knowledge from leaving the company, it is often embedded in the product anyway. In Hong Kong, Taiwan, South Korea, and elsewhere, companies buy products on the open market to "reverse engineer" them into their raw components. The cost of reverse engineering is usually a fraction of what was spent in perfecting the original design. A company spending millions—even billions—of dollars in a new product may be displaced by near-identical clones spilling forth from rival competitors.

As a result, the next two decades will witness a boon for businesses specializing in James Bond paraphernalia: briefcases with concealed tape recorders, pens with radio transmitters, umbrellas that gather sound from far-away conversations. US department stores Macy's and Bloomingdale's have already opened spy departments.

"Info-brokers" will seek out anything on everything and sell it to the highest bidder. They will scour trash Dumpsters looking for discarded customer lists, purchased parts, dictation tapes, typewriter ribbons, and blueprints. Computer hackers will conduct clandestine "robberies" of corporate databases and voice-mail systems from the comfort of their homes.

Even governments are getting involved as information brokers on behalf of their resident companies. As the competitive pressures of the Service Age loom, it is no longer just the KGB's infamous Department X that seeks to steal foreign knowledge. Now nearly every government on earth has soiled its hands in corporate espionage. National spy apparatuses are discreetly shifting to corporate espionage— wire-tapping board rooms and telephones, planting spies—to learn what new service offerings will be forthcoming. Israeli secret service sought to buy clandestine blueprints to a top-secret spy camera. To get clandestine coating samples, Japanese and Russian agents scrape metal filings off their shoes after Silicon Valley plant tours. The French government even bugged first-class passenger seats on Air France flights to monitor talkative executives and to plant moles in the European offices of Texas Instruments, IBM, and other foreign electronics companies.

But most companies need not go to such extremes. They will learn to exploit the information already available in public filings, patent applications, court records, credit databases. Employees recruited from competitors can be tapped. Even more important, the field sales force is—if their corporations would only ask them—chock-full of delicious nuggets of information. It is the field sales force that is in daily contact with the concerns of customers, the offerings of competitors, the services of other suppliers. This information—all of it—needs to be collected, compared, and synthesized, and corporations that fail to do so will be outfoxed at every turn by those that do.

Mobility of knowledge will create the fundamental challenge in the Service Age. Each time an employee changes jobs, she takes a bit of her knowledge from one employer to another. Each consultant and vendor visiting a Silicon Valley firm takes a few tidbits away to the next door. The Japanese busily comb patent filings in North America and Europe to keep their pulse on the world's knowledge base. The companies offering the best services in the twenty-first century will be those that gather and interpret information about their rivals, to the point of becoming information junkies.

"INFO-CENSORS"

CORPORATIONS WILL COMPETE ON the basis of their "info-edge." Like feudal castles in the Middle Ages, they will attempt to construct ever higher walls and moats to keep company secrets from leaking out. They will undergo massive efforts to guard trade secrets, customer lists, and R&D discoveries from falling into rivals' hands.

Corporations will monitor more closely what gets published in their own newsletters, and who goes on plant tours. The lackadaisical approach to voice-mail and E-mail will be replaced by sophisticated levels of security protection. Consultants, and perhaps full-time in-house information specialists, will track the level of information needed for each task in the corporation. Employees will routinely be asked to sign nondisclosure statements on their first day of work and will be given an exit interview on their last; on both occasions, they will be diplomatically threatened with legal consequences if they open their mouths.

Information on computer systems will become compartmentalized, with access to proprietary sections only on a need-to-know basis—and only with the right passwords and security clearances. Computers will track who logs in which databases and for how long, with log records archived for a decade or more. When job tasks change or employment ends, the electronic locks will be changed.

Every written word leaving the company—public documents, sales presentation, advertising, even letters—will no longer be reviewed just by corporate attorneys but also by "info-censors" to make sure that disclosures are not too revealing. Even patent applications for new inventions will seek to obtain key legal protection, without also publicly disclosing secret processes or aspects of design.

In the Age of Everything-Everywhere, the distinction between *inside* a corporation and *outside* is fast eroding. What the engineers tell the sales personnel spreads into sales presentations to customers and competitors. Vendors and consultants incestuously visit rival companies carrying with them new ideas and processes. In the Placeless Society, secrets will be guarded by erecting fire walls *within* the organization.

But for all this secrecy, the corporation of the twenty-first century is pulled into an inescapable dilemma. By building fire walls within itself—by limiting employees' access to information—the organization also limits its effectiveness by not exploiting its knowledge base to its maximum potential. Often, it is the serendipitous matching of chaotic knowledge within an organization that leads to innovation. This tension between controlling the flow of information and the need to let it run freely will be the major organization challenge of the twenty-first century. Today's management has little understanding of it, yet it is a delicate balance that may well decide who wins in the competitive corporate battles just ahead.

COUNTING BEANS

EQUALLY UNKNOWN IS THE issue of measurement. How can companies manage themselves if they do not even know how to measure the Pollution Barrier and the new Service Barrier that now confront them? The classical corporate financial statements are rich in excruciating details about what is no longer important: capital, labor, and raw materials. For instance, accountants' balance statements balance out the corporate physical assets with the capital needed to get them, and income statements itemize labor and raw materials purchases. All the while, they ignore the keys to wealth in the Placeless Society.

We are, for the most part, out of control upon entering the Placeless Society. While the twenty-first century is closing fast, we lack the basic tools needed to measure the very factors that will decide victory in the emerging corporate battlefield: service and the environment.

How do we measure the quality of customer service, assistance hot lines, and instruction manuals? Of what value is a well-trained workforce? And what is the value of knowledge and information, which underlie service? If a BMW engineer learns to increase the mileage of a car just by changing a few wires and hoses, what is that knowledge worth? How do we measure it? What is the value of a trade name, a customer list, warranty registrations? The frightening truth is that we have no idea. We guess.

This also applies to pollution issues. Today's accountants have no way of measuring the "cost" of pollution; the variables are too many. What is the cost of acid rain? Of an endangered species? Of toxin-based cancer? Of a polluted aquifer? Is it a cost only when a lawsuit is filed? Only when there is a price imposed by government regulation?

Today's bean-counter methods are outdated. The corporations that succeed in the Placeless Society will need to find ways to account for the new constraints to wealth—tools we just do not have today. Over the next decade, the result will be a major revolution in how corporations weigh profits and track success. The ones looking at "profits" as gauged by twentieth-century accountants will be swallowed by those who see, measure, and react to the new barriers to wealth.

In the last several chapters, we have seen a fundamental shift in the building blocks with which the houses of wealth are built. The limiting factors have shifted away from the three Industrial Age constraints of labor, capital, and raw materials; wealth in the Placeless

Society will be built by those who can leap the twin barriers imposed by service and pollution.

It is no longer a question of *if* these changes will occur. They already are upon us, and happening so fast that they will likely turn hundreds of behemoth corporations into dinosaurs. The circumstances of the twenty-first century favor a new species of corporate philosophy. Organizations that understand the dynamics of *service-prods* are already stealing business away from thing-oriented manufacturing companies that do not. And rising *environmental* costs have already affected mighty giants, from Exxon and General Motors to Occidental Petroleum and Manville Corporation, and are increasingly affecting every auto mechanic, dry cleaner, and print shop—soon every office—in the world.

The revolution of change in creating wealth will not stop there, for the twin barriers are largely *external,* so we turn next to radical *internal* changes already taking place in our corporations—changes that strike a dagger through the very heart of corporate structure as we know it today.

Part Four

THE HOUSES
OF WEALTH

8

THE CORPORATE
TENTACLES

MIKO KAWASAKI ENJOYED her new job, but she was a bit confused. As the countryside blurred outside the bullet train, she thought about her roots and how she fit into the world.

As a devout Shinto Buddhist, she always sought to respect ancestors and elders. She learned from her parents to submit to authority and follow directions without questioning. In school she practiced teamwork but also never to draw attention to herself. Her university never prepared her for today.

Her boss seemed to have come from another planet. She giggled inwardly in her job interview, as he spilled out Berlitz-Japanese phrases with a Texas accent. She'd read a few best-selling books on how to understand Western foreigners in business but she didn't get it. Why do they do what they do? Was her boss crazy or was it a cultural thing?

At age twenty-four, she was product manager of the Cajun Hickory Catsup line. What use do the Japanese have for catsup? How do we promote Cajun cuisine to a people used to rice, fish, and sake?

Miko's American boss had asked her to prepare a strategy for marketing the product in Japan and to advocate her particular view. Even though many of her colleagues were older, she was expected to ignore

135

that fact and argue her opinions rather than go for diplomatic consensus dominated by wise elders.

As her train pulled in, she felt a lump in her throat. Another thirty minutes and she would begin her presentation, in a style that was completely alien to her cultural heritage.

——

It was Friday night over dinner when Wilhelm Kassel got the call. He put the kitchen phone down, thought for a minute, and ran into the study to find out if it was true.

His computer scoured the company's worldwide E-mail, pulling out all field sales force communications about recent lost bids on skyscraper elevators. The system indicated a recent tripling of company communications in Western Europe, about competitive bids lost to a new rival, Phoenix Technologies, that six months earlier did not even exist. The name also came up frequently in communications from Asia and North America.

Then he found it. A saleswoman in New Jersey had managed to get a text of the Phoenix proposal from a close customer. Product blueprints, pricing, options, installation schedule—everything to understand the new competitive threat was there.

He recognized it as a state-of-the-art system, the kind he had only dreamed of: magnetically suspended, it gave a frictionless ride and finer speed control. Equipped with a "face-recognition system," it would "remember" which passenger went to which floor. The injection-molded elevator cars brought the costs down too. Unless Wilhelm's company reacted immediately, Phoenix would win the highly competitive battle for elevator sales worldwide.

Wilhelm immediately combed the corporate computer database and assembled the best talent. From a Japanese division came superconducting linear motors, from Germany came visual recognition systems. He found the advanced materials in the United States, a voice-recognition system in Sweden, and he called in sales representatives who knew the Phoenix system.

Connected electronically, the global team worked through the weekend, hammering out the specifications and costs. By Monday morning, product specifications were distributed electronically to the field sales force worldwide. The Phoenix threat was contained.

———

Tommy Patton was red-faced. He had built his political fortune speaking out against foreigners, cheap imports, and the displacement of local workers. By stoking nationalistic fires, he thought he had just the ticket to gain entrance to the US Senate.

Then came the news. For twelve years he had aligned himself with large American companies to beat out foreign ones in local government contracts. Whenever an American company had a bid, he would favor it over the foreign rival. Now it was coming back to haunt him: the "American" companies were selling equipment made with foreign labor, while the "foreign" companies were producing domestically. Confused, Tommy was realizing that no products were made entirely from inputs from a single country. *Everything seemed to come from everywhere.*

———

In the twenty-first century, our local economies will be global. The pace of global commerce will be so feverish that we will lose track of where a product is made. The concept of national origin will become as irrelevant as the need to know which city or province a particular product comes from today.

The new realities will force business enterprises to conduct themselves as if national borders did not even exist. The successful ones will integrate the best global talent, technologies, and costs into one global resource. Our multilingual colleagues and bosses will carry passports from other countries, and those who get promoted will often be the ones adapting best to a multicultural, multinational environment.

ECONOMIC PROMISCUITY

WE CAN SEE THE dramatic changes that have already occurred. We no longer live in parochial economies where the lumber comes from nearby forests, rocks from local quarries, and bread from neighborhood bakeries. Almost everything we use in our lives comes *from* somewhere else; everything made is shipped *to* somewhere else.

That "somewhere" is global. We sip wine and bottled water from France and munch on cookies from Denmark. We wear sweaters made in Iceland, our toys come from Hong Kong, our cars and cameras from Japan, our radios from Korea, our coffee pots from Germany, and the coffee in them from Brazil.

World trade accounts for nearly $8 trillion in goods and services a year, a number that is still growing fast. In the United States, the proportion of the economy involved in trade has doubled in the past two decades and represents one-sixth of total GNP. A quarter of US agricultural product is sold abroad, and one in six American manufacturing jobs depends on exports.

While the United States is dependent on foreign trade, it pales by comparison with the rest of the world. The average country is twice as dependent on world trade as is the United States. One-half of the value of the economies of Germany, France, the United Kingdom, and Canada consist of imports and exports. In nineteen countries the level of annual trade is so great that the value of products clearing its ports exceeds its GNP; Singapore, truly a "distributor nation," ships products in and out at such a frenetic pace that they equal nearly five times its national income. Without international trade, national economies simply stop.

This reality of placeless commerce, our mutual dependence on one another, is the primary force tearing down centuries-old administrative barriers between our countries. The average worldwide tariff has fallen from nearly half the value of an imported product in the early 1950s to less than 5 percent today. Passenger cars, foods, and pharmaceuticals are standardized to enable them to cross borders without administrative hurdles. More and more, commerce is conducted in a borderless world.

While protectionist politicians flex their muscles from time to time, our world economy has grown so interdependent that it would be impossible to reerect barriers between countries without causing their economies to crash. Nations are no longer insular economic blocks acting on their own, but integral threads in a vast fabric. The world's economy can no more return to isolated nation-states than Europe or Japan can return to medieval feudalism. The forces of placelessness integrating the world economy are just too strong to let us slide backward.

GLOBOCORPS

AS WORLD TRADE HAS grown, so have its captains: the multinational corporations. They cross national boundaries so freely that the major cities of the world have the same business directory, products, and services: Agfa-Gevaert, Amoco, Barclays Bank, Bayer, Canon, CIBA-Geigy, Citicorp, Citizen Watch, Club Med, Coca-Cola, Conoco, Du Pont, Esso, Exxon, Ford, Fuji, General Electric, General Motors, Gulf, Hewlett-Packard, Hoechst, Honda, Hyundai, IBM, Kodak, Levi Strauss, Matsushita, Maxwell, Mazda, Mitsubishi, Mobil Oil, Monsanto, Nestlé, Nippon, Nissan, Procter & Gamble, Ricoh, Sanyo, Seagram, Sharp, Shell, Siemens, SmithKline, Sony, Sumitomo, TDK, Texaco, Texas Instruments, 3M, Toshiba, Toyota, Unilever, Xerox, Yamaha—even McDonald's.

These and 37,000 other titans expand unimpeded in a global market and now rival nation-states on the rosters of world power. One-third of global trade is conducted between diverse branches *within* the same corporation. The companies account for over one-fourth of global production and often dwarf the economic power of the countries in which they operate. Even in 1990, of the top 125 economic entities (whether government or corporate), over half were multinationals. In 1992 the revenues of General Motors would make it the largest "country" in Africa and the second largest in South America. The entire GNP of oil-rich Saudi Arabia is only slightly larger than the revenues of Exxon. All Venezuela fits easily into IBM. Toyota and Daimler-Benz each produce more than the Philippines. Holland's Philips, Switzerland's Asea Brown Boveri, and Sweden's Electrolux all practically dwarf the countries that contain them.

Rather than be intimidated by these commercial giants, each country now seems to court them to gain their favors, dismantling bans against foreign-owned transnational corporations. Canada, India, Russia, Mexico—even Cuba and China—are opening their markets and liberalizing ownership rules. And the multinational corporations come.

The nature of multinational corporations is also changing. Not only do they have distinct operations in two or more countries, but they also are managed as if countries did not exist: there is only *the world*.

The term *multinational* is out of date because it implies that nationality is relevant. It is like calling ozone depletion, AIDS, or weather patterns multinational instead of global. Many economists now use the term *transnational*, but that misses the point too: the idea of national classification is steeped in nineteenth-century notions of economics and power. The titanic entities that live among us do not see "nations."

They take the best from around the world, ignoring lines on political maps. When necessary, they blend chameleonlike into the local landscape, owing no allegiance. Like a headless amoeba, the corporate headquarters could as easily be in one country as another, or not be confined to place at all. This new engine of global wealth is perhaps best described as a *globocorp*.

THE NEW QUEST

THE PREDECESSORS TO modern-day globocorps include the millennium-old vessels that plied the Mediterranean or South China Seas, and later celebrated trading companies like the Dutch West India or the Hudson's Bay Company. The globocorps of the twenty-first century are different from the trading companies that existed up to the Industrial Revolution and the multinational corporations that characterized much of the twentieth century. The reasons lie in why they exist.

Historically, businesses that engaged in commerce outside their home country were on a quest for cheap labor or raw materials. The seventeenth century Dutch East India Company, for example, acted on a global basis in bringing spices to the Netherlands. The Hudson's Bay Company brought Canadian furs to England. Others brought African slaves to operate plantations in the Americas. Companies went global to tap low-cost labor or raw materials, or to bring products to a cash-rich home market.

These patterns largely continued through the late twentieth century. Even today, Mexico's low-cost labor attracts worldwide corporations by the hundreds into its *maquiladora* program. In Malaysia, American-based RCA, Motorola, and Texas Instruments accounted for over half of Malaysia's electronics industry, sending back over $300 million in semiconductors to the United States. Japan's corporations are outsourcing to Indonesia, the Philippines, and China. Other globocorps are attracted by the cheap labor in Thailand, Bangladesh, Ghana, Guatemala, and Bolivia.

But the globocorps of the twenty-first century will be distinct from the multinationals of the twentieth. In the Placeless Society cheap labor and raw materials will decline as a motive force, because, as we have seen, they are less important for competitive production. As automation displaces labor, the cost of an hour of labor becomes less relevant in determining overall costs. The labor-cost advantage that once made the Second World so interesting, is dwindling in importance. In some cases automation is once again making it economical for manufacturing to return "home" to the United States, Japan, and Europe, despite higher *hourly* labor costs. Labor and raw material costs are becoming irrelevant as a means for one corporation to beat out another.

Increasingly, globocorps are going global for reasons barely under-

stood by their multinational predecessors. Rising environmental regulations in the First World, for instance, are driving polluting industries to the Second. Many industries (petrochemicals, plating, tan-
ning, dyeing, smelting) flee to the poorest corners of Africa, Asia, and
Eastern Europe where the investment is welcome, the tax rates low,
and environmental enforcement almost nonexistent. The results are
open pits and rivers flowing with benzene, chloroform, toluene, xy-
lene and PCBs. Mexico's *maquiladora* companies generate some 20
million tons of hazardous waste each year. In India, one in ten workers in foreign lead plants has lead poisoning.

Far more corporations, however, will go global for a more noble
cause: knowledge that will enable them to better serve their customers around the world. Being in multiple countries has a strategic advantage, since ideas developed in one place can be used in another.
By sharing knowledge, the global corporation can develop winning
business ideas unmatched by any single-country operation.

This practice is demonstrated by Levi Strauss. Twice a year, Levi
managers worldwide gather to brainstorm and review local Levi television ads that have aired all over the world. One ad for stone-washed
denim had a young man throwing stones into a washing machine with
a pair of Levi's to the tune of Marvin Gaye's "I Heard It Through the
Grapevine." It made such a smash that Levi managers everywhere
adapted it to their local markets.

Sometimes the geographical diversification of globocorps helps
them piece together complex products from the best technical expertise across the globe. When managers at United Technologies' Otis
Elevator sought to design a state-of-the-art elevator system, it put together a world team: its French division supplied the door systems,
the Spaniards worked on the small-gear components, the German
group turned out the electronics, the Japanese came up with the
motor drives, and the US division handled the integration. The development time was cut in half, saving about $10 million in costs.

Having a widespread global operation also helps to cover the extraordinary development costs of many cutting-edge products. Simple box cameras have given way to video recorders with sophisticated

imaging software, distance sensors, variable lens, and audio systems. Developers of integrated circuits can spend hundreds of millions of dollars on design work and production facilities for just one type of chip. While the cost of making the first unit can be in the *billions* of dollars, the second unit is almost *free*. As the up-front investments mount, the need for ever larger markets grows stronger to cover cost. Without a global market, many of the new miracles of technology may not have been created.

Take the pharmaceutical industry. In the 1970s in the United States, it took around $15 million, and four to five years, to develop a new drug. By the 1990s the entry cost rose to $250 million and up to twelve years, and by 2000 it will likely be higher still. Industry lobbyists point to higher regulatory scrutiny as reasons for the higher costs and delays. But even without regulations, scientists appear to have saturated the possibilities of finding new uses for old chemicals. Just so many things can be done with tree bark or bean extracts, and the new technologies, such as gene splicing, are extraordinarily expensive undertakings. Only a global market can support the heavy investments required to break new ground. No major pharmaceutical company can contemplate developing anything short of a global blockbuster product.

COCA-COLONIZATION

THANKS TO THEIR DISPERSED operations, globocorps gain insight into local customers, competition, and trends. Japanese automakers routinely set up automotive design centers in the United States to determine the tastes of their largest export market. Italian chipmaker Dynamit Nobel Silicon opened a plant in the United States just to be closer to customers.

The rewards of global marketing are even sweeter considering the rapid pace of world population growth. Every three years, the world population grows by more than the US population. In the next ten years, world population will grow by a billion new people—almost the current populations of North America, South America, and Western Europe *combined*.

This growth creates tremendous strain on our global environment and urban infrastructures, particularly in poor, war-torn countries. But through the mist, the globocorps see fresh opportunities for building desalination plants, hydroelectric dams, and airports. They know that even poor countries have an affluent middle class. India alone has a well-educated middle class double the population of France. Even five-dollar-a-day workers in Mexico have their Sony Walkmans. We in the First World often view the industrialization process as over, but most of the industrialization of the world is yet to come.

As the poorer two-thirds of the world's 5 billion people rise from the mud, the globocorps are eager to provide them with soaps, medicines, cameras, and radios, a form of industrial "Coca-Colonization." With much of Asia, Latin America, Africa, and Eastern Europe just beginning to build their economies, the globocorps—many say "globalopolies"—are ready.

As these liaisons mature, they offer tremendous advantages over their competitors who operate in single countries. To cut costs, standardized parts can be shared across multiple regions. Purchasing can be consolidated from key suppliers, and from the best-deal countries, to get maximum price concessions. Resources—management teams, technology, production output—can be shifted around the globe overnight like giant chess pieces, to outwit competitors trapped in single nations.

It is no accident that of the top 100 US globocorps, two-thirds of profits come from *foreign* operations or that three to four times as many companies are engaged in multinational operations as two decades ago. When national companies and globocorps are pitted against one another, the globocorp has no peer.

TICKETS TO GLOBALNESS

THE SHIFT TOWARD globalization will create new challenges and opportunities. Globocorps are already so numerous and powerful that some firms specialize in selling services to *other* globocorps. Ogilvy & Mather's strategy is to develop one-stop shopping for its globocorp clients doing worldwide advertising. It was the first Western company to set up advertising behind the Iron Curtain, and it maintains nearly 300 offices around the world.

The very company that provides communications to globocorps is itself global. Intelsat (International Telecommunications Satellite Organization) is a consortium of 122 countries. The system comprises a cosmic highway with seventeen satellites transporting telephone, facsimile, telex, computer data, and television signals, at the speed of light. Intelsat enables Citibank to monitor its global capital flows, IBM to talk to its suppliers in Japan, and Hewlett-Packard to implement state-of-the-art products on a global scale.

Start-up companies also think globally before they even make their first sale. Once, high-tech start-up companies like Apple Computer or Microsoft could be launched in a garage, ignoring international markets until after the domestic one matured. Not today.

One Silicon Valley computer start-up company, the Momenta Corporation, reasoned that, to prosper, it needed to grow quickly and to masterfully combine the best skills available in the world. In its business plan, American engineers would shoulder the system architecture, Europeans would furnish the styling and ergonomics, the Japanese would provide components and packaging, Taiwan and Singapore would assume high-volume production. Each region supplied what it did best. As a baby globocorp grows, it can raise further capital wherever the terms are the most favorable—perhaps in Taiwan or Singapore. While such globalization may add extraordinary organizational costs for a young company, as the Placeless Society matures, such strategies will become commonplace, even necessary, to compete.

Companies that grew mellow in a protected national market find themselves unwittingly competing on a global stage as foreign goods flood domestic markets. In the Placeless Society, many of these local operations will be forced to somehow merge geographically dispersed operations, or face extinction. An avalanche of mergers, acquisitions, and joint ventures will take place as each smaller corporation seeks to find its niche in some larger global organism.

Not *every* industry will be affected by the move toward globalization. Some products and services can be provided locally and gain little benefit from being associated with a larger organization: mowing lawns, cutting hair, sweeping streets, or building houses. But many more industries will not be exempt from a need to globalize.

In hundreds of industries, an increased globalizing shakeout will, in many cases, leave three to five economic entities dominating each industry. We already see this in computer chips, software, and consumer electronics, and we will soon see it in automobiles, banking, pharmaceuticals, publishing, washing machines, and zippers. The winning organizations will be difficult to unseat because they will provide the most advanced product designs, the most streamlined manufacturing, and the best customer service. New ideas developed anywhere in the world will instantly ripple through the global network, improving performance everywhere.

In preparing for these new realities, operating divisions are already traded among globocorps, like baseball cards, to create a proper power base for global markets. Whirlpool bought control of Philips's $2 billion European appliance division. Cash-rich Siemens snapped up Bendix Electronics, Nixdorf, Rolm, and a piece of Plessey. Bristol-Myers and Squibb merged, and Roche got Syntex and Genetech. US-based Philip Morris Companies snapped up Swiss confectioner Jacobs Suchard and Norway candy giant Freia Marabou. Nestlé sponged up Perrier. Hongkong Shanghai Bank Corporation acquired Midland Bank, just as Holland's ING bought up Britain's Barings. The ebb and flow will follow periodic business cycles, but the long-term trend is that more global consolidations are yet to come.

SEÑOR MITSUBISHI, S'IL VOUS PLAIT

AS THE BATON OF economic power passes to the rising globocorps, global managers are waltzing through world cultures with grace. This new breed of multicultural player glues together projects whose teams span the globe. The recent head of General Electric's computing tomography group illustrates this trend: born in *Morocco* of *Jewish* parents and schooled in *France,* he received his PhD in *California,* married an *American,* worked in *Paris,* and headed up GE Medical Systems in *Wisconsin.*

During the 1980s the board of directors of the world's major corporations shifted toward an international composition in preparation for the new realities. Britain's Imperial Chemical Industries illustrates the shift. In 1982 ICI's sixteen-person board was all British; by 1989 it included two Americans, a Canadian, a Japanese, and a German. Of the top 180 executives of ICI, over a third are now foreign. Whirlpool International, headquartered in Italy, has a six-person management team with executives from Sweden, Holland, Belgium, Germany, Italy, and the United States. The eight-person board of Switzerland's engineering giant Asea Brown Boveri is made up of four nationalities, and their executive committee is made up of five. IBM has five nationalities among its top executives, Unilever has four, and Shell Oil has three. Japan broke ground when Sony appointed an American and a German to its board. With competition like this, the large corporations that fail to diversify their top management are unlikely to flourish in the world we are entering.

Globocorps are so supranational that they feel little loyalty toward the nation-state where they are headquartered, and global managers reflect this new reality: they are not to promote a particular country but to undertake activities that enhance the globocorp's profitability, market share, or stock price. The global manager who fails to seize an opportunity will lose to another who does. Each manager must find ways to skillfully combine the best research, designs, manufacturing, markets, and financing from around the world, into a well-tuned social machine, regardless of national borders.

Those who can span cultural chasms will be able to write a job ticket to anywhere in the world. Needless to say, managers have to adapt to *corporate* culture, but the diversity of the *world* culture can be even trickier, with each country having extraordinary idiosyncrasies. The stories are many: the English, for example, prefer to have a "personal space" of several feet, whereas Venezuelans prefer to touch one another during conversation. Americans believe in human effort, schedules, and control; Middle Easterners and many Northern Africans rely on Allah's will; Germans and Swiss start meetings when the second hand sweeps past the appointed hour; Latins and Africans may or may not meet on the appointed day; Europeans believe in individual actions; Latins, Asians, and Africans promote group collectivism. Americans boast, Brazilians interrupt, Asians respect silence, and Arabs speak loudly. Such is the challenge for the manager of the future.

Equally confusing is the subtlety of language. In the United States, a *billion* means a thousand million; in Britain it means a million million—three more zeros. In America, *to table* something means to postpone discussion; in Britain it means to discuss it right away.

In Japanese, *hai* literally translates as "yes," but it actually means "yes, I'm listening," not "yes, I agree." In Bulgaria, nodding one's head up and down means "no," not "yes." When "Come Alive with Pepsi" was originally translated into German, it came out closer to "Come Out of the Grave with Pepsi," and in Asia, it became "Bring Your Ancestors Back From the Grave."

Even simple things like people's names can become a labyrinth of confusion: in America and much of Europe, Blaise Pascal is Mr. Pascal. In China, Zhou Enlai is Mr. Zhou, not Mr. Enlai. In Latin America or Spain, Miguel Ortega Gonzales is Señor Ortega, not Señor Gonzales.

The key to working in a multicultural environment is to read about the specific culture in order to understand its customs, history, religion, and language, including body language; to remain alert; and to discuss cultural differences with coworkers.

THE FOREIGN DOMESTICS

BECAUSE OUR GLOBOCORPS and their managers seek to act as though borders do not exist, it is impossible to classify a corporation by its national allegiances. Corporate nationality is a dated notion. At one time, Ford was clearly American, and Volkswagen German. Management, employees, shareholders, production facilities, even key suppliers, were all from the same country. Globocorps don't follow such simple rules.

Today, it is hard to tell an American globocorp from a European or Japanese one. Their "nationality" is as meaningless as the "nationality" of the clouds blowing across the sky. Consider IBM, the jewel of "American" know-how: headquartered in Armonk, New York, with research facilities in Switzerland and operations in forty-six countries, it purchases components from Japan, assembles them in Singapore, markets and services everywhere. Almost two-thirds of IBM's revenues are *outside* the United States; its stock is traded in the major exchanges of ten countries; its list of shareholders include Saudi Arabians, Koreans, and Belgians; and it pays taxes everywhere.

Even the national companies set up by European governments after World War II have turned their backs on economic nationalism. Britain's largest glassmaker, Pilkington, has joined forces with Nippon Sheet Glass in Japan and Saint-Gobain in France. Italy's Olivetti is working closely with Japan's Hitachi. Daimler-Benz, Germany's largest and most powerful industrial group, is courting Mitsubishi and Fujitsu and has acquired Britain's ICL. These global pioneers are charting new territory in a new world, disregarding the favors of parochial politicians.

Xerox is thought to be an American company, yet half of its 110,000 employees are outside the United States, just as half of Sony's employees are outside Japan. Digital Equipment is headquartered in Massachusetts, yet *less than half* its revenue comes from the United States.

When Sony bought Columbia Pictures and CBS Records, did this make *Sleepless in Seattle* a Japanese film, or Michael Jackson's music Japanese? Although the shareholders who ultimately benefited are in Japan, most of the financial benefit stays in Hollywood: the 30,000 employees, management, stars, and producers are predominantly American.

Most Americans regard Toyota, Nissan, and Honda as Japanese. Yet Toyota Camrys are churned out of a plant in Kentucky, and Nissan Altimas come from Tennessee. Honda—with its popular Accord and Civic—manufactures and sells more cars in America than in Japan, and exports cars from America. It may be only a matter of time before Honda's worldwide headquarters are moved to Marysville, Ohio, leaving a subordinate branch in Japan.

The nationality of products is even confusing US municipalities wishing to "buy American." Over half the products manufactured in the United States have foreign components. Los Angeles is learning this the hard way. The water district bought forty-eight new American Ford trucks—with engines made in Brazil. The work gloves were made from California cotton but sewn in Asia. The city typewriters were assembled locally, but the supplier is headquartered in Japan. Likewise, a municipality in New York rejected a $40,000 dirt excavator from Japanese-owned Komatsu in favor of an "American" John Deere model costing $15,000 more. It didn't know the John Deere unit was manufactured in Japan and the Komatsu model was made locally.

Politicians too often mix up corporate and national welfare, not realizing that the competitiveness of national corporations has little to do any more with the competitiveness of the nation. The corporation has vaulted into the Fourth Dimension, while countries are still held captive to geographic place.

When Japan's prime minister asked his countrymen to buy more American products, the imports surged for Del Monte ketchup, Kleenex tissues, and Wilson tennis rackets. But these "American" products were all made in Taiwan, Portugal, Hong Kong, and Japan—everywhere but America. Political maps of the world bear little relation to the realities of commercial activity.

IMPERIALISM COMES HOME

WHILE GOVERNMENTS COMPETE with sweet deals to attract free-flowing globocorps, there is a risk: their goals are divergent. Governments strive to increase *local* standards of living and offer full employment, whereas globocorps strive to maximize *worldwide* market share, profits, and shareholder values. While international business is surging ahead in a supercharged "turbocapitalism," the political world is being left behind in the dust. In many ways, the economic system is becoming entirely decoupled from the political structures that once controlled and regulated them.

The fluidity of globocorps gives them a power edge over rigid government structures. The more corporations globalize, the less authority and control is left to local or national governments. Corporations can play off one regional government against another and dictate the terms of their involvement. This is happening in tax concessions, infrastructure subsidies, and enforcement of pollution and worker-safety controls. Power is inexorably shifting from nations to newer economic engines.

The history of multinational corporations over the past 200 years provides key insight into the globocorps of the next century. When multinational trading companies grew in prominence in the seventeenth and eighteenth centuries, "primitive" peoples were impotent to negotiate with these technologically superior entities that came with guns, ideas, and jobs, making offers that could not be refused. Their ships left with slaves, gold, silver—anything the trading companies deemed of value that could be sold elsewhere.

By the twentieth century, small industrialized nations began to feel the pressures of multinational corporations usurping their sovereignty. Finland, Costa Rica, and Malaysia, swimming in a sea of corporate giants, currently have little autonomy. As nations, they lacked a critical mass in language, technology, or economic muscle to compete successfully without surrendering sovereignty. For decades they had to give up any notion of autonomous development; their economies were largely at the pleasure of nimble globocorps looking for the best deals.

What was first true for poorer regions, then small industrialized countries, is now also true for the giants: Germany, France, Japan, and the United States. Once, US multinationals "invaded" Latin America; now, the United States feels an invasion by the Japanese, and Europe feels the presence of the Americans. Today, even the superpowers are losing their freedom to set interest rates, pollution controls, tax rates, or social programs. Unseen forces of globalization seem in control, pitting one set of national programs against another, forcing them into a common battle to attract globocorp trade. The last vestiges of do-it-alone national sovereignty have nearly vanished.

THE MINDANAO SYNDROME

THE SECOND WORLD OFFERS a glimpse of what the future may bring if current trends are left unchecked. The government of the Philippines was more than happy to accommodate key globocorps in setting up export industries in the Philippines. Dole, Del Monte, and United Brands quickly pitched agricultural operations on the island of Mindanao, but in so doing, peasant farmers were displaced, forced to move up to the rocky hills overlooking the globocorp estates in the fertile valleys. The Philippine military and private armies are used to suppress unions, while crops are exported and scarcely any is left for the local people to eat. As a result, although the Philippines is one of the top dozen food producers in the world, three-quarters of its children are malnourished. While the globocorps do not *control* Mindanao, they clearly tip the balance in determining public policy.

This "Mindanao Syndrome" is infecting industrialized countries as well. As early as 1976, the managements of Exxon, United Brands, Gulf Oil, and Northrop admitted to making secret payments to foreign government officials to tip policies in their favors. Lockheed Aircraft was caught bribing officials in Italy, the Netherlands, Japan, and Turkey.

In America, politicians look the other way while accepting millions of dollars in political "contributions." The donors' list reads like a *Who's Who* of international business, including Switzerland's CIBA-Geigy and Nestlé, Canada's Seagram, and Hong Kong's Marine Midland Banks.

Globocorps routinely hire high-powered Washington lobbyists (often former government employees) to push the right buttons along Pennsylvania Avenue. In 1987 and 1988, when Toshiba faced US trade sanctions for selling sensitive materials to the Soviet Union, Toshiba reportedly spent $30 *million* on lobbyists. In 1982, when Tennessee Senator James Sasser supported buy-American automobile legislation, Nissan executives held a fund-raiser supporting Sasser's opponent. If sovereignty means controlling one's political system, countries everywhere are losing their sovereignty. Governments and democracies will survive, but unless they adapt to the realities of world globalization, it is the globocorps that will govern.

WHAT'S THE SCORE?

THE NEW STRUCTURES CALL for entirely new ways for national governments to look at the world, and almost none have got it right. American politicians want to place "American" companies in Japan. What for? President Bush's trade mission to Japan in 1992 featured his visit to Toys "Я" Us to congratulate a successful American beachhead. Yet, except for a handful of US managers, the operation does not affect Americans: almost everything sold in the store is designed and made outside the United States.

Politicians and economists are still preoccupied with trade balance, imports, and exports. But the bulk of these items consists of the shipment of things from one place to another place. They have little bearing on the economy that we are just now entering. For example, "imports" used to be a simple concept: products from another country. But today's imports to Korea, for instance, include items assembled from components that were originally *exported* from Korea in the first place. A fifth of the total imports to the United States are from subsidiaries of American companies. "Imports" and "exports" as a way of keeping score are dated concepts left over from nineteenth-century economics.

The old scoring system not only measures the *wrong* variables, it measures them inaccurately. In the old order, the value of imports was easy to measure: a ship would arrive with x tons of timber or y yards of cloth. In the new age, wealth springs from service and its kindred knowledge, not things. We trade intangible services impossible to value: engineering, design, marketing ideas, management— often transferred across national borders within the same globocorp. US customs values a computer tape according to the number of square inches, although the data itself may represent millions of hours of imported man-hours done abroad. Even if the customs service knew its true value, it could not stop it from being zapped across borders by telephone or corporate satellite link, or even be aware that it had happened. Products of the highest value today are invisible and intangible. Nation-states are at a complete loss in the new economy.

What is the answer? The effective economists of the twenty-first century will start by throwing away nineteenth-century concepts of "nationality," "physical products," and "country of origin," and focus instead on regional development: jobs, training, and local investment. It sounds simple, but economists have few tools to effectively manage our economies in the decades ahead.

In time, they will come to view globocorps not as corporations—for the corporate aspect operates largely outside the scope of any single national government—but as projects. Governments should look at specific proposals put forth by globocorps and evaluate them on the basis of local regional development. What are the amounts and types of local labor used? Will there be job-training features to advance the skills of the people? Are suppliers to the project likely to be regional companies or from far away? Will the project act as a magnet, attracting related suppliers and schools? Will the likely tax receipts offset the added costs of highways, schools, and public services? And on and on.

While the evaluation process is complex, in the end a small region like central Ohio—or a large region like America—may well prefer a Honda manufacturing plant in Marysville, to a General Motors manufacturing plant in Mexico. By looking at beneficial interests rather than the nationality of the company involved, politicians and economists will have begun to grapple with the Placeless Society.

We have seen how globocorps no longer operate in multiple nations, but ignore national borders altogether. Yet paradoxically, as our businesses become more global on the outside, inside the forces of placelessness are gnawing at their very structures. The cracks in their façades are already showing.

9

THE COMING AMOEBAS

TAKASHI KUBOTA LOOKED up from his mahogany desk out to the pool where his grandchildren were playing. His day-dreaming took him back to the days after he left college; as a young engineer, he was recruited into a giant kitchen appliance company with 12,000 employees. His skill enabled him to rise quickly, first as a team leader, eventually with responsibility over 650 people.

However, Takashi was always frustrated at the hierarchical rigidity of the company. It took *years* to get new technologies into old products; the marketing department would reject great ideas because they "didn't fit the existing product line," or were "inconsistent with our channels of distribution." When his boss finally told him to just focus on what he was asked to do, he decided to quit to start his own company, knowing he could do better.

And, at age fifty-eight, he did. He started Novaproducts with five hand-picked engineers; all six were equal partners. In eight years, his company's revenues swelled to a fifth of his former employer's, with only two dozen employees. His management philosophy was: have as few employees as possible, don't invest in expensive equipment, and outsource *everything*. Novaproducts coordinated the existing talent, production capabilities, and market opportunities that already existed.

Outsourcing—using subcontractors from manufacturing to packaging, from administration and finance to marketing and sales—enabled Novaproducts to use any technology, any production method, and almost any channel of distribution, wherever it was in the world. The key was to conceive the right products at the right time, and make sure the right people were involved and well coordinated. Takashi knew that the emerging technologies of communications, computers, and high-speed transportation would tie his global network together.

The flexibility allowed him to develop new products in half the time it took his behemoth competitors, and by contracting with manufacturers around the world who had the right tooling and idle capacity, he was sometimes the lowest cost producer. His experience taught him that the megacorporation would fall into extinction amidst nimble competitors.

━━

Sergio Lombardelli was huddled in front of the green glow of his battery of monitors.

Transfixed to the monitors like an adolescent at a video arcade, his hands frantically fingering a music keyboard, he studied the images of what would be the next model Ford WarpCoup XT. Sergio, the leading automotive designer of his generation for Ford, GM, Chrysler, Nissan, Volkswagen, BMW, Toyota, and others, had become one of the wealthiest 100 people in the world.

A disembodied voice boomed out from the speaker behind him, "That's good, hold that!" It was Jean Rodin, from Ford's design center in Cologne, Germany. A second voice, that of a woman from Dearborn, Michigan, pierced the air from another speaker to suggest a smoother flow on the tail fin. On the screens, Sergio molded liquid metal before everyone's eyes, as designers, auto experts, and engineers huddled over his shoulder electronically.

Sergio's proprietary design equipment, combined with his uncanny skill at creating award-winning designs, enabled him to see a car from any angle. With his magical keyboard, he could race the car down a mountain road, go inside and alter the sheen on the beige leather seats, open the hood and change the "look" and layout of the engine compartment. He simulated crash tests to see how the structure would survive an accident.

As he altered the cosmetic features, his high-speed computer systems were testing for best-fit off-the-shelf parts available from worldwide auto vendors. As the external appearance of the car shifted, the computer designed the underlying parts and produced detailed diagrams regarding assembly. In the corner of a monitor, the computer continually tracked the unit cost as the design changed.

Sergio worked alone from his fortress house outside Siena, Italy. His state-of-the-art system was built inside a vault high atop an ancient medieval castle. As a backup, carefully encrypted copies of his "top secret" software were kept in a bank vault in Lucerne.

When the design was accepted, Sergio snapped the "send" key, and specifications of the body contours down to ashtrays and harness wiring were downloaded to Ford's computers worldwide. Within seconds of receipt, Sergio was automatically transferred his second $12 million installment for payment of yet another accepted design.

It was with some trepidation that Elizabeth McCracken had quit her job as a graphic designer with an advertising agency. Everybody loved her talents, but the daily grind of her commute to work was killing her. She was fed up with the rush-hour traffic, with arriving drained and late due to bad weather or some unexpected accident. By the time she got out of work, picked up her daughter at day care, and ate dinner, she was ready to collapse in bed to get up early the next day.

And the bills were killing her. No sooner had she paid for insurance and monthly parking fees, child care and gasoline, than she needed to replace her brakes, or the entire transmission. The day her car broke down and she couldn't pick up her daughter after work, she quit her job.

Lately, though, she couldn't have been happier. The two hours a day she spent driving are now relaxation or play time with Chelsea. The money saved on commuting, child care, and work clothes goes to pampering her daughter.

Elizabeth set up office in a bedroom, with the best equipment she could afford, and continued design work for her clients at the firm; even her ex-employer gave her new assignments. Between the electronic videophone, computer network, and same-day package delivery services, she got more work done than before—*without leaving her home.*

She designs in the evenings and weekends without feeling guilty for neglecting her daughter; and her growing list of clients, including a few overseas, attest to her increased creativity.

———

Randy Nadir's attorney wasn't sure what they should do next. Randy's wife had died of carbon monoxide poisoning a few years earlier, caused by a faulty clothes dryer. The attorney had identified over a hundred other victims who had died, or suffered permanent brain damage, as a result of the bad device. A class action suit of this scope would normally require billions of dollars to settle.

Who should they sue? The companies that installed the units were small, independent distributors scattered everywhere; they had since gone out of business, some to escape liability for the deaths. Records showed that the "manufacturer," Kenmarla Industries, was now a defunct assembly operation that once worked out of a rented warehouse, assembling pieces purchased from multiple offshore vendors. The owners used assumed names and were long gone. The attorney acknowledged that none of the *pieces* were faulty; the problem lay in how they were put together. As for the offshore vendors, they had no local presence and were beyond the jurisdiction of the law.

———

Welcome to the wonderful world of the fragmented corporation.

In the last chapter, we saw how the myriad forces of placelessness are propelling organizations unwittingly onto a global stage. Organizations will compete by combining the best talents and resources from around the world, to produce the most innovative, cost-effective products and services. In this chapter, we unveil a seeming paradox:

the Placeless Society will favor organizations with a global view, but not large monoliths. Quite the contrary. The winning organizations of the twenty-first century will be highly fragmented, "multilocal," with minuscule corporate headquarters, or even clusters of tightly coupled groups and individuals scattered throughout the world.

No longer will divisions, departments, and individuals in an organization be "subordinate" or "superior" to one another, but each will interact as part of a dynamic, ever-changing team focused on a common endeavor, coordinated through the technologies of placelessness. The role of the individual will be not unlike that of the cells in a growing plant: each contributes to the others and is necessary for the robustness of the whole.

Many of today's industrial giants may continue to have a monolithic external *appearance* to the public, but the underlying organization will have broken up or hollowed out, overtaken by more agile forms of economic organization. We are on the edge of a new economic system whose very structure will be unrecognizable to us in a few decades.

COLLAPSING GOLIATHS

THE GIANTS THAT WE'VE grown up with, and accepted as household names (IBM, General Motors, Hitachi, Daimler-Benz, Procter & Gamble), are the icons of the twentieth century, the companies to emulate. But placelessness is methodically tearing them apart. What seemed initially to be a cyclical downturn, or some idiosyncrasy of a particular industry, is in truth a broad set of structural changes sweeping the world. The giants are being replaced by a new species more adaptable than anything that has preceded it in the evolution of corporations.

To understand why, let us look at how the giant corporate structures evolved in the first place. The large corporation became the role model to emulate in the Industrial Revolution. The new textile mills needed power to operate, which they gained first from water wheels, and later from steam engines. Once these power sources were in place, various belts and pulleys conveyed the power to a great many individual machines. This in turn led to large *concentrations* of people working efficiently under one roof, because different parts of the production process required close interaction. Industrialists began to grasp the rather new concept of "economies of scale": the larger a textile plant, the more efficient and profitable it was. In the ensuing competitive battles, the smaller enterprises were ground under by their larger rivals. *Bigger* became equated with *better,* and the paradigm of organizational gigantism was born.

Gigantism got its second wind in the wake of World Wars I and II. As each country prepared for battle, the centrally orchestrated command-and-control style of the military campaigns translated into effective mobilizations and powerful victories. When the war ended, celebrated "Whiz Kids" like Robert McNamara and "Tex" Thornton brought their command-and-control styles to the corporate board rooms and business schools all over the world.

In parallel with the hierarchical management style, corporations the world over kept growing bigger. The goal for many was to become a diversified conglomerate—in Japan the *zaibatsu*—with tightly centralized control.

Before the Placeless Society, the spirit of gigantism reigned; in the twenty-first century, the spirit of individualism will flourish. Overgrown corporations are "downsizing," spinning off unrelated business units, decentralizing. Board rooms are yielding power to remote managers; corporate "headquarters" are becoming anachronistic; middle managers are being slashed. Corporate structures that have evolved for over a century are being turned upside down, no longer managed from above but from below, all the way "down" to the customer.

Technology is the reason. Before placelessness, the best way to manage large pools of resources and deploying personnel was through very structured hierarchies. Each person had a fixed role to perform, and groups were rigidly organized under nearby managers. These in turn reported to other managers, who reported to the top boss, the one who decided the "war plan." Before the electronic age, rigid hierarchical structures were the cheapest—if not the only—way to coordinate human resources.

Computers and communications changed all that, allowing ad hoc teams of people to be assembled, organized, disassembled, and reassigned at will, depending on the task at hand. It no longer matters *where* someone is physically—a team can easily consist of an engineer in Germany, a programmer in India, a marketing guru in California, and an accountant in Japan. The important thing is that they be the best combination of people to solve a particular problem. Once their goal is reached, the group dissolves and each individual can be redeployed to another project.

The companies exploiting the technologies of placelessness are simply able to beat their competitors who are not. The behemoths that performed well in a static world are proving unadaptable to a changing marketplace, dizzying technologies, and dynamic consumer tastes. They are too inbred, unwieldy, and cushioned from competitive pressures. Hierarchy and centralized control are collapsing. Bigger is no longer better.

Take IBM, the hierarchical giant who "owned" the computer industry, supplying large-scale computer systems to its behemoth clients. In 1977, when Steven Jobs and Stephen Wozniak started combining off-the-shelf gadgets in a garage to form Apple Computer, executives at IBM dismissed the new "desktop" computer as a useless toy. But as the "toy" began to steal market share from IBM, it didn't know how to react, having no "department" to deal with the new realities in the marketplace.

IBM realized that their giant corporate hierarchy could never react to the growing Apple threat. Thus, they set up an "independent business unit" with hands-off autonomy from the corporate headquarters. Within a *blitzkrieg* eighteen months, this autonomous group designed, manufactured, and got to market the IBM PC. Its success later caused IBM to completely disassemble its hierarchy into scores of independent business units, each operating with autonomy, but under the IBM flag.

Corporations are preparing for the future by decentralizing decision making. GM realized that, to produce an electric car ahead of its
competitors, it needed an autonomous team of 200 people to work
outside its command hierarchy. Well-run companies in the automobile industry are giving responsibility to youth-led teams that even the
CEO cannot easily override.

THE RISE OF McSPAGHETTI

EVEN THE CORPORATE HEADQUARTERS, once the sacred citadel
from which marching orders were chanted, have been sacrificed to
the gods of the twenty-first century. They are often lilliputian compared to the size of the whole operation and limited to the broadest of
strategic decisions, leaving operating decisions in the "field."

When RJR Nabisco, with 48,000 employees, moved its global headquarters to Atlanta, Georgia, the city fathers expected an imposing
skyscraper from which Nabisco would rule its global empire. Certainly it would be a boon to local employment. Little did they know
that Nabisco had already entered the Placeless Society, with a small
staff of a few hundred people working out of leased space in a subur-
ban development.

Switzerland's Asea Brown Boveri—the world's largest producer of
industrial equipment with 240,000 employees worldwide—has only
100 professionals in its Zürich headquarters. Swedish CEO Percy Barnevik explains that the Zürich headquarters are just where the mail
arrives before important letters are faxed to wherever he happens to
be. But the headquarters could just as well be in Chicago or Frankfurt—or nowhere. Power is blurring so rapidly away from the center
to the periphery that global enterprises will soon have no formal
"headquarters" as we know them today.

Companies in the new era may have several global headquarters,
with each business unit focused in a different place. The head of
Hewlett-Packard's personal computer business is in Grenoble,
France. Siemens moved the head of its medical electronics divi-

sion from Germany to Chicago. Honda's power-products division is headed in Atlanta.

In the 1960s, the operation of multinational corporations was simple to understand. Worldwide headquarters were in one country, with all international operations bowing to the central command. Products, pricing, research and development, capital flows, and markets were all centrally determined. Foreign operations were set up to extract raw materials, exploit local markets, or clone successful business ideas from the headquarters' country. As commands flowed from the center to the periphery, profits flowed from the periphery to the center.

In the 1980s, the world turned upside down. Key elements of product design, manufacturing, marketing, and finance shifted to the periphery. But in the everything-everywhere world, even the notions of "center" and "periphery" became obsolete. The Japanese refer to this phenomenon as "glocalizing"; to McDonald's, it is "multilocal"; United Technologies calls it "multidomestic"; and Levi Strauss follows the mantra "Be global, act local."

In most Japanese companies today, the head office often makes decisions for product design and research, but local offices focus on packaging, marketing, and advertising. Japan is so successful because its companies study the global markets before designing a product. Whereas Americans often design products for a domestic market, then attempt to peddle them abroad, the Japanese hone careful specifications to international standards, then focus corporate and national policy to win acceptance in global markets.

Although the Japanese drive on the left side of the street, not one of their standard models shipped to America has had a steering wheel on the right side. General Motors, Ford, and Chrysler complain that the Japanese do not buy American cars; they have been too slow to understand that a 7-foot-wide Buick with the steering wheel on the curb side and a speedometer measuring miles instead of kilometers has no appeal in Tokyo, where streets are narrow and parking is impossible.

Levi Strauss, the most globally oriented apparel maker headquartered in the United States, has a dozen facilities placed strategically

around the world so that it can react quickly to local fads. Its marketing is left strictly to local managers, who know the niche markets in
each culture. Best-selling fabrics, colors, and sizes in Germany and
England won't sell in Florida and California. Brazilian women like
them tight-fitting, the Japanese wear them loose, the Europeans buy
them expensive. The multilocal approach has paid off handsomely:
Levi's foreign sales account for nearly two-thirds of corporate profits.

United Technologies actively strikes local joint ventures and part-
nerships, even acquiring family-run companies. This approach allows
UT to disappear into the fabric of the country. Over half its sales are
foreign; of the 47,000 employees in its Otis Elevator division, only
7,000 are American.

McDonald's, with 1994 revenues of $8.3 billion, is a successful role
model for the globocorp of the twenty-first century, being well
adapted to local environments. Its 9,300 locations in the United States
have nearly saturated the country, causing it to look abroad for additional growth. For the past few years, of the three outlets it adds each
day worldwide, two are outside the United States. Already, McDonald's operates 4,700 offshore restaurants in 70 countries, and the majority of its revenues and assets is now outside the United States.
McDonald's secret is that it is multilocal. In the United States, it sells
Coke; in France it serves wine and cooks French fries in nongreasy
vegetable oil. Germany offers beer, and the Philippines feature
McSpaghetti. In Japan one can get chopsticks and green tea, and in
India it has plans to make hamburgers from mutton instead of beef.
The company makes great efforts to find *local* suppliers, partners, and
staff; only a few dozen Americans work in the 4,700 outlets outside
the United States.

GOLDEN MARRIAGES

WHILE CORPORATIONS decentralize and fragment, the individual
pieces are reassembling in new constellations of power that will be the
hallmark of the twenty-first century: the units are forming alliances

with detachments from other corporations—even their competitors. Boards of directors in the last centuries would have shuddered at the thought of such alliances, but they will be as common tomorrow as fax machines are today.

Two factors are driving the alliances. First, people and physical facilities no longer need be in the same place to function. It doesn't matter if one's coworker is in the next office, across the country, or working for another company. What's important is that the task get accomplished as quickly and cheaply as possible.

The second factor is technological obsolescence. The accelerated pace of technological development, made possible by the rapid exchange of information, means that any piece of technology must be utilized *right now*. Cutting-edge technology is as perishable as a truckload of ripe bananas: it's worth a fortune today, but if not used quickly, it becomes worthless.

To fully exploit a new technology, a company joins up with others, even competitors. The new team has the necessary know-how, resources, and marketing clout to get a commercial product out the door before others invent a superior technology. From the standpoint of each member of an alliance, it is better to have a piece of a great project than no project at all.

The intense pressure to get the best product on the market at the most competitive price drives many companies into "incestuous" pacts. Joint ventures and ownership are so widespread that it is difficult to tell where one company begins and another one ends. For instance, Ford Motor Company owns 25 percent of Mazda; Mercury distributes Mazda's Tracer, designed by Mazda but manufactured by Ford in Mexico. Ford designed the Fiesta, but it is made by Kia in Korea. Ford will use its Ohio plant to make a minivan designed by Nissan, to be sold by both. In Latin America, Ford and Volkswagen have merged operations to build trucks for exports—to the United States.

When Motorola wanted to build its worldwide wireless global telecommunications network known as Iridium, it knew it would be a daunting task. To make the system work, Iridium would have to juggle dozens of low-orbit satellites, innovate leading-edge technologies, come up with extraordinary amounts of capital, and sell the services throughout the Americas, Asia, and Europe. *And,* it had to do it all in record time, before some alternative system captured the market first.

Motorola could not build such a network on its own, but found a solution in the Placeless Society: it formed a consortium of a dozen partners such as Sony, Mitsubishi, Bell Canada, Sprint, and groups from Russia and China. The broad base gave Iridium access not only to leading-edge technology but also to foreign markets, with a minimum of resistance from nationalistic telephone monopolies.

CORPORATE *DÉCOUPAGE*

STILL MORE DRAMATIC than the growth in strategic alliances and joint ventures is the surge in outsourcing (subcontracting to other companies), which corporations will experience in the near future.

Somewhere deep in Tatarstan (in the former Soviet Union) is Kamaz, a truck manufacturer that could be one of the most self-contained companies of its type. At one end of the factory are dumped steel, glass, rubber, and other raw materials; out the other end pop road-ready trucks complete with windshields, tires, engines, frames, doors, and handles. Kamaz still ascribes to the mid-twentieth-century school, where the goal of an enterprise was to control even its sources of raw materials.

In contrast, Chrysler, one foot already in the twenty-first century, purchases 70 percent of its materials from outside vendors. Chrysler's Concorde, Intrepid, and Eagle Vision consist of only ten distinct sections: Chrysler makes the engine, transmission, and metal skin; outside vendors make the other seven. The interior is in four sections: Textron provides the doors and instrument panels, Johnson Controls produces the seats, and Prince provides the ceiling module. The pieces come ready-assembled, ready to clap in place.

Subcontracting the pieces forces the subcontractors to provide the most innovative technology at the lowest price to keep Chrysler's business. The subcontractors make the product cheaper than could Chrysler in-house, since they make similar parts for *other* automakers and can afford the specialized tooling and R&D that any single automaker would not find economical.

The advantages of outsourcing are such that automakers will focus on what they do best—engineering, styling, and marketing—and leave manufacturing entirely to others who can do it more cheaply. In the twenty-first century, the world's automakers will no longer manufacture cars, but merely snap together modules purchased elsewhere. The manufacturing giants of today will become mere "snapufacturers."

The trend toward modular manufacturing is firmly around us today, yet few of us are aware of it. Computer "manufacturers" like Dell of Austin, Texas, don't manufacture a thing. Outside vendors supply circuit boards, disk drives, components, and shipping boxes to Dell's strict specifications, and Dell simply clicks them together in its warehouse before shipping. The Apple PowerPC is actually delivered to Apple from Solectron's plant in Milpitas, California, fully assembled and packed in a shipping box bearing Apple's distinctive logo. And IBM is moving in the same direction.

Lewis Galoob Toys takes the concept of the "hypermodular organization" one step further. It receives design ideas for new toys from outside entrepreneurs, then sends the design outside to contract manufacturers who make the product and package it. Yet another agency dreams up the advertising and promotion. Outside agents sell the product, and contract vendors do the data processing and billing. Outsourcing enables Lewis Galoob to do what it does best—the screening of innovative ideas—and to leave others to their specialties. The result is that the toy company has sales of $170 million with a mere 250 employees.

Riding ahead of the wave, a new class of companies actively seeks outsourcing business. The most famous is perhaps Ross Perot's original Electronic Data Systems (EDS), a computer-service giant with close to $10 billion in revenues. In a $3.2 billion deal characteristic of the twenty-first century, Xerox agreed to outsource its critical computer and telecommunications operations to EDS, transferring almost 2,000 Xerox people to EDS. The transaction allowed EDS to focus on what it did best: it provided better quality services for Xerox, immediately saved Xerox money, and freed management time to focus on their core business.

Seattle-based Stratos Product Development Group is also out in front. Taking on tough design problems, it provides a fully engineered, ready-to-manufacture product to its clients, in record time. When Stratos tackled a portable workstation for Automatic Data Processing (ADP), it got the job done in just nine months, compared to two years had ADP done it in-house. Stratos provided British Airways with an in-flight video-playback system, in three months, compared to Lockheed's one year estimate as prime contractor. Again, when Microsoft needed a design for their BallPoint 2.0 mouse, Stratos did the job in less than a year. Each time, Stratos had the staff, equipment, and expertise to tackle state-of-the-art design problems in record turnaround time. Listening to client specifications, they act, for each one, as an in-house design team. That they are *physically* remote from their clients is of no concern to anyone.

A typical corporation, say Procter & Gamble, has numerous diverse employees: data processors, accountants, lawyers, mail clerks, cafeteria workers, janitors, security guards, copywriters, artists, nurses, and others. While each of their jobs is important, in the fluidity of placelessness, their tasks will most likely be performed by outsourcing to third-party entities offering greater efficiency and sophistication in the future. None of these personnel are central to the so-called core competency of Procter & Gamble, which is the design and marketing of consumer products. Outsourcing to specialist contractors at lower cost would allow Procter & Gamble to better focus on its core business.

The reality of placelessness enables diverse groups from different corporate umbrellas to work together in a common organization. In other words, the *corporate* body (the legal entity that writes the paychecks) will be decoupled from the economic *organization* (the working entity that creates wealth). The implications of this are astounding. As we will see later, these hypermodular organizations even call into question the role of the corporation, which has been the centerpiece of wealth creation in industrial societies for the past 200 years. We will also see that these organizations render irrelevant much of modern financial accounting, and, most significantly, undermine the very power of governments in regulating economic activity.

But before getting into that, we need to examine the now well-accepted collapse of hierarchy in corporations all over the world. . . .

GOING TOPLESS

THE FORCES THAT ARE resculpting corporations into hypermodulars are also tearing apart classical corporate structures. The predominant corporate structure of the twenty-first century will be scarcely recognizable to the industrial titans of the now anachronistic twentieth century. The problem, of course, is the collapse of hierarchy as we have known it, as characterized by the traditional corporation. Individual power was determined by one's position in the hierarchy, not by one's knowledge. Each person had a boss, and each boss had a boss, some distant figurehead that everybody read about and nobody saw.

The actual *work* of the corporation was performed by legions of pawns out in the field selling, or in the factory welding, or in the R&D labs designing. Policies and strategy were set out by some ivory-towered group who coveted the offices with the corner windows. In between, an army of middle managers acted as a conduit between what was happening in the field and what was desired by the top. The middle managers were high-priced messengers who would ferry papers up and down the hierarchy, a sort of all-purpose organizational lubricant keeping all the pieces moving.

In the Placeless Society, this is all being torn apart as workers are finding new, more efficient paths to coordinate their efforts. "Smart" computers, telecommunications, videophones, overnight and same-day package delivery collude to displace the messenger and the coordination function once provided by middle managers. In its place, nebulous teams, regardless of where they are physically or which department they are nominally assigned to, work on common problems. The groups expand and contract organically, and each member is aware of what the others are working on. If some members don't carry their own weight, everyone knows it. If a person excels by superior knowledge, ideas, or natural leadership, the group defers to her for guidance, regardless of whether she is a seasoned twenty-year veteran or a new engineer just out of university.

In this system, colleagues will no longer ask "what is your position on the corporate ladder?" but "what can you do?" Project leadership will be a constant negotiation of skills: an individual at the top, because of knowledge relevant to the tasks at hand, may have only a tangential role on the next project, or participate in several at a time. Teams may last for years, or be disbanded and regrouped anew with high frequency. It all depends on what is needed.

THE BORDERLESS COMPANY

THE COLLAPSE OF HIERARCHIES and the mixing and matching of resources from multiple companies allow us to sculpt at will organizations that defy any description in place: the placeless organization.

It can be a collaborative effort of a few people, or 10,000 people, linked together via electronic networks enabling them to work together in what computer junkies call "real time." The workers can be in the same city, or spread out in Manila, Munich, and Miami, yet because they are connected and aware of one another, decisions are collective and collaborative. Thus there is no need for a "headquarters." In the extreme, the organization may have a contact with the outside world only through a post office box, or everything-everywhere 800-number phone lines.

In the mid-1980s, the placeless office would have been considered a fictional notion, yet it has become mainstream among young, nimble enterprises. The next decade will see more companies like Telemorphix, an interactive TV production company of twenty-five employees with no headquarters and no office. Each person works from home, connected to a central computer physically located at the president's house. Employees know who is performing and who is not, and they often work on weekends and evenings without leaving the house. The company saves on office rental, the staff on commuting. When needed, telephones, faxes, and their in-computer network can set up conferences within seconds.

Placeless corporations also exist in the form of tightly coupled distinct corporations that act as a single entity. Mainstream businesses are already striving toward virtual manufacturing, operations so tightly intertwined with suppliers all the way to the end customer that it becomes irrelevant where one company ends and the next one begins. Each person concentrates on operating the whole chain of entities as efficiently as possible.

Innovative companies like Levi Strauss are linking their computers directly to their retailers' point-of-sale systems. The manufacturer knows *immediately* when an end-user purchases a size 8 pair of blue jeans and instantly adjusts cloth purchasing, production, and delivery schedules accordingly. The early information also gives Levi Strauss advance warning of trends and of how effective its regional advertising is. By merging manufacturing and retail operations, both become more responsive, agile, and profitable.

Some companies are so adamant about the strategic advantage found in the Fourth Dimension that they will not do business with those who don't make the journey with them. The British supermarket chain Tesco won't buy from suppliers who are not a part of its expansive computer network that links each store to suppliers electronically. The system tracks inventories, makes automatic orders, provides three-month forecasts, even pays the vendors—all automatically—and choreographs 1,200 diverse companies to act as a sole, highly streamlined organization.

The placeless organization will soon become mainstream as competition pressures corporations to enter the Fourth Dimension. Because the new form is so different from the classical "Corporate

Form," the challenge in the early twenty-first century will be in establishing new paradigms for strategy, management, organization, finance, and regulation. The emerging form of organization, distinct
from anything we've seen before, takes hypermodularity to the extreme in breaking components down (occasionally, down to the individual person) and is for the most part ignorant of place.

I call this new form of organization the "Amoeba Form" because,
like the jellylike blob of cytoplasm seen under the microscope, it is
amorphous, changeable, and conforms in shape to its environment; it
is difficult to distinguish where one ends and the next begins. When
an amoeba grows past a certain size, it merely splits in two, each going
its own way.

Clearly, the Amoeba Form will invade some industries faster than
others. It is built on the premise that people no longer need to be
physically together, or under the same corporate umbrella, to work as
a team. Resources can be mixed and matched on an infinitely dynamic, ad hoc way, to create economic wealth. And because the
Amoeba Form can grow and shrink to fit the problem, and adapt to
any challenge, it will prove superior to any corporation with ossified
bureaucracies.

Placeless technologies, by allowing anyone to work directly with
anyone else, have completely redefined the nature of "market." Markets are places where buyers and sellers come to get matched up. We
all know about the markets for products, stock markets, commodity
markets, financial markets, labor markets, even marriage markets.
With the advent of low-cost placeless technologies, we now have organizational markets where resources, ideas, people, and opportunities
can merge, match, and rematch in ways unimaginable ten years ago.

Stanley Baldwin, the three-time prime minister of Britain in the
early 1900s, remarked that if there was one lesson from history, it was
that society moves from status as measured by rank, to contract where
market value is the key. We have seen this in the political realm,
where feudalism gave way to mercantilism, and later, when economies based on markets thrived over centrally controlled ones.

In this context, where even the once-mighty Soviet Union has col-

lapsed and politicians are touting the advantages of market economies, the one place where socialism and a command economy still
rules is in the largest worldwide corporations. Too many are still buried in central planning. Their MBA's decide what "prices" ought to be
between departments, what gets produced and what does not, how
many people to employ and where, what capital equipment to purchase and from whom, who will get promoted and who will get
sacked. The hierarchic form is rich in misunderstandings, with little
choice for affected participants.

For all their good intentions, the corporate planners and central
planners suffer the same handicaps: lost is the individual entrepre-
neur; buried are the brilliant ideas germinated in the trenches; unknown are the fine details discovered organically in the field; unnur-
tured is a new technology used in a novel, or seemingly "crazy" way.

For this reason, forward-looking corporations have already introduced "markets" within their umbrella, and decentralized power.
*Intra*preneurs are allowed to be creative and autonomous, departments are treating one another as customers and suppliers, managers
are given the freedom to outsource, even when the capability is available in-house. Everywhere, markets are replacing hierarchy.

THE FIRST TO EVERYWHERE

SHIFTING TOWARD THE Amoeba Form of organization affects not
just the companies involved, but indeed transforms the very structure
of the economy. Many of the resources of our twentieth-century
economy are spent on *place:* office buildings, carports, highways,
cars, gasoline, auto insurance, even retail stores. Once organizations become decoupled from place, most of these expenses disappear, as do the supporting industries: janitors, building maintenance,
gasoline-station attendants, office space, secretaries, heating bills, and
construction workers. Although the result is displaced workers who
must scramble to hone new careers, society becomes much more productive and streamlined. In the end, the societies first able to weave

their multiple enterprises into the realm of placelessness will be the most productive and wealthiest in the highly competitive global economy.

No culture can move there overnight; the transition will be slow and awkward. In making the shift, the United States has some key cultural advantages, such as more desktop computers and telephones per capita than any other region on the Earth. Its strong entrepreneurial and individualistic culture, and a natural inclination to disregard hierarchy in favor of merit and ability, are essential traits in making the Amoeba Form of organization work to the fullest.

In contrast, European society works against entrepreneurial spirit, is suspicious of personal profit, and respects age, title, and position over raw ability. The Germans in particular have a rigid code of hierarchy that pervades their culture. All of this runs contrary to the free-form fluidity required of amoebic organizations.

The Japanese have a strong teamwork approach to problem solving, but their culture often thwarts individuals who seek to stand out. Until recently, the Japanese have favored fixed-term jobs with a fixed constellation of work colleagues for life. This contrasts sharply with the transient nature of the Amoeba Form. Ironically, despite their genius in commercializing things electronic, the Japanese have surprisingly few desktop computers in their households, and even office E-mail is not prevalent.

Despite certain advantages of its culture, the United States is also severely handicapped. The American educational system—so vital to the abstract problem solving of the Amoeba Form of organization—is sorrowfully unprepared for the challenges ahead, and ranks at the bottom of industrialized societies. Even more problematic, the US culture is lawsuit happy; instead of solving contractual disputes by compromise, Americans are too quick to enter into costly legal litigation. Because the Amoeba Form *is* contracts—and millions of them—the United States' legal system and culture need a major overhaul if it expects to remain competitive.

The United States may be in the lead *entering* the Fourth Dimension, but without a comprehensive change in industrial policy to better fertilize the nascent Amoeba Form, the race with Europe and Japan will be close.

A THOUSAND THOUSAND COMPANIES

THE CORPORATE FORM will decline because its original purpose has run its course. Law students are fond of defining corporations as charters granted by the government for a specific purpose: an enterprise becomes a "person" who can enter contracts, sue and be sued, pay taxes, et cetera. In English law, corporate charters were first granted by the king to limit the liabilities of the owners. If an exploration company hit the rocks, the loss to the owners would be limited to their investment; nobody was going to take away their family estate. Charters grew in popularity with the Industrial Revolution as the method of choice to set up a business enterprise. Today, they are *de rigueur* all over the world.

But does the Corporate Form limit liability, or does it magnify liability?

Is not a corporation, particularly in the United States, viewed as a large pot of money to be sued? Civil attorneys delight when they can weave a large corporate litigant as a defendant into a big-claim lawsuit, no matter how remote their actual responsibility. If a driver is hurt in an auto accident, sue General Motors for a safety lapse; if a person is sick from asbestos poisoning, sue the Manville Corporation; if it's lung cancer, sue Philip Morris; if the problem is somehow linked to synthetic materials in a medical implant, sue Dow Corning. Clearly we *should* hold corporations accountable when they are responsible. But can we expect the captains of industry to set themselves up as targets?

Is not the Corporate Form also an easy target for government regulators to effect controls on whatever suits them—taxes, pollution controls, affirmative action, environmental cleanup, safety regulations, and on and on? While governments necessarily amass regulations to control society's destiny, it is the omnipresent Amoeba Form that will provide the escape valve for business.

Over the next two decades, business strategists will question the wisdom of the Corporate Form, which will be seen as a lightning rod for lawsuits, government regulations, unionists, perhaps terrorists. The worldwide shift to the Amoeba Form will call for fresh challenges for governments everywhere.

Unfortunately, the governmental structures that have evolved over the past two centuries are not equal to the task. Because of its decentralized, ever-changing structure, the Amoeba Form will be uncannily unwieldy for regulators to get a handle on. Lest there be any doubt, look at one industry that comes closest to the Amoeba Form; it operates in every large urban center in the world and is infinitely adaptable to changing market conditions. Unquestionably the most profitable industry on the globe, with estimated retail sales at $1 trillion a year worldwide, it is the illicit drug trade.

The drug industry is as complex as any other, perhaps more so. The cocaine sector alone is believed to "employ" as many as 1.5 million people in *production* as growers, harvesters, laboratory processors, buyers, pilots, accountants, and gunmen. An additional uncounted army is involved in *distribution:* smugglers, regional distributors, retail sales agents, and money launderers.

The worldwide drug network has many characteristics of the Amoeba Form. While some clusters of individuals in the drug industry are more powerful than others, the notion of a well-organized cartel is exaggerated in the press. In reality, the industry is highly fragmented and decentralized, since each individual (or cluster of individuals) is an autonomous business that provides specific services to other industry participants. The network operates by market forces and is governed by its own code of ethics, verbal contracts, and internal self-policing.

So tightly choreographed are all the independent "contractors," that together they create the appearance of a single megalithic organization. Law enforcement agencies and the press like to think that once the "top ringleaders" are crushed, the whole network will tumble. However, the Amoeba Form is the most resilient of economic

organizations: no sooner does the government cut down one operation than two more emerge, like Hydra heads, to take its place. There
is no top or bottom, only a flexible network. Conforming to new realities at once, it alters supplies, transportation corridors, shipping "containers," prices, and distribution tactics, in a hostile environment.

The lessons to government regulators are as clear as they are frightening: If the technologies of placelessness encourage the Amoeba
Form in mainstream industries, how will rules be enforced? Traditionally, government regulators could monitor 20,000 employees scattered over a dozen manufacturing sites with relative ease by filing a
single complaint to the company president. In its place are hundreds,
thousands of "amoebic clusters" that can, if need be, slip out of existence overnight to reemerge somewhere else. The fluidity of the
Amoebic Form makes it difficult to pin responsibility for environmental regulations, product liability, taxing, and auditing. It is precisely for
this reason that the drug industry evolved toward this nonhierarchical
system.

In the Amoeba Form it is virtually impossible to place responsibility on any large corporate body, because none exists. Today, it is hard
enough to prove that, say, a feminine hygiene product caused cervical
cancer. But what if the same item were produced under the Amoeba
Form? What if thousands of tiny one-person "companies" networking
together were involved in the conception, design, testing, manufacturing, quality assurance, packaging, warehousing, advertising, and
distribution? Which one would be responsible for the cervical cancer?
All of them? None of them? And what if they were too small to have
any significant assets, or they just closed the door and went out of
business?

In the new reality of the twenty-first century, economic organization under the Amoeba Form is so fragmented that it will prove
nearly impossible for nation-states to regulate. Governments still immersed in the Third Dimension will be outmaneuvered at every turn
by commerce operating in the Fourth. For this reason, the first two
decades of the twenty-first century will likely see a frenzy of unfet-

tered global turbocapitalism, until governments can catch up.

AMOEBA MANAGEMENT

THE TRANSITION INTO THE Amoeba Form, and the ability of diverse people to work from their homes, will also occur at different speeds for different tasks and industries. The most affected jobs will involve one-on-one client interaction in the field: insurance adjusters, field sales personnel, real estate agents, retail stockbrokers. Next will be areas where groups of professionals work together to solve specific problems: accountants, lawyers, architects, graphic artists, computer programmers. At another level will be the information-intensive industries: government, sales orders, customer service, teaching, insurance processing.

Clearly, the activities least affected are the ones where the work has to be performed *in situ* due to the practical limitations of physicality. These laggard industries—mining, shipbuilding, automobile assembly, janitorial services, and equipment repair—are nonetheless likely to become amoebic in that the value chain will increasingly fragment and specialize, with more tasks shifting to subcontractors.

Some corporations will make the transition into the Fourth Dimension better than others. In some instances, we don't yet know how to transform staid, hierarchic enterprises into a streamlined amoebic organization. Some are spinning off businesses outside their core competency, while others are breaking up internally, giving full operational autonomy to divisions.

Such breakups are in the right direction, but too often the division managers brought up in the school of the twentieth-century corporation stop short of making a full transition to remove the next layers of hierarchy. In truth, any department or individual should be free to contract services elsewhere, and the price of services provided in-house should be explicit. If the business and product make sense, the various "departments" should move in sync as a team.

The forward-looking manager will identify the organization's core competency—what they do best in the world beyond anyone else—and redefine the business's *raison d'être* around that core. Employees, tasks, or departments that are not in the core area might better be outsourced. In some cases, existing departments can be spun off as independent business units, supercharged by employees who would now have the magic of ownership and the incentive to make a difference.

As for the areas of core competency that remain, the wise executive will seek amoebic relationships with other entities, even competitors, to leverage that competency to the fullest. It was this principle that pulled AT&T from being only a telephone company to become a credit card company: AT&T's core competency was transaction processing, combined with a world-class brand name associated with integrity and reliability.

Our society will not *leap* to the highly fragmented Amoeba Form, but will evolve there. Some of us will be affected overnight by a closing factory overtaken by more nimble competitors. Others will find their old familiar jobs now conducted on an unfamiliar keyboard: the manufacturing workers whose instructions come on a diskette, the personnel director who needs to scan a database to find the right talent, the salesperson who places orders by modem on a car phone. We will all be affected differently. But we will all be affected.

Our inexorable movement away from the Corporate Form toward a free-flow Amoeba Form will call for new skills on the job market. Managers will face particular changes: the importance of title and position will erode. The new leaders will no longer be like ship captains but rather like candidates running for office. In the evolving market-based organizations, they will be masters at negotiating, at selling ideas to others, at putting the right teams together and getting them enthused. (As we enter the twenty-first century, we'll witness a steady rise in the popularity of books and courses on the art of negotiation and team motivation.) The skillful leaders will also get people to reach a consensus and resolve disputes before they flare up.

Decentralization works best with self-motivated and self-monitoring individuals. The successful Amoeba Form workers will be able to see a problem and figure out solutions on their own, without being told what to do (those jobs can be automated).

Our vocabulary will change. To be "at work" or "at the office" will no longer describe a *location* but an *activity*. *Where* will no longer matter, as long as the work gets done.

In the twenty-first century, more people will work autonomously; no one will be there to watch them. As a result, the emphasis will shift from the motions of work to its result. Individuals involved in the Amoeba Form of organization become like a corporation under the Corporate Form: they are valued and compensated on the quality of their output. They become service workers, whose service is adding value to a physical product (as an automobile-assembly worker) or to the group (as an insurance adjuster). They may have one or more suppliers or one or more customers, but either way, everybody is a client.

New, market-based compensation systems will evolve. In the old economy, "job slots" were often paid within rigid limits: two secretaries would earn the same income, even if one was far superior to the other. Assembly workers with the same seniority would get identical pay regardless of creativity, conscientiousness, or contribution. The system was interested in easy measurement (the number of hours worked) and paid accordingly. A "bonus" always fit within a tight predetermined range designed to be a small fraction of the base salary.

Under the Amoeba Form, our compensation will not be related to the number of hours worked but to the value of our work to the collective effort. Contracts will resemble those of rock stars or movie celebrities who are compensated according to their likely impact on ultimate box office revenues, or who are paid a royalty based on the commercial success of the end product. Bill Gates at Microsoft already pays his top programmers "celebrity" salaries, plus a royalty on the sales of the products worked on. He knows that good talent can make or break a product; if he doesn't pay accordingly, someone else will. In the age of the Amoeba Form, talent flows easily to the highest bidder.

The reward for superior talent will define the job market of the twenty-first century. In the command-and-control economy, the creators of organizations extracted extraordinary profits from the value chain: the suppliers of raw materials, workers, and capital providers were largely compensated at "standard" rates based on prevailing commodity prices, wages, and interest rates. If the entrepreneurs put together a well-tuned organization, the "excess" profits would go to the entrepreneurs—the organizers. With the Amoeba Form, they and the workers are likely to be one and the same, and the talented worker may earn an extraordinary income.

In the twenty-first century, income will be less apportioned to provide a "decent wage" (with upper and lower bounds), and more closely related to talent, energy, ability, and contribution. This is good news for the talented and the hardworking and those endowed with cutting-edge technological tools, but disastrous for those in the Second World and elsewhere without marketable twenty-first-century skills.

We have seen the forces of everything-everywhere dramatically change the rules of wealth and how our economy is organized. Now, in the next few chapters, we shift our attention to government and the breakdown of the most powerful force that has evolved in modern history: the nation-state.

Part Five

THE EROSION OF GOVERNANCE

10

THE GLOBAL TRIBES

NAIMA ABOU-HIND WAS taking her final exam. She always had a talent for drawing faces, for translating any shape into something full of feeling.

As she copied the tiny Greek statue on her desk onto paper, she thought of her family in Tunisia; but the institute in Cairo was everything she could ask for. She had received a scholarship from a wealthy family in Saudi Arabia who wanted Islam to regain world leadership in the arts. Instead of a live male model, she had to make do with the plaster-molded sculpture of Apollo provided by her teacher.

Naima was giving form to the thighs when her statue was snatched by a stranger in robes—it was the *mutawa,* the "morality police." She and her teacher were hurled into separate beat-up vans and taken to the police station for booking for their "crime" against the sacred *shari'ah.* This meant expulsion from the school. What punishment would she have to endure? Even if they let her go, how would she afford the trek back to Tunisia?

═══

Sergei Zvereva would have no need for the warm, furry *shapka* stuffed in the seat compartment in front of him. He had left Ekaterinburg with its blizzard-strewn landscape, and below, central Africa seemed to be rising up, close to his aircraft.

Clutching the Holy Book, he wondered if he was crazy to go off to this jungle land to preach Christianity to "pagans and animists." Sergei had been inspired by watching Christian televangelists with their bright-red carpets and dreamy choirs beamed directly from California.

He would convert people to what he believed was the true nature of existence. His trip was financed by wealthy contributors in Canada and the United States; it didn't matter to him. He would take a crash course in Kongo and have a hut in a village somewhere.

Sergei felt a certain comfort at being part of a global movement.

==

For the first time, Richard Amorose *belonged* where he was. He had always felt different from his classmates and was shunned by them. Even home was awkward: he was supposed to think and act like his siblings, and play their games.

The last week of high school and the prom were disasters; what a relief to clear out and be off to college. Richard's new world was much larger than the small midwestern town where he grew up, with different outlooks on life and philosophies. He met Michael, from Sweden, who thought exactly as he did. Gazing into Michael's pale blue eyes was like looking into a mirror. That night, he made a permanent transformation; he'd found his home.

Now, at the international AIDS conference in Montreal, he was a part of a global movement, a sort of nation of its own, with a common cause and purpose next to which nothing else seemed so important.

==

Some think that global commerce and mass media will create a bland, homogeneous world. In reality, the capacity of placelessness will more likely make the opposite true. One consistent thread of human nature is our primeval yearning for tribal affiliation—to being part of a group that is different from another—to coalesce into the "us" and the "them."

From the beginning of human time, when *Australopithecus afri-*

canus and *Australopithecus robustus* first squared off 1.5 million years ago, humankind has been grouped into opposing camps. The Old Testament is packed with stories of clan groupings; Homer's *Iliad* pits the Greeks against the Trojans in a battle imbued with tribal brotherhood and retribution.

Native Americans and Africans coalesced easily into tribes. The history of Asia and Europe is filled with ever-changing alliances, here a feudal lord, there a king, again a church, then a nation. In our own lives, we all remember the schoolyard cliques, the street gangs, our fraternities and sororities, the sports-team fanaticism, the tribelike affiliations to our country clubs, our professions, our neighborhoods. None of us has escaped its pull.

In the Placeless Society, the smorgasbord of options for tribal affiliation will be wider than anyone has ever imagined. Far from being homogeneous, the future world culture will be a dynamic one, with swirls of the Confucian East embedded in the Christian West, with pockets of homosexuality in a sea of heterosexuality, and groups of environmentalists mixing with industrialists.

Although the Placeless Society broadens our exposure to new tribal affiliations that are determined as much by choice as by accidents of birth, it places new stress on the old social fabric. Placelessness means that the people born into a given country are exposed to alternate ideas that compete with a monolithic national culture. The new ideas invigorate a culture, but at the same time create transnational allegiances that tear at the heart of parochialism, and radically change the rules of "self."

NATIONAL IDENTITY

IT WOULD BE DIFFICULT to deny the powerful effect of nationalism on our lives. As we approach the *fin de siècle* and look back a hundred years, it is clear that no institution has had a tighter grip on controlling the destinies of each of us—and for most of us, determining group self-identity—than the nation-state. Nationalism pulled all of humanity into the vortex of two world wars. Our nation-states controlled the flow of immigration at our borders, provided for our defense and security, printed our currencies, and regulated commerce and our economies.

We have all been touched by it, but few of us stop to think about what it is that makes a nation-state. A *nation* is a community that shares a common culture, territory, and language. Its people feel bonded to one another because they believe they share a common descent or racial origin, a religion, a common future, or a common enemy. We often think of nations as countries with a government, but that is not always so. For example, 25 million Kurds are torn among Turkey, Iran, Iraq, Syria, and Azerbaijan. The million-strong Basque nation in Europe straddles France and Spain in the Pyrenees Mountains. Strictly speaking, these peoples are nations, though they lack political control over their own lives.

A *state*, on the other hand, is a hunk of land with a sovereign governmental body, wherein the state sets the supreme law of the land, above which there is no superior legal authority. We usually think of *state* and *country* as one and the same. Within a state, there may exist multiple nations. The United States has approximately a million Native Americans living on or near some 300 "Indian" reservations. Brazil has some ninety nations. Even the name of the *United* Kingdom is a tacit acknowledgment that the country consists of multiple nations: the Scots, the Welsh, the Irish, and the English—now expanded to also embrace Pakistanis, Indians and West Indians, among others.

The modern nation-state is made up of the overlap between two concepts: the nation and the state. In the "ideal" nation-state, the nation and the state borders are matched. Although they are changing, modern-day France, Japan, Iceland, and Vietnam are nation-states that have people, government, and territory relatively well matched. In the former Yugoslavia, they are not.

When we look today at the constellations of power around us (the United States, Japan, Germany, France, Italy, Russia, Canada, China, India, and another 190-odd nation-states) we take them for granted as if they had always been in existence and always will be. In reality, the idea of *nation-state* has existed for only a mere speck of time in the history of human development.

The great empires—Roman, Ottoman, Mongol, Persian, and a hundred like them throughout history—ruled by brute force over conquered territories, disregarding the self-identity of their subjects. Alexander the Great from Macedonia was happy to conquer the Hindu population of northern India. The Hapsburg family passed around pieces of Europe to family members like wedding cake. Napoleon, a Frenchman, looked forward to conquering the Germanic peoples of Prussia and Austria and other diverse peoples in modern-day Spain, Italy, and elsewhere. The despots often invoked religious rituals to maintain their claims to absolute, unlimited power over their "subjects." The concept of government *by the people* was not at issue.

An early turning point came in England: the upwardly mobile commoners—the wealthy merchants and businessmen—had gone up the social ladder carried by the new wave of the Industrial Revolution. They resented the rigid social structure where mobility was an anomaly. In its place, they offered a new legitimacy of government dependent on the people, a new conceptual framework where each person became equal to every other member. This completely novel idea understandably caught hold in the public. It asserted that the only legitimate power of the state derives from the people, who have the inherent right of self-determination.

By the end of the nineteenth century, the Industrial Revolution also built roads, canals, and railroads, to tie vast geographic areas together. The evolving trading patterns lent geographic form to a new concept of self-identity that spread over large areas of land.

With the American and French Revolutions completed, the new nationalistic fervor spread like fire, consolidating a decentralized Italy under Mazzini, a fragmented Germany under Bismarck. By the end of World War I, the Hapsburg and Romanov empires had collapsed into the nation-states of Austria, Hungary, Czechoslovakia, Poland, Yugoslavia, and Romania. Nationalistic fervor swept India under Mahatma Gandhi, China under Sun Yat-sen.

The nation-state as the dominant form of tribal affiliation had come of age.

PLACELESS TRIBES

HISTORY SUGGESTS THAT PART of the human condition is to seek a self-identity and to join with others who share that identity. There is a sense of "us" versus "them" in this, a sort of soccer-match mentality in group membership. German nationalism does not exist except in the context of France, Poland, Italy, and the United Kingdom. American nationalism does not exist except in the context of Japan, Europe, and others.

In each country, we are fond of idealizing the national character that sets us apart and therefore makes "us" better than "them" somewhere else. The Americans have their raw individualism and personal freedoms; the Germans boast their meticulous efficiency and clean streets; the French have their *joie de vivre,* epicurean culture, and spirit of debate; the Japanese pride themselves on their collective discipline; and Greece has its history as the cradle of Western civilization. Each culture has its *something,* a certain combination of beliefs, customs, features that make its members believe they are superior.

Nationalism is comforting for each member born into the culture of the nation. It allows each individual's meaning to be understood with only an economy of words or a nod of the head. Each person's belief system is in sync with those around him. It is these nuances of national character that make so many of us feel "at home."

But placelessness no longer confines us to parochial tribalism defined by mere state boundaries. It broadens our freedom of association, our knowledge of competing ideologies. The world watches MTV, and our work colleagues come from remote corners of the planet. We are more and more aligned with global—instead of national—interests and causes.

Placelessness is facilitating tribal affiliations between individuals of common interests, beliefs, and cultures, but in diverse lands. The world is becoming a marketplace of ideas where group affiliation and ideological interest no longer depend on place but on free choice. Self-identity and dignity are no longer associated strictly with one's country of birth, but according to one's global tribe.

THE FLAME OF ALLAH

THE SIGNIFICANCE OF THE tribe is demonstrated in the power of Islam.

The phenomenal rise of Islam easily traverses national borders, spreading across Algeria, Tunisia, Egypt, Lebanon, and Turkey, and affecting the Sudan, Kuwait, Saudi Arabia, Jordan. Its swelling body of a billion adherents reaches into Indonesia, Malaysia, Pakistan, Bangladesh, and great swaths of India. Its shadow falls as far away as France, England, and the United States.

Of course, Islam is not new. What *is* new is a grass-roots solidarity among Muslims from Djakarta to New York, from Khartoum to Birmingham. In the Fourth Dimension, they are keenly aware of threats to their dignity *wherever* they are in the world. When Salman Rushdie's *Satanic Verses* offended Muslim fundamentalists, riots erupted in Pakistan and India, Muslims in England took to the streets burning books, discussion groups opened up in mosques in Los Angeles. Throughout much of the Islamic world the book was banned. Such a vast global fraternity could never act as a single organism so spontaneously except for the realities of placelessness.

Global communication networks envelop the world: the Gulf War, with Saddam Hussein against the rest of the world, was watched on television monitors by Muslims everywhere. Cassette tapes by Egypt's imprisoned Sheik Omar Abdel Rahman and Tunisia's exiled Rachid al-Ghannushi are traded in New York and Tunis. Mosques are interconnected by a network of telephones and fax machines: a worldwide citizens "army" of a billion Muslims can be made aware—if need be—of attacks against Islam on just a few hours' notice.

Laced across this grass-roots, decentralized network are more formal organizations—the Islamic Group, the Islamic Jihad, the Hezbollah, Hamas, the Popular Front for the Liberation of Palestine, and dozens more—each group connected by secret memberships, international bank transfers, telephone, and global couriers. In the fundamentalist movement, no one person or group of people has control: the Fourth Dimension allows individuals to link up with others in a decentralized way without hierarchy, making it impossible for any government to quell the quest of Islam for status as a truly global tribe. For each leader crushed, jailed, or exiled, two more take his place.

When Islamic fundamentalist leaders met in Khartoum in 1991, their announced goal was to create a transitional "Islamic Belt" stretching from Iran through the Middle East and North Africa, ignoring existing nation-states. Vast sums are transferred between mosques and militants linking Iran, Saudi Arabia, Sudan, and Afghanistan, to support fundamentalists in Algeria, Egypt, Tunisia, and elsewhere. These sinews of camaraderie have ancient roots, but in the Placeless Society, they have the potential to multiply, amplify, and strengthen as never before.

The fuel that is flaming Islam is understandable in the context of a quest for dignity and self-identity. The West has demeaned the once-proud people of Arabia as barbaric infidels. By the nineteenth century, the French and British had managed to control the area, eventually trading great swaths of territory among themselves, with utter contempt for natural, cultural, or ethnic boundaries.

The leaders that were installed by the West sought to maintain power by autocratic rules, intimidation, torture, and corrupt policies. As the nominal leaders in Jordan, Iraq, Syria, Libya, and Palestine grow older, the baby boomers swelling the demographic ranks will view them increasingly as out of touch. In several countries, two-thirds of the population is below age twenty. A third of the people attending the mosques are unemployed. The clerics at the mosques are eager to offer an alternative to the failures of the national governments, which are seen as set up by the West. In place of what they regard as decadence and materialism, the clerics offer spiritual values based on their interpretation of the Koran.

Islamic fundamentalism will continue to sweep the Second World in the twenty-first century in the same way that the promise of personal dignity and self-identity has molded much of world history. When the First World—the rich countries—speaks of building "infrastructure," it means fiber-optic links, satellite communications, a computer superhighway, a supersonic airport. In the Second World, it means repairing the bridge that got washed out in last year's flood. The First World builds universities equipped with billion-dollar cyclotrons and libraries whose volumes are counted in the millions. In the Second World, "education" often means a tin-roofed hut with a parched soccer field outside.

Even worse, we in rich countries are finding our *own* labor force less in demand, since we are able to make more with fewer people and less raw materials. As the thrust of the Fourth Dimension carries us forward, we leave the Second World further and further behind. Unlike the early days of capitalism, when the rich could always hire the poor, today's rich countries have no use for poor countries or their raw materials.

At some point, we need to ask ourselves a question: If all of Pakistan and Bangladesh, with a quarter billion people, were to disappear from the face of the earth, would those glued to the Dow Jones Industrial average or those in the citadels of power of the First World even notice? The question needs to be asked regarding the half billion souls who populate Nigeria, Indonesia, Sudan, Ethiopia, Tanzania, and others elsewhere. It could well be that the gulf between the haves and the have-nots is already so great that if the Second World were to disappear, the First World might falter briefly, but within three months it would be onto other problems.

This looming reality has not escaped the notice of the Second World. What is the unemployed Algerian parent of five to think when he sees pictures of unimaginable wealth and luxury on television? What of the thousands of people who live in Cairo's dusty shantytown—"City of the Dead"—with clothes lines stretched between hovels, and children kicking discarded cans among medieval tombs— what are *they* to do?

The green banner of radical Islam offers them an alternate path to self-respect. Defining Western values as decadent and adopting the Koran allows the people of Islam to surpass the West by their own ideological standards.

THE BUILT-IN COLLAPSE

ISLAM WILL RISE ALL over much of the developing world. If history is any guide, however, by midcentury their chosen path will collapse. The parallels between today's Islamic fundamentalism and the 1917 Bolshevik Revolution are unmistakable. Both grew out of an ideological fervor to create a utopian world by yielding individualism to a higher good: socialism for the Bolsheviks, Allah for the fundamentalists. Both require strict conformity to ideological norms. Both systems have their inner circle of ideological experts who issue decrees to the faithful based on supposed ideological values. They view the rest of the world as satanic and worthy of conversion, even by force, and use the need to invest in global expansion as an excuse for further sacrifice at home. Both systems are a reaction to the unprecedented wealth created elsewhere, and an attempt to foster autonomy while suppressing foreign interference or ideologies.

But of the two, it is fundamentalist Islam that may eventually pose the greater challenge to the West. In the area of economics at least, Marxism and capitalism agreed on much more than they disagreed over. They both accepted the value of material wealth and the importance of industrialization. Where they differed was on the distribution of wealth between those who furnished labor and those who contributed capital.

Islamic fundamentalism, in contrast, does not even accept that material things are necessarily good. The zealots further seek to control *every* aspect of personal life: how one dresses, eats, or prays; how one courts and makes love. Yet for all their advice, the fundamentalists offer no cogent theory on how wealth is to be produced—a particularly egregious problem considering the abject poverty in the countries where it is most likely to bloom, and considering the exploding number of mouths to feed, bodies to clothe, and families to house.

Many interpretations of the Koran run contrary to sound economics. Property rights being very insecure and tenuous, incentives for investments are practically nonexistent. It is no accident that few corporations in the Islamic world are larger than family enterprises; contracts between businesses or between employers and employees are not enforceable in any meaningful way. Since the Koran outlaws "hoarding," undeveloped land cannot be owned. Even charging interest for loans raises eyebrows. Simply put, Koranic teachings argue that striving for profits is corrupt.

Part of the problem stems from what *shari'ah* scholars acknowledge as "the closing of the gate of *ijtihad*"—the application of reason to seek truth—in the fifteenth century. Any new interpretation of the Koran after that time is simply disrespectful of the earlier jurists. Thus, while the rest of society—its customs, organizations, laws, and structures—is free to adapt to the challenges of the Fourth Dimension, the sacred *taqlid* of Islamic interpretation potentially freezes a billion people in the Middle Ages.

In the end, as Islamic fundamentalism will rise and standards of living plummet, fierce battles for power will occur between fundamentalists and moderates. When the dust has settled—as with world communism—the peoples affected will find their living standards further behind and the rest of the world further ahead. As for now, the Islamic fundamentalists are only forestalling the inevitable: when the dam bursts, it may well spill a torrent of humanity—and perhaps a fresh wave of global terrorism—across the Mediterranean into Western Europe, North America, and throughout the world.

THE CHILDREN OF ABRAHAM

WORLD JUDAISM ALSO ILLUSTRATES how global tribes operate in a placeless society. In its current embodiment, Judaism is a curious nation, one *not* defined strictly by language, ethnicity, blood lines, origins, or religion.

While Hebrew has been revived for use in modern Israel, millions of Jews can utter little more than "Hanukkah" or "bar mitzvah." The diaspora around the world speaks everything from Hungarian to Spanish, the lingua franca being English as much as anything else.

Genealogical blood lines are also irrelevant. While the Torah makes a case for the Ethiopian Jew being genealogically related to Lithuanian Jews through a multimillennium grandparent in Abraham, the link is more academic than real. Further, is not a convert to Judaism Jewish? So it is not blood lines that define the Jew, and religious belief is no longer the binding force either. Throughout Israel, the United States, and elsewhere, many secular Jews—or atheistic ones—have no less fervor for Jewish holidays, rituals, and customs than religious ones.

If there is a common thread uniting world Jewry, it is perhaps the dark force of anti-Semitism. It occurs in Ethiopia, Europe, the Middle East, and America, both North and South. Few Jews living today have been untouched: Hitler in a single genocidal war murdered one-third of the world's Jewish population; others lost property or migrated. Today, everywhere, beneath the thin veneer of civility, the threats, jokes, and innuendoes go on.

The common cultural beliefs stemming from the Torah within, combined with the common threats of xenophobia from without, have created a powerful cohesive glue uniting the otherwise diverse peoples of this world diaspora. This unity has always existed, but the novelty in the Age of Everything-Everywhere is that the Jewish people of the world can now *act* on their unity and need no longer be in isolation from one another.

True, Israel may exist as the "capital" of the Jewish people, but the

Jewish "nation" in the Fourth Dimension goes far beyond that. The Russian-speaking engineer from Moscow, the Spanish-speaking secretary from Buenos Aires, the Holocaust survivor in Tel Aviv, are part of a global fraternity, a people connected in the Fourth Dimension.

When Israel has been threatened, thousands of Jews have dropped their work to flee to Israel to pick up arms in its defense. In times of peace, they send their sons and daughters to live on *kibbutzim*. When Jews are attacked anywhere in the world—such as the bombing of a Jewish cultural center in Buenos Aires in 1994—the Israeli Mossad is immediately there (whether or not Israeli citizens were involved). In every way, the Jewish people are a nation defined more by an *esprit de nation* than by place.

COUNTRYLESS COUNTRIES

THE IDEA OF A placeless nation was also demonstrated by the Palestinians prior to their regaining a toehold in the Middle East. Expelled from their land for nearly half a century, they dispersed throughout Arabia. In time, the Palestinian Liberation Organization was recognized internationally as the government-in-exile of a dispersed nation without a state. With a budget and an army, the "virtual state" of Palestine set up headquarters first in Jordan, then Lebanon, then Tunisia.

Throughout the region, governments identified who the Palestinians were and extracted a "Palestinian tax" of 5 to 7 percent of a worker's income—all remitted to the PLO government office in Tunis, who in turn dispatched the funds to banks in New York, Geneva, and elsewhere. The process of tax collection and investment completely bypassed the problem of place.

The money would finance state business, Palestinian families on welfare, hospitals, universities, community centers, and newspapers for Palestinians still in the "occupied" territories, even when the Palestinians had no sovereignty over any country or territory.

At the time, the PLO also operated a placeless army of fighters—

individuals who carried out the battle for liberating Palestine on a global basis: here a kidnapping, there an airplane hijacking, again a mass murder. Regarded as fanatical terrorists by the outside world, the PLO was actually engaging in a sophisticated, well-financed form of warfare in a placeless society. It was a battle without a battle front or enemy lines, but no less effective: the world would have forgotten the Palestine problem without it. In the end, Palestine has recovered some of its lost territory, but it probably would have been unsuccessful had it not first operated in the realm of placelessness.

The Palestinian placeless government evolved over multiple decades, yet the like can be formed overnight.

When Kuwait was invaded on August 2, 1990, it became an "offshore country" in one day. It had an offshore population living in luxury apartments from London to Riyadh, a seat in the United Nations in New York, over $100 billion in an investment trust in London, real estate in California, a public relations firm and lobbyists in Washington, an offshore airline, and an Olympic team. It had everything a country needs, except a country.

Kuwaiti businesses were no less mobile. The day of the invasion, a bank manager faxed critical bank records out of the country. The bank reopened in Bahrain the next day, outside Saddam Hussein's grasp, without missing a beat. As we have seen, communications technology has made the location of a business increasingly unimportant.

While exiled governments are as old as the Greeks and continued to embrace the Gaulist government in France during World War I, what is new in the Placeless Society is that the governments-in-exile can perform virtually every function that governments-in-place do.

Before the Information Age, a "countryless" country, such as Kuwait in 1990 or the PLO before its reconciliation with Israel, would have been inconceivable; a century ago, to control the borders was to control the country. In the new age, borders are less important in defining a nation, or managing a state.

THE UBIQUITOUS DRAGON

THE EFFECTS OF GLOBAL tribes are felt as well in the realm of commercial power. China—a country of 1.2 billion inhabitants—has demonstrated spectacular economic growth over the last fifteen years, and promises to become a major economic juggernaut in the twenty-first century.

While economists and political scientists seek to understand the "Chinese miracle" and apply the lessons to other Second World regions, they have not grasped the underlying realities of the Chinese people. By drawing a line around 1.2 billion Chinese and calling it a country, they have arbitrarily excluded the *real* China that exists in the Fourth Dimension.

The analysts seem to forget that for centuries, the square-sailed junks of the South China Sea plied the fertile waters for fish, and in time set up trading posts on the protected harbors around its perimeter. The Chinese were able merchants, and in time some came to settle in the Philippines, Malaysia, Indonesia, Thailand, Cambodia, and Vietnam—every land that forms the South China Sea basin. The Chinese diaspora further spread under the yoke of European colonialism, and to North America, where poor peasants came as coolie laborers.

Ethnic Chinese now dominate trade and investment in every country in eastern Asia except Japan and Korea. They have the most capital, the best connections, and the best access to information to put regional deals together, superior to any other group in the world. These dispersed Chinese are the backbone of a new and vitalized regional economy. Today, 55 million ethnic Chinese live outside the Peoples' Republic of China, and while they have developed into distinct cultural groups, each sporting somewhat local characteristics, the sinews tying them to a common "Chineseness" remain strong. Almost all of Hong Kong and much of Taiwan is Chinese; so are three-quarters of Singaporeans. The most progressive economies in the area have powerful Chinese driving the domestic economies forward: the Philippines, Indonesia, Thailand, and Malaysia.

In the Philippines, ethnic Chinese form only 1 percent of the population, yet their companies comprise 35 percent of the sales of Philippine companies and two-thirds of the fifty largest enterprises. In Indonesia, the Chinese are just 2 percent of the population, but they account for up to three-quarters of private domestic capital and control seventeen of the twenty-five biggest business groups. In Thailand, the Chinese account for just one-tenth of the population, but they own 90 percent of the commercial and manufacturing assets and half the capital in domestic banks. In Malaysia one-third of the population is ethnic Chinese, and they retain tight control of the economy. For decades, the government attempted to force transfer to the majority Malays before finally giving up. Taken together, the Chinese diaspora represents just 4 percent of the population of mainland China, yet their "national" income is about two-thirds as large.

The labyrinth of business deals and commercial ties between their diverse outposts are so complex and interwoven that few outsiders have been able to penetrate it. This success is due partly to the commercial structure adopted by the offshore Chinese community: the highly adaptive Amoeba Form of organization. Businesses are mostly small and family operated, but the key is in the *guanxi*—networks—involving family members or village clan members, and spanning thousands of miles across the Pacific. The bonds of kinship, dialect, or common roots to a particular clan or village are so strong that multimillion yen contracts are often struck verbally in a matter of days. In the West, they would take months of legal hocus-pocus to finalize.

Collectively, the result is a highly decentralized business organization operating so seamlessly that, for all practical purposes, the boundaries of the nation-states do not even exist. The flexible—even secret—business arrangements make it all but impossible for governments to regulate the commerce. For example, when Taiwan sought to have foreign-exchange controls, Chinese merchants could deposit large sums of cash with a neighborhood gold shop in Taipei, and a relative or business colleague could withdraw it the next day from the gold shop's collaborator 1,200 miles away in Vietnam. When a Thai tax collector wants his due from a local factory, the factory owner simply asks his supplier in Hong Kong to overbill for equipment, with the difference sent to an offshore bank account—or gold shop—in Indonesia.

More important, the Amoeba Form allows ten of thousands of Chinese businesses to act, interact, connect, and reconnect in flexible ways to adjust to the global economy. And while the Chinese bonds tether decentralized business entities across vast distances, these businesses, in turn, interact in intimate ways in the local economies. They supply the Malays, the Philippines, the Thais, the Singaporeans, the Indonesians, with jobs and access to a global economy.

A Chinese writer once described the highly decentralized Chinese business structure as a "tray of sand," compared to the monolithic structural "block of granite" characteristic of the Japanese form. In the twenty-first century, the West may well try to emulate the decentralized, informal Chinese *guanxi,* leaving the well-known hierarchical Japanese *zaibatsu* in the dust of the twentieth century.

ECO-TRIBES

THE GLOBAL TRIBES WE HAVE discussed—the Jews, the Muslims, the Chinese—all relate to placeless memberships that bind a dispersed people. But the twenty-first century is also bringing a new class of powerful tribes whose membership is by pure ideological choice, having little to do with language or birth. The most obvious example is *environmentalism.*

The current wave of environmentalism sweeping the planet is born from our individual experiences: from the parent in Baton Rouge fiercely upset about her son's breathing disorder stemming from the neighborhood incinerator, to the fishermen along the Volga, Rhine, or Pechora Rivers who can no longer fish—or at times even get near the rancid water. There is the child in Mexico City who can barely see her school down the street through the smog, or the family in Kenya at a loss to find any remaining trees for shade or firewood. Most people adapt, but others react and join eco-organizations.

Starting out small, with odd names like Wyoming's Pollution Posse, or clever acronyms like SAVE, RESCUE, and PANIC, they have grown from neighborhood fringe groups barely noticed by the press in the 1960s, to powerful global organizations causing industries to tremble and nation-states to cower.

The National Wildlife Federation's directory displays over 2,000 conservation groups in the United States alone. Tens of thousands more are scattered like so many stars—some large, some barely visible—across Europe, South America, Africa, Asia, even Antarctica. As we enter the Placeless Society, these "dots" are forming constellations, each connecting with the other to act toward a common goal.

Some of these organizations are downright militaristic and do not eschew violence to get what they want. Earth First! openly endorses eco-terrorism anywhere in the world: *any* means justifies saving the environment (some members say even murder). Earth First! operates through a network of 15,000 members, among them some 2,000 hard-core "guerrilla" fighters. Members have been known to fell high-voltage electrical transmission towers, destroy bulldozers and earth-movers, torch buildings, and attempt to shut down nuclear power plants. To foil investigators, Earth First! has learned to operate with a lean and highly decentralized structure, and avoids keeping formal membership rolls.

The Sea Shepherds, a detachment of the growing worldwide eco-navy, operate with volunteer pirate crews. Their take-no-prisoners approach has led to three commandos sinking eight whaling ships, submerging a tuna drift-net ship, ramming half a dozen others, and blockading the Canadian sealing fleet. With each successful attack, their membership, bank accounts, and following only grow.

Greenpeace, the world's largest environmental group, has grown so powerful that even nation-states have learned to keep their distance. It achieved martyrdom in 1985 when French government agents sank the *Rainbow Warrior*, which was protesting nuclear testing in the Pacific. One person was killed. The French government paid an $8 million fine to New Zealand, and donations to Greenpeace tripled. Since then, leaders shudder whenever a detachment of the powerful

Greenpeace armada approaches one of their naval vessels. Their strongest weapon is the video camera that connects them with the evening news worldwide.

Greenpeace International has offices in twenty-seven countries, more than 5 million members, a multimillion dollar budget, and numerous high-priced lawyers and lobbyists. By staging dramatic telegenic stunts—climbing nuclear smokestacks, plugging industrial sewage pipes, sailing inflatable boats into nuclear test sites—Greenpeace has sparked the public imagination to support its views. But success in outflanking powerful nation-states is perhaps best illustrated by Greenpeace's ban on whaling.

The International Whaling Commission was established in 1946 to prevent overhunting of whales. Japan, Iceland, the Soviet Union, and Norway—all supporters of whaling—were the powerhouse countries, but any nation-state willing to pay the $30,000 annual membership was welcome to join. Greenpeace targeted poor nations like tiny Antigua, St. Lucia, and Panama, and fronted their membership fees, even filling out the necessary applications. After packing the commission with half a dozen Greenpeace-controlled delegates, it got an astounding three-fourths majority, outmaneuvering the big whaling states to get a global moratorium on commercial whaling.

An Icelandic company, which continued whaling in defiance of the ban, had its critical computer room mysteriously trashed and two whaling ships sunk in Reykjavik harbor, all on the same day. (The emerging eco-tribes have powers to pass laws *and enforce them.*)

As it turned out, Greenpeace's hands were clean; it was another group, acting on its own initiative, that wreaked havoc in Reykjavik. But the scuttling of the ships in Iceland points to a trend in the eco-wars ahead. In the Fourth Dimension, the various eco-tribes will work together, each with its own strength or specialty, yet interconnected, exchanging ideas and personnel on a global basis in a common war against a complex and multifaceted enemy.

Thanks to the technologies of placelessness, environmental lapses are immediately relayed to the administrative group best geared for a response. Ecological Action of Quito, Ecuador, linked up with counterparts in Canada to investigate the Canadian firm that had authored a suspicious environmental report. A tip-off from Germany that radioactive fuel rods were headed to Scotland for processing via Holland allowed Greenpeace to mobilize dock workers in Rotterdam; they refused to handle the ship carrying the uranium. In Africa, groups have linked up with Earthroots to tap their considerable experience with Canadian reforestation. In the Age of Everything-Everywhere, eco-organizations are no longer insular but act in concert in a global orchestration.

They showed unity of purpose in 1992 in Rio de Janeiro when the UN-sponsored Earth Summit evolved into the *largest international conference ever held.* For nearly two weeks, it attracted 35,000 people, among them 17,000 delegates, 10,000 representatives of private organizations, and 8,000 journalists. The significance of the Earth Summit is not that any issues were resolved, but more importantly, that all of the splintered bands of eco-warriors and interest groups were able to come together. This movement is steadily growing and will, in time, expand into a formidable eco-tribe able to wield powerful influence in the twenty-first century.

BLACK, GAY, AND FEMININE

CONSIDER ALSO THE Christian fundamentalists buying up the airwaves in Russia. Look at the Mormon missionaries penetrating deeply into Latin America. Consider the Pope's encyclicals against birth control to a Catholic "nation" nearly one billion strong.

It is to be expected, too, that new global cults will emerge with doomsday prophesies along the lines of the Branch Davidians in the United States, or the Aum Shin Rikyo in Japan. Although most will be local phenomena, many will enter the Fourth Dimension and make their presence known around the world.

View the worldwide Black community. It is impossible for the United States—a nation-state with thirty-three million Blacks, to ignore the plight of Black South Africans, Black Haitians, or Black Equatorial Africans. The tribal undercurrents run deep, and the screams of apartheid and racism are no longer felt just by an individual but also by a people. These cries resonate in a global nation that will rise to a new level of dignity and heightened self-awareness.

Look, too, at global feminism. Subjugated for millennia under the yoke of male self-importance, women have opened the doors of liberation. If 2,000 women in Istanbul rise to protest their lot, it is done with the knowledge that in the West women are treated equally (or more equally) under the law. Women are reaching the highest ranks as prime ministers, engineers, authors, business leaders; each role model encourages others to claim their due. The free-flow of information—movies, television, magazines, word-of-mouth, universities, books, travel—spreads these ideas. Women in France are incensed at the sexual mutilation (clitoridectomies) still practiced in numerous cultures on millions of young girls. Women in Sweden and Canada cry out for their compatriots in Latin America restricted from access to birth control, or over the subjugation of Islamic women, kept hidden from view like prisoners. Women everywhere feel a common global bond in the plight of their gender.

The gay community—once a set of closeted individuals living in secret in their own communities—are finding that there are millions like them worldwide. What was once shameful has become a source of pride and activism. Pushed initially by discrimination, the global AIDS epidemic has catapulted gays into the Fourth Dimension with computer networks, international symposia and conferences, and an unprecedented political activism at every turn.

The traditional states defined by place will continue to exist because, even in the Placeless Society, place continues to exist. But it loses its primacy, and must yield to other factors that shape emerging tribal affiliations.

The new realities create allegiances that compete with the once-monopolistic nation-state. They erode the unity of purpose that once gave it vitality and undermine the military institutions that gave its people security. For as we see next, the powerful military machines of the nation-states may be outflanked by a new species of tribal "supranation," opening the door to a fundamental shift in global warfare.

11

THE NEW WARFARE

JOHN MUIRLESS WAS ABOUT to make one last phone call before his flight. He had just spent eighteen months with a small band of operatives working in a dozen countries.

His colleague in Panama was anonymously sending faxes to twenty-four news organizations around the world. Their militant group, the Gaia Warriors, sought to save *Gaia,* the Earth, from destruction by one of its evil species, humans. The rising world population coupled with increased consumption had already stripped the planet of its topsoil, its ozone, its rain forests. Four hundred species a day were disappearing.

John knew he would never again see his basement office in the First Interstate Building—Los Angeles's tallest—where he had a short-term lease. He thought about the filing cabinets packed with C-4 plastic explosives shipped to him in air-tight plastic bags by his colleague in Bonn. A tiny wire went from behind those cabinets along the wall and into the back of a desktop computer; another wire led out of that computer and plugged directly into the worldwide telephone grid. Everything was ready for his call.

John scrolled through his auto telephone dialer. "Atlanta: C&S Plaza," "Chicago: Sears Tower," "Frankfurt: Messe Turm," "Hong Kong: Bank of China," "London: Natwest Tower," "New York: Chrysler," "Paris: Tour Elf Aquitaine," "Tokyo: Ikebukuro Office

Tower," "Sydney: MLC Centre," "Toronto: CN Tower." He pictured each one, with its heavy filing cabinets, telephone, computer. He didn't even know the names of his counterparts; they thought it better to build "firewalls" of protection between themselves in case one got caught. Only John knew the details of how extensive their network had grown, and they took every precaution not to be traced.

He punched the auto-dial code to his office computer, took a deep breath, punched a second code to activate the system, and hung up. As he casually walked toward his plane to Rio, he calmly took the batteries out of his auto-dialer, erasing all records of names and telephone numbers, and tossed it into the trash.

As the plane taxied down the runway, John looked at his watch. Hong Kong's 1,209-foot-tall Bank of China building would be first, completely flattened within three minutes. For the next three hours, horror would sweep the world. Every fifteen minutes, one monument of capitalism after another would turn into a twisted rubble of steel, concrete, glass, and flesh. By now, all clocks were synchronized and ticking, and what was set in motion by one phone call could not be stopped by any power on earth.

John looked forward to his meeting in Brazil to plan their next assault.

———

Jokar Ausmiyev had the straps of his rucksack fastened snugly around his shoulders. His load was much lighter than when he left Berlin, carrying a few apples and four plastic bottles of "drinking" water for the journey.

He dropped the first bottle twenty minutes into the Chunnel as he passed from one train car to the next. The contents seeped under the black vinyl floor cover where the wagons connected, allowing the colorless liquid to drip down over 5 of 10 miles of track, as the train streaked deep under the Strait of Dover connecting England and France.

In London, he let the second bottle leak from his hand as he walked the length of tunnels connected to the King's Cross subway station. It was linked to the Victoria, Northern, Metropolitan, Piccadilly, and Circle lines: tens of thousands of commuters passed through these points each day.

Jokar caught the next train to Charing Cross for his third bottle. He was one of the last members of the Zikr Gazavat, a splinter group of the Chechen militia seeking to gain international support for their autonomy struggle from Russia. Each water bottle contained a sugary syrup with 50 grams of concentrated Pulmonary Anthrax, Type E, a genetically mutated form of *Bacillus anthracis* for which there was no known cure.

Nearly every person who passed through the Chunnel, and any of the miles of tubes connected to Charing or King's Cross over the next three days, would likely suffer hidden blisters and pussy cankers in their lungs within days. The scabs would spread to the lips and ears, and within weeks, 95 percent of those infected would be dead. The underground tunnels were perfect, because each passing train acted like a tight-fitting piston pumping the invisible spores throughout the labyrinth of tunnels. He hoped that within a day every train car, every seat in the system would be infected.

Each person would carry the highly virulent bacteria on his or her clothes, to offices, churches, and homes. They would spread it on buses, through coins and bills and the hands they touched, the children they hugged. The disease would travel silently throughout the island, completely undetected. Yet in two weeks, over 100,000 English men, women, and children, including Jokar, would be dead.

He smiled as the train lurched to a stop at Paddington Station, his last bottle of anthrax on his back. Jokar had never accomplished much in life; he relished the idea of finally doing something worthwhile.

———

In Kinneret, Mohammed al-Hussein, age twenty-three, picked out a small fishing boat with a sturdy gas motor. On this clear day, he could easily see the Golan Heights across the Sea of Galilee. This was the first time he had ever been to Israel, or even seen the occupied territory of Syria.

Unemployed in Tunis, he looked forward to adventure in Israel. The decadent West and the destabilizing force of Israel were responsible for the hardship of his family, because they were the enemies of Allah. Mohammed believed that Allah was punishing Tunisia with a drought because it had not done enough to fight the forces of Satan.

Beneath his boat, the water was cool and clear. He pulled the detailed map out of his vest pocket and skillfully spied the shore with his binoculars and compass. Casting several times, mapping the direction of water currents at different depths, he maneuvered the boat here and there before dropping anchor.

He slowly dropped his large tackle box over the side, watched it sink to exactly 8 feet, and float slowly in the currents toward the intake to the Kinneret-Negev Conduit. Within thirty minutes, the sides of the box would spring open, releasing a demitasse of very fine plutonium dust, the most toxic chemical known to man. It would forever shut down the vital aqueduct that quenched the thirst of 6 million people.

———

In the Placeless Society ahead, the classical rules of warfare will forever change. Wars won't be fought to control territory, and the idea of a military "front" will become passé. Aircraft carriers and rocket systems, "Star Wars" defense systems and thermonuclear bombs will be largely useless. The giant military machines that evolved over the past century will become anachronistic and of little purpose.

With the means of warfare, the purpose will also change. State governments will face new foes armed with technical knowledge and once-exotic materials. The guerrilla and terrorist wars of the future will ignore the primacy of national boundaries and the distinction between soldier and civilian. Their most powerful weapon will prove to be raw fear . . . on us all.

LESS IS MORE

IN THE DECADES AHEAD, military planners will have to throw away their two-dimensional war maps and face a new form of tribal warfare devoid of clear-cut lines. The future battle plans are more likely to resemble the genocide of the former Yugoslavia, the anarchy of Sierra Leone and Somalia, the assassinations and explosions in Cairo, Algiers, and Caracas, the street fighting in Chechnya, the arson and looting of the Los Angeles riots.

Until the close of the twentieth century, power and wealth were defined by territory, on which one controlled the raw materials and had access to laborers and markets. The larger the domain of one's hegemony, the better.

But the Placeless Society threatens to collapse the very motivation and objectives of armed conflict as we have known them throughout history. Since labor, raw materials, and capital no longer unlock the doors of wealth, territory is no longer key. In our global economy, tiny countries have an equal footing with the giants.

It is no accident that today's largest empires—Russia, China, and India—are among the poorest on a per-capita basis, even though they control nearly half the world's landmass. Even the United States has overextended its empire: the cost of military hardware and personnel to maintain a global reach can exceed its return, in time impoverishing the nation. This is what military historian Paul Kennedy calls "imperial overstretch." We now understand that the two former superpowers of our era raced down the wrong track. They invested in territorial hegemony instead of raw productive horsepower in accordance with the new rules of wealth.

We live in an inverted world that Alexander the Great, Caesar, and Napoleon would not recognize: the richest countries are among the smallest. Size of a nation is no longer a key to per-capita prosperity.

In the new economic order, wealth is created not by acquisition of territory but by the proper application of human knowledge. The United States would have little to gain from taking over Mexico. Germany would gain little by annexing Poland; Japan would lose by acquiring China. In each case, globocorps *already* have access to human capital, resources, and markets, without the attendant liabilities of national medicine, education, and social security. A country can gain far more by lowering tariff barriers than through military conquest. No longer is sheer bulk an advantage.

We now know that the *quantity* of economic activity is not as important as its *quality*. Pakistan has a GNP comparable to New Zealand's, but with thirty-three times as many people doing the work. What counts is not the value added, but the value added *per person*. This in turn depends on education, infrastructure (communications, roads, utilities), and policies (taxes, business regulations)—not brute size. The five countries with the highest per-capita income are Switzerland, Finland, Norway, Sweden, and Luxembourg—not the United States, Germany, Japan, France, or Italy. The two largest countries, China and India, are among the poorest.

In the global economy, even dwarf-sized nations have equal access to raw materials, markets, and technology. Communications tie them into the global fabric.

Massiveness may even be detrimental. While a factory owner in Kansas City becomes complacent in a large *national* market, his counterpart in Taipei, Seoul, and Helsinki has to study *global* markets. The countries with the fastest growth rates are often the ones looking outside their borders.

In many cases, globocorps have already achieved what armies and bloodshed could not. What Japan failed in its military attempt to control eastern Asia, it has accomplished through trade five decades later. Germany also lost the "battle" of World War II, but in retrospect won the war as an economic juggernaut on the world stage. In the global economy, one no longer needs to control territory to have access to its fruits. Wars over territory will continue in the early twenty-first century but will be confined to those parts of the world still untouched by the Fourth Dimension. A placeless world has no use for fighting over place.

DIFFUSED POWER

PLACELESSNESS IS ALSO changing another dynamic of war. It has been said that no major wars in the twentieth century have been started by democracies. At best, a victorious war may help a politician win reelection, but more often than not, the placelessness of television brings blood, refugees, and destruction into the living rooms of too many everyday folks. For a "television democracy" to be the aggressor in any long-term protracted war, the reasons have to be compelling, and such reasons are increasingly rare.

And placelessness is making democracy difficult to avoid the world over. The long-term trends favor democratic principals, especially where the Fourth Dimension is already blossoming. Power used to be a secret chessboard where only a few knew how to move the pieces. The ubiquity of information in our present society has unmasked the mysteries behind power. We now know our leaders more intimately, the names of their lovers, their tax scandals, their election-time motives behind foreign-policy moves. A public appearance, a speech, a meeting, a shuffle in high-level appointments is there for all to see. The leader thus stripped naked is weaker in many ways, more given to democratic pressures, and more accountable for his actions.

TOPSOIL AND DEAD RATS

IN THE PLACELESS SOCIETY, the thirst for democracy is heightened, the greed for territorial expansion is lessened, and the horrors of war are more public. By all accounts, then, the borders of the nation-state ought to be more secure than ever.

Yet, as we will now see, a new set of challenges are rising just as the old demons seem conquered. If left unchallenged, they may pull every corner of the world into an epoch of unmatched brutality, destruction, and human suffering.

The new wars will be placeless, without boundaries, battle fronts, fleets of ships, columns of soldiers, or tanks. Intercontinental ballistic missiles will be of little value, dancing satellites beaming lasers to and fro entirely frivolous. The wars of the twenty-first century will be fought in our streets as new pressures, alliances, technologies, and the mobility of personnel bring a complete realignment to this thing called war.

What are the conflicts just ahead? We have described the world moving into the Fourth Dimension as a land of everything-everywhere, full of new opportunities for the innovative, a sort of happy never-never land. In reality, while most of us in rich countries will be thrust forward into the twenty-first century, the vast bulk of humankind will be left far behind. The disenfranchised will fail to grasp the lifeboat of technology; worse, their living standards will continue to erode dramatically.

The reasons for this stem from the rising barrier to wealth discussed earlier: the environment. In a debate raging since the 1960s, the neo-Malthusians claim that population growth will outstrip the world's capacity to produce, whereas the non-Malthusians argue that technology will save all. We now understand that they are *both* right. Regions that have embraced technology continue to be *too* productive in their ability to create food. They are already working on the next phase of food production: how to make apples redder, how to make strawberries sweeter. The basic problem of having *enough* apples and strawberries is no longer an issue. But most of humanity will not enjoy the cornucopia of the Fourth Dimension. For these people, recent events have made the argument of the neo-Malthusians just too compelling to ignore.

A drive down the coast of Guinea yields an ugly sight: zinc-roofed shacks assembled from rusted shipping containers, bits of wire, and cardboard. In the streets of rutted mud, garbage is strewn, mosquitoes breed, children have protruding bellies and scant clothing. The muck beach exposes an abandoned car here, a dead rat there. While the population is projected to double by the next generation, entrepreneurs are stripping the forests of hardwood as precious topsoil is washing into the sea. With average incomes scarcely more than a dollar a day, the people keep borrowing from the next generation.

No wonder that in nearby Sierra Leone, all sense of order has broken down. The "nation-state" government controls the capital by day, but by night, bands of looters roam free. Half a million Sierra Leoneans are displaced, half as many have fled to neighboring Guinea and Liberia, even as half a million Liberians have fled to Sierra Leone.

Sierra Leone is a microcosm of what is happening in much of Africa: the collapse of the nation-state. In Somalia and Rwanda, where the gunshots are the sounds of a people at war with themselves, there is no battle "front," no attack from without, just a placeless chaos cutting from within.

The underlying stress springs from too many people on a land depleted of topsoil, arable water, and open air. AIDS and resistant strains of malaria and hepatitis weaken an already broken people. Much of Africa is a time-bomb set to explode within half a generation, with perhaps more human misery than has existed in all prior wars. And Africa may be only the harbinger of a Second World forgotten in technology's wake.

While many in the wealthy countries dismiss Africa as too remote to merit concern, it would be a mistake for them to be smug. The cruel reality is that the wrenching change occurring even within rich societies is rather like a crashing surf: a minority catches the wave and effortlessly rides it, while the vast majority gets buried in the wave with faces ground into the sand.

Those embracing fundamentalist Islam are not alone in being left behind. Throughout Europe and the Americas, technology displaces workers, or leaves them with nothing to do. In the Placeless Society, they are pitted against one another in a global pool. The under-educated ginger-farm worker in Sierra Leone will do little better in Frankfurt, Chicago, or Taipei, because his skills are just not needed.

In the First World regions, those who have no significant skills are competing head to head with their counterparts throughout the Second World. In the Age of Everything-Everywhere, the Second World is no longer a place one can circle on a map, but a group of people, spread throughout the globe.

The Second World is already present in one of the richest countries on earth: the 1992 riots in Los Angeles were not *caused* by the racially charged Rodney King trial; that was only the fuse. The underlying problem was social deprivation, joblessness, discrimination, poverty, urban decay—a Second World people isolated in a First World country. Within an hour of the trial verdict, Los Angeles became a microcosm of Sierra Leone: utter lawlessness, looting, arson, beatings. White against Black against Korean against Latino, the whole fabric of society unveiled its underlying fragility.

Within hours, television coverage of Los Angeles spread the condition to Las Vegas, New York City, and Miami. Within a week, Toronto, Canada, flared with White, Black, and Asian youths on a rampage. In Nigeria rioters torched government buildings and banks protesting inadequate public transportation. Panama's Colon was ablaze for two days with 3,500 demonstrators demanding government action against a collapsing city infrastructure. In our electronic world, a fuse set in one city can trigger aftershocks all over the globe. Distance and borders no longer provide a firewall against the spread of ideas.

In such an environment, tribal affiliations crystallize. With the rich technocrats against the poor and unskilled, the enthused environmentalists against the polluting capitalists, the fundamentalist Christians and Muslims against the decadent majority (and each other), the Serbs against the Croatians, with the Bosnians in between, the Blacks and Browns against the Whites and Yellows, the world becomes Sierra Leone.

The challenge of the Placeless Society will be to bring all of humanity to the same table, for those in the First World to help pull the Second World forward. It is essential not just for altruistic reasons but out of self-interest as well: at stake is social order, without which the promises of technology's bounty cannot be fully realized. The reasons lie in the reality of warfare in the twenty-first century: *terrorism*.

WAR WITHOUT RULES

THE POWER OF TERRORISM was demonstrated a few minutes after 10:00 P.M. on May 21, 1991, in India. Rajiv Gandhi—the leading candidate to become the prime minister of India's 850 million people, was killed by a Tamil separatist. The man who was to lead the world's largest democracy was "eliminated" by a flower girl wearing a blue denim belt.

Three thousand miles away, another demonstration of terrorism was made against the US Marines stationed at a barracks near the Beirut international airport. One October morning, a two-and-a-half-ton truck crashed into the lobby of what the marines jokingly called the "Beirut Hilton." The four-story building "disappeared" into a crater 40 feet wide and 9 feet deep, in what the FBI later called the largest nonnuclear explosion *ever*. Two hundred forty-one marines were killed.

The United States, with trillions of dollars invested in military hardware, intercontinental ballistic missiles, thermonuclear bombs, submarines and aircraft carriers, spy satellites, squadrons of fighter aircraft, and armed forces of over two million personnel, was turned out of Lebanon by one man in a yellow truck.

With such victories against such improbable odds, who among us is safe when a death warrant is issued by an enemy tribe? How can society protect itself? How do we stop the subway gas attacks in Tokyo? Or the bombing of the World Trade Center in New York, the Federal Building in Oklahoma City, or the metro in Paris? There are just too many targets, too many places, and too many people. And perhaps the technology of terrorism is too widespread.

We often discount terrorists as fringe groups of lunatics who kill indiscriminately. But these groups know exactly what they want, and often get it. Politicians deliver public speeches against giving in to terrorists, but in the back rooms, they yield arms or cash, or think twice before announcing policies likely to arouse terrorists' passions.

The new reality is that terrorism is a war fought by and among disenfranchised tribes in a placeless society. Over the centuries of armed conflict, states have developed a "civilized" set of rules for killing each other that has become "international law": no attacks on civilians, no hostages to enforce agreements, no bombing of hospitals, no attacking of neutral territory, no wanton destruction of cultural or religious property, no pillage or rape or torture, no killing of captives, and no biological warfare (though atomic bombs are acceptable).

Terrorists argue that these rules were made for the convenience of the nation-state. In the terrorist wars, anything goes, any means justifies the ends. And worst of all, the technologies of placelessness favor the highly mobile terrorist-warrior over the nation-state. New technologies will give small bands of terrorists unprecedented power that can affect millions of people with a single act. The worst may be yet to come.

TOOLS OF TERROR

THE ULTIMATE WEAPON, whose power stayed even the superpowers, is the atomic bomb. Its design involves untold billions of dollars of research and testing, significantly limiting membership in the once-exclusive "nuclear club."

But knowledge has a way of diffusing, and what is learned cannot be unlearned. What started with the United States and then the former Soviet Union, has expanded to France, the United Kingdom, and China, followed by India, Pakistan, Israel, North Korea, Libya, Algeria, Argentina, Brazil, and South Africa. All have either completed a nuclear bomb or have programs to develop one. Revelations about Iraq in the wake of the Gulf War illustrate that, for all the international monitoring and export controls, a country determined to build a nuclear bomb can do so, virtually without detection.

The design of the atomic bomb is no longer a secret. Pakistan and Iraq demonstrated how easy it was, in the global economy, to bypass export controls. China has provided information freely to Pakistan and nuclear power technology to Iran, while rogue former Soviet scientists are said to be employed today in Libya and Algeria.

Even plutonium, the most toxic chemical known to man, is entering the Age of Everything-Everywhere. International authorities are simply unable to plug every possible leak from among a thousand nuclear sites around the world; 100 pounds of plutonium are already missing. Russia has 1 to 2 *million* pounds of weapons-grade plutonium and enriched uranium, over hundreds of sites. All that is needed for a good bomb are a few pounds (for a Hiroshima repeat, just a few ounces). How do we know that there is not, right now, a nuclear bomb set up in a van snaking through the narrow streets of Tokyo, or in the trunk of a taxi in Washington, DC, or in a private "office" in Paris?

Terrorist organizations *already have* significant amounts of bomb-grade plutonium because it has turned up in government raids. If just a few grams of highly toxic plutonium (or even readily available cobalt-60 or iodine-131) had been included in the World Trade Center bombing, it may have rendered New York's financial district uninhabitable for generations.

But terrorists need not resort to atomic exotica to make a point. As early as 1972, American agents uncovered nearly 100 *pounds* of botulin, a powerful toxin that strikes the victim dead in microgram quantities. Pulmonary anthrax kills 99 percent of the people it infects, and can be grown safely in one's garage.

The advent of genetic engineering multiplies the risks of biological warfare a thousandfold in the twenty-first century. Imagine a version of the lethal HIV virus as contagious as the common cold. Imagine bacteria that exacerbate hereditary diseases endemic only to certain "racial" groups, such as sickle cell anemia (Blacks), or Tay-Sachs disease or Niemann-Pick disease (European Jews). Think of a virulent airborne virus that would kill all in its path, except those inoculated. Would not a fanatical anti-abortionist delight in "perfuming" abortion centers? Would not a national airline be an easy target for a terrorist, who could cause a few thousand deaths (just a handful of flights) by contaminating the air-recirculation system with poison? Everyone in the US Congress, the Tokyo Stock Exchange, and the UN Building could be infected the same way before anyone knew what happened. How do you stop that which you cannot see?

Bio-terrorism need not even be high tech to work. California's rich agricultural industry has been repeatedly set back by the Medfly epidemic. Although officials like to keep it secret, there is strong evidence that a few individuals calling themselves "the Breeders" are growing Medflies on rotten fruit and releasing them by the boxload to protest California's agricultural practices. This results in tens of millions of dollars in crop losses and periodic bans on California's exports all over the world.

Terrorists worldwide have access to a whole playpen of paraphernalia. It is no longer difficult to purchase Stinger hand-held rockets that allow the user to knock out an airplane with virtually no training. Computer viruses pulse through the global computer webs each day with yet newer mutations, making them ever more difficult to detect. "Liquid metal embrittlement" (LME) agents, applied on metal with a felt-tipped pen, cause critical parts on trucks, aircraft, or bridges to snap under stress. Now, widespread plastic explosives like C-4 are so powerful that a simple manila envelope, powered by a tiny watch battery, can send a mighty Boeing 747 and the nearly half-thousand individuals on board cartwheeling to the ground.

MADISON AVENUE

BUT FOR ALL THE SOPHISTICATED tools, placelessness is the terrorists' best friend. It allows airplanes to take them anywhere to stage their attack. It allows their money, information, and ideas to flow through our banking system and electronic networks.

The bombing of Pan Am Flight 103, which killed all 259 passengers, involved an electronic detonating device made in Switzerland, purchased by Libya, checked into the "airline grid" in Malta, transferred to Germany, retransferred to England onto an American jet, which blew up over Scotland. And, of course, the passengers were from *everywhere*. More Americans and Europeans were killed in this operation than from battle deaths in the Gulf War.

The new armies move undetected among us, through our borders, our aircraft, and our subways. They watch our sports arenas, concerts, and theaters; they drive over the aqueducts and bridges that feed our cities. The easy spread of knowledge and materials, the rich coffers of today's global tribes, give them the means to deliver on any promise. For each roadblock a government erects, the terrorists have a thousand options. With their technology, it takes but one warrior to harm the many.

More important than the placelessness of terrorist movement and destruction is the placelessness of knowledge of the act—through satellites and television.

For any act of destruction committed, the promise of more to follow injects the most fear into men's hearts. When the World Trade Center was bombed, when Pan Am 103 fell over Lockerbie, when nerve gas attacked Tokyo's subways, or when a truck bomb exploded in Oklahoma City, television reproduced the event a million times, replaying it over and over, allowing each of us to touch the victims, to hear the cries of family members.

If the business of terrorists is terror, there is no better conduit, no greater amplifier than television. It tells each of us that *we* may be next: the next plane we board, the next building we enter, the next aspirin we take or glass of water we drink.

Television drives terrorists to seek the daring and spectacular. In the Placeless Society, professional terrorists may act like Madison Avenue media experts looking for the perfect timing, the exact vehicle, and the most dramatic execution. The numbing aspect of television will drive each terrorist group to outdo the latest horrendous act, or else risk losing the world's top billing.

Placelessness—the ability to move undetected, the ubiquity of tools of destruction, the access to our minds to instill fear—is what gives terrorists potency. Former US Defense Secretary Caspar Weinberger once labeled assassinations, kidnappings, and terrorism the "most immediate threat to free-world security" over the decades just ahead. In the Placeless Society, his vision may be more chillingly pre-scient than anyone dared to dream.

KEVLAR CARS

THE TERRORIST PROBLEM is not one easily solved because, in the end, it relies not on technology or resources, but on the spectacular. Just as we tighten airport security, can we also do the same at every building, schoolroom, bus, movie theater? Can we protect every politician and business executive from assassination? Or their spouses or children from being kidnapped? At some point, the cost of protecting a lamp post from getting vandalized is more than the lamp post is worth, and, unfortunately, society has to limit how much it can spend to protect even innocent children.

The incidence of terrorism is likely to rise over the next few decades as people in the First World advance, while many in the Second World slip further behind. Pressures on the environment will pit naturalists against industrialists. Wanton consumerism will pit fanatic spiritualists against capitalists. In the new millennium, doomsday cults will emerge all over the world with a message of Armageddon— and will seek to bring about their own prophesies of mass murder and suicides. The pressures of change—for all of us—will pit neighbor against neighbor. The fault lines of conflict will no longer be along geographic borders, but within us, tearing at the soul of civilization.

Then what is to be done? It is not clear that the nation-state of old can react, because the battle is not *against* the state but *within* it. The future may look like Colombia, where the central government bowed to the powerful drug cartels, obliging a frustrated citizenry to form vigilante squads to help out the police.

Perhaps the nation-state has grown too bureaucratic and inflexible to deal with this new nimble foe: the terrorists roam the world while the arm of the state affected is short. The state seeks to follow the "civilized" rules of warfare while terrorists ignore the distinction be-tween civilian and soldier in indiscriminate slaughter. The twenty-first century will likely see governments "subcontracting" independent hit squads, seeking to attack terrorists on their own level: assassinations, mysterious explosions, kidnappings.

We will also see governments dealing more closely with other governments to exchange information and round up suspects for extradition. There may well be strain placed on individual liberties regarding access to travel, free passage, the seizure of goods, the tapping of phones, and the scrutiny of electronic payments in the digital age. In a Faustian bargain, we may have to trade off freedom from terrorism for freedom from government surveillance.

Private security services will boom. Researchers are already looking for new materials to make concrete and glass more shock resistant. Special censors will abound, searching for molecules that burn, explode, or radiate; or instruments that cut or shoot. More and more businesspeople will wear suits and drive cars reinforced with Kevlar. Police departments will train special quick-response commando units. The distinction between war and crime will become obsolete.

For all these changes, the nation-state will lose its most compelling *raison d'être:* to protect its people from the military threat of other nation-states. In the placeless warfare of the twenty-first century, we will more likely find nation-states working *with* one another, as placeless bands of terrorists, or tribal affiliations, slice easily through once-rigid national boundaries.

As we see next, the rising weight of terrorism will be the last straw to snap the back of the once-mighty nation-state.

Part Six

THE EMERGING
WORLD ORDER

12

THE END OF THE
NATION-STATE

XABIER GARAIKOETXEA SAT DRINKING a cool iced tea at the sidewalk restaurant. He never knew a flag could be so beautiful.

The day before, in the Bilbao plaza, bands were playing and folks were dancing. The Basque people had finally been granted independence from Spain, and the new nation, Euskadi, was immediately recognized by the European Union and the United Nations as its 278th member state.

Xabier explained the struggle to his two grandchildren. Spain's constitution had already granted limited autonomy to the Basques even before the children were born: for years, schools were taught, and road signs were written, in their revived Euskara language. Euskadi grew comfortable in making its own laws and limiting tax remittances to Madrid. Yet *full* autonomy was forever withheld.

As a former team member in the San Sebastián ETA unit, Xabier was picked up a number of times by the Spanish Civil Guard and occasionally tortured, but he never revealed how much he knew. The ETA had killed about 1,000 people in car bombings, assassinations, kidnappings, extortions, and random murders. Half as many were in Spanish and French jails before Euskadi was recognized. Full war amnesty was miraculously granted.

Xabier loved telling these stories, but one thing still puzzled him: when the ETA was at its peak in the 1980s, independence was not granted—yet it happened in the more recent peaceful times, as if Madrid had finally decided on its own.

———

The Victorian lampshade gave a green hue to the room where Jean Fontaine sat down to review his taxes. It had been three years now since La République de Québec was carved out of the enormous Canadian landmass. Jean had always voted with the separatist Parti Québecois out of pride. But he was never sure whether the economic doomsayers were right.

Every day, there was a new article in the newspaper, a new problem: if Canada divided, who would be left with the extraordinary national debt? What about military or terrorist hostilities between the two nations? Wouldn't a new currency disrupt investment in Quebec? There were predictions of economic chaos and mass migrations south to the United States.

Yes, the transition had some unexpected problems, but the changeover occurred more smoothly than anyone had imagined. Quebec was immediately admitted as the fourth member of the NAFTA trade block, gaining a new status as an independent, dynamic nation ready to cut investment and trade deals in the international arena.

More important, Jean felt that his new national government was more responsive to his needs and those of Quebec, unlike the bureaucratic "foreign" government in Ottawa. While the federal government was negotiating timber laws for British Columbia, or sending troops to Africa, or engaging in wasteful studies and bloating the national debt, Quebecois were concerned about their schools, crime, and taxes.

Since autonomy, his "local" government had been more efficient in attracting foreign investment and in solving real problems. Jean gazed outside to see two cargo ships inching down the St. Lawrence River with the currents. He pushed his taxes to the back of his desk, and went outside to tend his garden.

There is now little question that future historians will mark the twenty-first century as the closing act of the large nation-state drama.

As we enter the Placeless Society, the large nation-state of the last hundred years will become an anachronism. Vast "empires" like China, Russia, and India will break up into bit-sized chunks. Africa will break into perhaps 75 to 100 administrative units.

The European Union of the twenty-first century will consist of more nations than anyone anticipates, not because the East will be knocking at its door, but because the traditional nations—the United Kingdom, Spain, Italy, and Belgium—will be under pressure to devolve power.

In North America, Canada will be disunited, perhaps Mexico too. Even in the current federation of the United States, power will devolve from the central government to the individual states, which will, in turn, fall under piecemeal separatist pressures of their own.

One by one, the peoples of the world are flexing for autonomy. It will come peacefully through referenda, and it will come through violence. But either way, the world is—even now—splintering into multiple pieces.

FROM CASTLES TO COUNTRIES

TO UNDERSTAND WHY THE power of nations will devolve, we need to first review how they evolved. What caused the small feudal structures to coalesce in the fourteenth and fifteenth centuries into large empires, usually headed by a powerful monarch? More than anything, it was the technology of warfare. Gunpowder and the new siege cannon could turn a fortress into rubble in a matter of hours. As a result, feudal structures could no longer be preserved with a small group of soldiers. It took larger armies to defend territory, and the cost of security went up. The only way to maintain peace was for power to unite at a higher level, to have larger political groupings.

Three centuries later, the consolidation of political power got another major impetus—again from technology—in the Industrial Revolution. Canals and railroads allowed people, ideas, and goods to move freely, expanding the self-concept of a people over a broad area. The wealth of the Industrial Revolution allowed European powers to amass unprecedented navies and armies, which set their compasses for Africa, the Americas, and Asia in a fervor of global partitioning.

Before the advent of the siege cannon around 1500, about 500 political bodies existed in Europe. By the dawn of the twentieth century, Europe and its colonies had coalesced into twenty-five powerful nations effectively controlling 84 percent of the world's landmass. In some ways, the control of the many by the few had reached its zenith.

But in our century, this has all been unwinding. In the wake of two world wars, colonial imperialism withered. At the close of World War I, Woodrow Wilson boosted "self-determination" to the world stage. In his view, all peoples, even colonies, have "a right to choose the sovereignty under which they shall live." By 1945 the principle was formalized in the UN Charter.

One by one the great empires, kingdoms, and republics were dismembered. Africa, once carved into European domains, was cut loose piece by piece. The British Commonwealth of Australia, India, and Canada was all but dismantled. The giant Ottoman Empire was partitioned to eventually become today's map of the Middle East. The powerful Austro-Hungarian Empire collapsed into the tiny nations that comprise much of today's Eastern Europe. As for Russia, it expanded into the Soviet "Empire," and more recently, shattered into still-uncounted fragments.

The United Nations has expanded from 52 member states in 1946 to its present count of around 190, and has not reached its upper limit. The main reason is that technologies that once gave the large political units their power are now shifting to favor the smaller state.

DAVID AND GOLIATH

IN THE AREA OF SELF-DEFENSE, for example, larger countries with powerful armies may not be better off: the extraordinary expenditures of the superpowers in the Cold War did more to impoverish them than enrich them. For decades, the Soviet Union funneled its top scientists, engineers, and industrial workers into "warcraft," leaving its commercial economy in shambles.

The United States did likewise and will be paying the price for decades, even generations: an unpaid national debt of $54,000 *per household,* millions of soldiers under lifetime pension, nuclear toxic leaks now entering its aquifers. Meanwhile, countries like Japan and Germany, who ironically were stripped of the right to field armies, invest methodically in industry and education to capture the true global prize.

In some cases today, small countries that are able to develop even two or three nuclear bombs, are keeping their larger neighbors at a distance. We see this with Pakistan's ability to keep nearly-billion-strong India at a distance under a nuclear threat. We see it, too, with Israel, where technology has contributed to a small state's survival against all odds. Technology has shifted the calculus of war; we no longer live in a world where sheer military size translates into tangible economic benefits or strategic benefits on the world stage.

In the case of underpowered secessionists who have sought to break off from larger countries—the Eritreans, Latvians, Chechens, Bosnians, and others—the "national defense" umbrella that they enjoyed under a larger empire was not worthwhile: rather than protect them, the guns pointed *at* them. For those with a national border between them and their former oppressors, they enjoy the worldwide recognition of autonomy, and their load is lightened. International borders, when broadly recognized, do stay the giants.

Nor, as we have seen, is size of a national economy a prerequisite to high per-capita incomes. In the Placeless Society, an enterprise can tap into the global economy just as well in a small country as in a large one. In Europe, Switzerland, Denmark, Luxembourg—even Iceland—have richer citizens than do the "Eurogiants" of Germany, France, and Britain. In Asia, micronations like Singapore and Hong Kong have among the highest per-capita wealth, while supergiants China and India struggle to raise living standards. In Latin America, Brazil, Mexico, and Argentina don't have the wealthiest citizens; tiny Surinam and Uruguay do.

Placelessness brings with it the ubiquitous flow of raw materials, labor, and capital (the old pillars of economic wealth) and makes access to knowledge and information the foundation for our new economy. Even in Japan, a resource-poor volcanic island, people have among the highest incomes in the world.

To be part of the world economy is what counts. Daimler-Benz sells motorcars to a world audience; if Baden-Württemberg were to split off from Germany, its Stuttgart factories would hardly change one particle. If California were a separate republic, its sales of Hollywood films, carrots, and computer software might even improve.

Why improve? Because the smaller state not only has access to the same global markets, but more important, it is forced to *think* globally. Too often, California companies look at the lucrative US market and don't adapt their innovations to the peculiarities of countries with different languages, electrical currents, budgets, and tastes. Smaller, autonomous governments can dispatch foreign-trade representatives, engage in special treaties, and adapt immigration laws to local needs in a way not possible when constrained by the limitations imposed by a larger federation. In a placeless society, autonomy brings nimbleness.

We have seen how global capital has made it impossible for a lone central government to unilaterally set interest rates and exchange rates, or modulate the level of unemployment. Globocorps and the emerging Amoeba Form of business organization defy the nation-state to effectively govern. Even trade, once measured in tonnage that came in by cargo ships, is increasingly of a different sort: knowledge and information carried in computer diskettes in briefcases, or beamed by satellite into a four-dimensional world.

The old nation-state is simply an anachronism, a nostalgic carryover from an era now slipping away. For the first time in history, the world's economy has grown decoupled from the very governments that seek to tame it.

ONE WORLD, ONE MIND

FURTHERMORE, A GROWING CLASS of problems can no longer be adequately addressed at a nation-state level. Much like the sheriff's posses of western films who could not pursue bandits beyond the county line, modern nation-states are finding that many of today's problems are simply outside the jurisdiction of their sovereignty. They are utterly helpless in solving them.

Drug cartels set up Amoeba Form organizations that glide through our society on a global scale, moving vast quantities of chemicals, drugs, and cash. Global mafias and crime rings warehouse rocket launchers, assault rifles, and worse. Terrorist organizations easily pass borders with their ideologies, bombs, and bank transfers. Even BCCI, a once globally respected bank, exploited the idiosyncrasies of parochial regulators unable to look beyond their borders. Only when looked at as a whole were their operations revealed as fraudulent.

So, too, with global pollution. Individual nation-states are powerless to stem the degradation of the ozone layer, global warming, the pollution of international waters, and the destruction of hundreds of marine species each year. Sweden, Germany, Italy, and France could offer its citizens little to protect them from Chernobyl's radioactive rain.

Even global communications undermines the ability of central governments to control what its citizens think and know. This was demonstrated in the Tiananmen Square demonstrations in 1989. While the powerful Chinese government was able to literally crush *some* students under the weight of its tanks, it was utterly powerless to stop simple fax communications between overseas Chinese and domestic Chinese students, without pulling the plug on the entire national telephone system.

Global communications turn international news into local news. What was once village gossip becomes global gossip. When CNN covers global issues—war, terrorists, tariff issues, the environment, or diplomacy—they commonly link correspondents from around the world as if they were conversing in a single room.

As a result, social consciousness is gradually shifting from nationalistic to globalistic. Deforestation in Brazil affects temperatures in Norway. Nuclear leaks in the Ukraine are linked to leukemia in the United States. An AIDS therapy in France affects longevity in Thailand. A real estate crash in Tokyo affects jobs in Ireland. A price hike in Saudi Arabian oil affects the price of fertilizer in the Philippines.

The rise in global consciousness—a common knowledge of our shared problems—provides a common frame of reference for the people of the world. This, in turn, makes arbitrary national borders less meaningful.

IMPERIAL BOOKKEEPING

AND BORDERS ARE INDEED arbitrary.

If a Martian were to come to Earth, the alien would have a tough time understanding the nature of the Earth's geopolitical boundaries. There is little sense of proportion in size. Out of the 190 or so countries in the world, only 6 administer half the world's population, while the smallest 60 nations *together* have fewer people than France.

Equally bizarre to the Martian visitor, unrelated landmasses half a world away are managed by the same country. Lisbon, Portugal, administers Macao in Asia (until 1999), while Amsterdam still controls islands offshore from Venezuela. Tiny Denmark "claims" Greenland, giving it more territory than Germany, France, Italy, the United Kingdom, and Spain combined. Moscow controls islands offshore from Japan and Alaska, ten time zones away.

Washington, DC, holds hegemony over Puerto Rico and the Virgin Islands in the Caribbean, oil fields in the Arctic, and over 2,300 islands in the Pacific, stretching through Hawaii to Wake, Guam, and

Palau, nearly half way around the world. Paris controls a chunk of South America, islands ten miles offshore from Canada, and countless other islands in the Pacific, Caribbean, and Indian Oceans. For decades the British Union Jack flew over Hong Kong, and London still oversees Gibraltar, the Falkland Islands, and places in the South Pacific, Caribbean, and Indian Ocean where the French and American flags don't reign.

The enormous variety in size and scope of countries is often due to inertia. Historic boundary lines and offshore territories are left over from long-forgotten wars, treaties, and collapsed empires. Or they are determined by geographical "barriers" no longer relevant. Boundaries throughout Africa, the Middle East, India, the Americas, and much of Asia, are often based on arbitrary lines drawn by colonial conquerors who have long since withdrawn. Many European boundaries were largely settled by treaty among the victors, following two world wars.

As a result, national boundaries disregard today's trading patterns or ethnic affinities. They arbitrarily tore through African tribes, or left groups like the Kurds scattered among many nations. Other times, divergent groups were haphazardly thrown together, as illustrated by the former Yugoslavia or Czechoslovakia, which have since split apart.

Such unnatural administrative groupings are inherently unstable. Political boundaries do not match the ideal condition of national groupings of individuals with a common destiny, who often share the same speech, history, religion, or enemies. In the new age, the most stable political units may be the smallest ones, not the largest. As Germany's *Die Zeit* concludes, "The happiest European lands are the smallest: Liechtenstein, San Marino, Monaco, and Luxembourg. The larger the state is, the stronger the tensions between homeland and nation."

For these reasons, the notion of autonomous regions is gaining momentum. Regions have common problems and interests, generating more cohesion than classical nation-states. Rural Northern California is one region, urban Southern California is another. Regionalism explains the terrorism in Northern Ireland and the Basque provinces, the tensions in Corsica, Sicily, and Catalonia. It explains the Scottish nationalists, the meltdown of the Soviet Union, and nearly every war in Africa for the past five decades, and the five decades to come.

Political maps, with their bold uniform colors, are a legacy of the European Renaissance, when specialists sought to classify and measure *things*. To the early colonists, country maps were a sort of imperial bookkeeping to keep track of who owned what. But the dividing lines are beginning to blur.

The maps of the twenty-first century will resemble holograms yet to be invented, in some four-dimensional space, with overlayered swirls of interests reflecting the complex tribalism linking customs, commerce, and language over vast chasms of space. A two-dimensional map cannot capture the realities of a four-dimensional world.

THE BEAR'S CHILDREN

UNDER SUCH A SETTING, diverse peoples are seeking to break away from the shackles of ineffective large nation-states. The new rules of power and wealth no longer favor the large over the small.

We see this clearly in the fate of the former Soviet Union. Its collapse in 1991 gave a tremendous boost to the idea of self-determination and regional autonomy. This improbable empire of numerous ethnic groupings had for centuries been suppressed. Each group was unable to express its underlying national aspirations until the USSR collapsed, cleaving into fifteen autonomous republics.

But, no sooner was Moldova independent of the Soviet Union than its three ethnic minorities—Russian, Romanian, and Turkish Muslim—sought to redivide into three pieces in bloody warfare. While the Ukraine and Russia squabbled over who should get Crimea, the latter tried declaring independence from both. Azerbaijan and Armenia got their independence, but Nagorno-Karabakh wanted out of the one and into the other. As for the Georgians, they became independent, but so did the Abkhazians—from Georgia.

The devolution will not stop there. The Bolsheviks once drew administrative lines within republics to *divide* ethnic groups, making each region easier to administer. These divisions form uncounted time bombs as some 200 ethnic groupings conflict with political ones.

Even Russia is under internal turmoil to break up further. Extending from the Arctic Ocean to the Black Sea, from Europe to the fingertip of Alaska, even with its territorial losses, Russia remains the largest country in the world, with one-eighth of the world's inhabited landmass. But it is far from monolithic: "Russia" is a patchwork of twenty-one republics and uncounted provinces, autonomous provinces, districts, autonomous districts, and territories. All have their special rules and exemptions.

If Moscow has invested an estimated $4 billion into crushing the back of tiny Chechnya—using cluster bombs on its own "citizens" and leveling its capital Grozny—it is because Moscow understands that the very disintegration of Russia is at stake. Were Chechnya to break away, so might other autonomous regions, weary of suppression by a distant Moscow. Resource-rich Komi, Karelia, and Yakutia might want to stop subsidizing their poorer neighbors to the south. The regions along the Volga, rich in oil, railways, and pipelines, also have registered their dissent. Tatarstan and Bashkortostan refuse to remit taxes to Moscow, and ten regions passed new charters contradicting Moscow's constitution.

The Russia that stumbles into the twenty-first century will have no real meaning as a cohesive nation-state. As each day passes, the centrifugal forces of some 200 ethnic groups set in 89 ethnic republics and regions add tensions to a cauldron of turmoil. Russia is unwinding; only lavish subsidies coupled with the threat of Moscow's army are keeping the empire together at all.

At best, Russia will devolve into a loose federation of autonomous regions adhering to one another only by economic self-interest and a mutual self-defense pact. At worst, the pieces will fly into a thousand pieces, a "Yugoslavization" on a titanic scale. Either way, Moscow is left with little more than Red Square and a bankrupt treasury.

With the Cold War ended, the world map has been unfrozen from a half century of suspended animation. As the sinews of superpower rivalry melt away, old tribal allegiances are joining new ones, and fault lines are emerging everywhere. The Second World countries that grew accustomed to superpower largess are under stress. Everywhere the race is on to catch up with the stark reality of the twenty-first century—the atomization of political hierarchy.

EURO-FISSION

FREED OF THE SOVIET THREAT to the east, and protected under the economic umbrella of the European Union, the diverse minorities of Western Europe are also straining for—and receiving—heightened regional autonomy.

Because small countries like the Netherlands, Luxembourg, Belgium, and Denmark are enjoying the protections offered by the Union, like-sized minorities in the large nation-states will want to do the same. Although the nations of Western Europe will not devolve as quickly as Russia, as bloodily as Yugoslavia, or as cleanly as Czechoslovakia, the devolution will nonetheless take place with its own distinct Western European flavor. Perhaps it will set role models for sensible power sharing to feuding minorities everywhere.

Ironically, the country with the deepest ethnic fissures is the country hosting the Euro-parliament: Belgium. This "nation-state" is an unhappy marriage among 6 million Dutch-speaking Flemings, 3 million French-speaking Walloons, and 1 million Italians and Germans. The hard-working Flemings, the majority, are seeking to be cut free from their poorer French-speaking countrymen. The national debt is out of control, the constitution is unstable, and the government has at least once been on the brink of collapse. The demands for separatism are growing on both sides. In the absence of national unity, inertia holds Belgium together.

The situation in Scotland is no less volatile: three-fourths of Scots want either autonomy from London, or outright independence. 25,000 Scots, hopeful that the framework of the European Union guarantees economic stability, and aware that England is "plundering" their North Sea oil reserves, marched against London rule when European leaders met in Edinburgh in 1992. While older Scots are concerned with their pensions and retain a small camaraderie with England through two world wars, the younger Scots are bolder in their separatist demands. As the Union matures and self-determination sweeps the globe, it is only a matter of time before Scots look toward Edinburgh, Brussels, and the world for cues, not London.

At stake is the United Kingdom. Continuously shrinking from the size of its Commonwealth in past centuries, London lost hegemony over North America, India, Africa, Australia, and the Republic of Ireland, giving rise to some forty sovereign nations. Even today, each concession made to Scotland, Northern Ireland, or Wales for autonomy emboldens the others to ask for even more. In the twenty-first century, terms like *United Kingdom* and *Great Britain* may fall, like the *Soviet Union,* into disuse.

In Spain and France, the Basques are arbitrarily divided between larger nation-states in the once-isolated Pyrenees Mountains. Over the centuries, these proud people repelled the incursions of Romans, Germanic tribes, Moors, and others. And the battle for autonomy goes on. The Basque Army, the deadly ETA, is no fringe group. French and Spanish prisons hold 500 ETA prisoners who have kidnapped, extorted, and bombed for the autonomy of Euskadi; all told, several hundred people have been killed by Basque terrorists.

While Madrid does not like to admit it, a million Basque people are by degrees winning the war; their territories have won considerable autonomy. The schools now teach in Euskera, the Basque language. Road signs in both France and Spain have dropped exclusive Spanish or French spellings, and traffic police are Basque.

As with the Scots, economic protections granted to minority states in the EU framework could create a favorable environment for Basque autonomy. But not just for economic reasons.

The rules of the European Union provide for free migration between its member countries: investors, workers, students, and vacationers move around a Europe without internal borders. Surveying a Spain teeming with Germans, Frenchmen, and Englishmen from the north and Arabs and Blacks from northern Africa, the Spanish-Basques of the twenty-first century are even less likely to identify with the Spanish—or French—culture. Rather, the Euskaldunak—a culture that has survived intact for a thousand years—will undergo a renaissance.

Spain with its Catalonians, France with its Corsicans and Bretons, Germany with its *Ost* and *West,* Belgium with its Flemish and Walloons, and the "Disunited" Kingdom—all are straddling potential fault lines. In Italy, too, the people of Sardinia, Sicily, Tuscany, Venetia, and Lombardy all have their unique cultures; most Italians still speak in regional dialects in their everyday lives. Groups in industrialized Lombardy are plotting to scrap the constitution and return Italy to its pre-Garibaldi days of autonomous regions.

Europe won't disintegrate, but "globalness" brings with it a paradoxical human need for "localness" and self-identity. The anonymity that comes with being thrown into a world sea, being reduced to a number in a computer, makes many of us want to preserve some special membership, some uniqueness. The coming Europe weakens nationalism at the nation-state level, but enhances it at the ethnic level, thus accelerating the demise of the nation-state.

THE POPULATION TIME BOMBS

PRESENT-DAY INDIA WILL be the most highly populated "country" on Earth by 2060. It is inconceivable that this ethnically diverse and impoverished region will survive population pressures without a political meltdown.

Like the former Soviet Union, India is a multiethnic powder keg waiting to explode, an artificial fusion of 600 independent states put together during British colonization. Today, the underlying nation has sixteen languages and a balkanized mixture of religious groups: Hindus, Moslems, Christians, and Sikhs. In the next millennium, India may well return to a precolonial subcontinent of multiple despotic states, each built around the primacy of one religion, caste, or language.

Free-market policies erode the ability of regional politicians to set aside ethnic differences to take bribes—"license raj"—for arbitrary business permits and licenses. With the Nehru-Gandhi dynasty ended, the binding quality provided by these founding families is all but dissolved.

India displays the signs of stress of a country too large for central management. Hindu fundamentalists show little tolerance for other faiths; several million Muslims in Kashmir seek independence; more than 20 million Sikhs are restless to form an autonomous Punjab nation. India's control over the region is so tenuous that, even when it deployed 250,000 soldiers to quell violence during a 1992 election, barely one in four eligible voters went to the polls; in many villages, no one came to vote. To assert its control, the central government dissolved the Tamil Nadu State government in the South, prompting riots and 23,000 arrests.

As population pressures mount, a billion hungry mouths of such extraordinary ethnic diversity will not for long tolerate a remote New Delhi or wait for solutions. India may not survive the twenty-first century intact.

Africa is in the same predicament. Five years into the new millennium, the continent's population will reach a billion, outstrip India, and by 2022 will be double the 1995 figure. Like India, the boundaries of Africa are largely the legacy of eighteenth and nineteenth century colonial cartography; they ignore natural, tribal, linguistic, or geographical barriers.

Moreover, Africa is the world's poorest continent. Centralized governments have no control over diverse ethnic tribes plagued by droughts, famine, and environmental degradation. Warring secessionists have little to lose when hunger looms. The stark reality of Africa is a people growing too rapidly, the quality of the land that feeds them eroding too fast, and technology with its life-giving riches passing the people by. As shifting weather patterns each year bring the scorching desert of the Sahara farther south, the permanent nation-state boundaries on colonial maps look like cages keeping a people from migrating to better grounds. The national governments monitoring borders—in effect maintaining the cages—will become the enemy. In such an environment, governments will collapse and political power will fragment.

The early stages of national disintegration are visible throughout Africa. Secessionists in Northern Somalia have announced a new country, the "Republic of Somaliland." Ethiopia has lost its northern regions of Eritrea and Tigre, and southern Ogaden is invited to join Somalia. Western Sahara is seeking to break loose from Morocco; Kasai and mineral-rich Katanga may secede from Zaïre; Biafran secessionists may rise again against Nigeria. Sudan may yet split in two, and South Africa, having already lost Namibia to secessionists, may attain peace only when its Zulus are given full autonomy.

And this is not the end. . . .

THE MIDDLE KINGDOM

WITH 1.2 BILLION PEOPLE, China enters the twenty-first century as the most populous country in the world. Beijing, however, has remained an empire only by the force of the gun.

Tibet, Xinjiang, and Inner Mongolia comprise nearly half of modern China's landmass. Each region, with its own language, culture, religion, and dress, is culturally distinct from Beijing. In the placeless world, so many tens of millions of people won't remain suppressed for much longer.

The shift from a centrally planned economy toward laissez-faire capitalism is also creating extreme rifts: the wealthy coastal provinces are sporting cellular phones and expensive high-rises while the interior is still growing rice in the mud.

The reformed southern provinces are bursting with economic growth. Guangdong's 63 million people make it a country within a country. In the 1980s, Guangdong's economy grew an average of 12.5

percent per year, making it the fastest growing region in the world; it may top $120 billion in production by the year 2000. Rickshaws have given way to plans for a six-lane tollway crisscrossing the province. As their power rises, Guangdong, Fujian, and other coastal provinces become resentful of Beijing's meddling in their success.

With a developing market economy, China's dynamism and culture are decentralizing, bringing individual choices in products, jobs, and lifestyles. The very notion of a choice-filled economic world brings forth a demand for political choices as well. The restless ethnic groups in the north and east, the disparity of income between the coast and the interior, the rise of a decentralized market economy, the increased knowledge of self-determination elsewhere, will all collude in the twenty-first century to undermine Beijing's power.

The Chinese social fabric is already unraveling with social disorder, lawlessness, and political corruption at every level. Crime rates have tripled in the past fifteen years. Divorce rates, joblessness, and suicides are up. Beijing may soon be unable to hold onto the reigns of power: the Empire of the Great Khan will not survive as one. The idea of China breaking up may seem odd to those still living the fiction that Taiwan and China will one day merge. Macao and nearby Hong Kong are being reunited with the mainland, yes, but they are microscopic in size and only transferred—unwillingly—because of "contracts" signed with their distant colonial powers eons ago.

As for Taiwan, it is already the fourth biggest economy in Asia and growing more powerful by the day. After decades of pursuing the myth of "one China," Taiwan and the mainland are reexamining it. The older Chinese who fled across the Formosa Straits are dying off, and the next generation of native Taiwanese is horrified at the idea of a Taiwan ruled from Beijing. China and Taiwan will never merge precisely because the smaller, richer entity—Taiwan—has everything to lose and little to gain that it cannot obtain in other ways.

Thanks to the German example, we now understand that the costs of reunification are staggering. Those in favor of the reunification of the two Koreas are still immersed in the nineteenth-century concept that sheer national girth somehow relates to a higher standard of living, combined with a nostalgia to go back to an earlier age. The two Koreas may yet reunite, but the dynamics are driven more by emotion than the new realities of the twenty-first century.

FRENCH BREAD AND IGLOOS

THE RISE IN REGIONAL autonomy is not confined to Europe, Asia, or India, but extends to the Americas. The most dramatic example is French-speaking Quebec in eastern Canada. With one-fourth of the population of Canada, it aspires to independence.

Canada offers little internal unity: there is English Canada, French Canada, western Canada, and maritime Canada, but no *Canada*. Trade seems to be more north-south (with the United States) than east-west (with itself). Quebec has culturally and linguistically more in common with France than with the rest of Canada.

While the autonomy of Quebec evolves in stages through negotiation, a small group of Canadians is considering armed violence. In 1991 the *Toronto Star* sported such headlines as "Can We Really Rule Out Civil War?" Quebec's pro-independence Parti Québécois has even drawn up a $5 billion national defense blueprint involving up to 50,000 soldiers, fifty multiple-use fighter aircraft, icebreakers, and patrol boats. By 1995, 40 percent of the population favored sovereignty for Quebec, and the possibility of an independent Quebec seems stronger each year.

Some speculate that the secession of Quebec could spark the disappearance of Canada altogether. In the wake of the North American Free Trade Agreement, Canada the nation-state is made somewhat obsolete for the peoples north of the forty-ninth parallel. An independent Quebec would isolate the eastern maritime provinces, which would more likely confederate with the United States than with western Canada. The Inuit-dominated north may have more in common with Greenland, where Inuit people also live, and the northern Lapp-populated regions of Scandinavia and northern Russia than with

Toronto (in 1991, the Canadian government carved out a landmass over half the size of India to give autonomy to the country's Inuit). British Columbia has more in common with Alaska, Washington, and Oregon than with Ontario and Manitoba, while Ontario is inexorably linked to the Great Lakes region.

Whether Quebec secedes or is given full autonomy under a new Canadian constitution hardly matters. The distinctions between "loose federations" and "autonomous nations" are increasingly blurred. Either way, power will progress from the center to the periphery, and global sinews will grow in place of regional ones.

THE DISUNITED STATES OF AMERICA

EVEN A TIGHTLY BOUND federation like the United States of America often behaves like a group of fifty autonomous nations. States compete against states and cities compete against cities to attract a bigger share of global commerce.

As in Canada, the forces of globalization have bound each region in the United States to an external global economy, making the *internal* bonds less vital. What helps one region often hurts another; new high-tech global industries rise in the West and South, leaving cities in the North and East in decline. Cars imported into California from Japan reduce employment in Detroit. Imported foods dethrone the Farm Belt from its near monopoly on national food production. The divergence in development patterns between regions makes a focused set of national policies all but impossible.

Despite its long-lived constitution, common language, and *e pluribus unum* slogan, there are signs that the United States is spinning apart. The United States has long been held together by a succession of unifying goals: first to throw off the yoke of England, later to conquer the West, then by the threat of two world wars and world communism. But now that the Cold War has ended, the United States suddenly finds itself victorious on the world stage with no more large military threats. The enemy that unites has been vanquished, and the country is left in search of a soul, a universal self-meaning. It is finding now that its own internal cleavages are deeper than anyone imagined.

The signs of decay in national allegiance are everywhere: two-thirds of Americans do not vote in midterm elections; people increasingly refuse to participate in the national census. Tax evasion has reached record levels; government-backed student loans are left unpaid.

Further, the United States incorporated diverse nationalities from all over the world, allowing each one to retain its cultural identity. Civil rights movements in the 1960s attempted to bring minorities into the mainstream, often by emphasizing pride in racial membership. But in the 1980s, the majority of Americans fell into one category or another of "disadvantaged minority," whether Black, Latino, single women with children, or handicapped war veterans. Affirmative action has wielded tremendous benefits for the disenfranchised while creating an allegiance to subnational loyalties. Today, "Americanness" has been subjugated to other "tribal" affiliations, from Vietnamese to Indian, ecologists to capitalists, fundamentalist Republicans to socialist Democrats, feminists to unionists. To be an American has been demeaned to mere national anthems sung at baseball games and dusty flags hung on gasoline stations—words and symbols bereft for too many of compelling meaning.

In the face of rising disunity, the central government is confronted—like large nation-states everywhere—with problems spinning out of control. Global capital flows prevent the government from effectively setting interest rates or controlling currency; competitive trade pressures prevent it from raising minimum wages or providing social programs; the global environment is beyond its grasp; illicit drugs and immigrants flow freely through porous borders. Added to these insurmountable constraints, the central government is boxed in by an extraordinary national debt, entitlement programs, a bankrupt Social Security system, and law upon law that no one could possibly grasp. Social problems have simply outgrown the ability of the large nation-state to cope.

Like the rest of the world, America is slowly atomizing; power is devolving away from central control. States have to supply services formerly provided by the federal government; cities are incorporating to break away from counties. James Crupi, president of the International Leadership Center, even suggests that "the US is on its way to becoming a nation of city-states." Alvin Toffler's *Powershift* ominously predicts that the widening disparities between regions "may well trigger an explosion of extremist movements demanding regional or local autonomy or actual secession."

DEVOLUTION HAS BEGUN

IN THE UNITED STATES, a backlash against the centrally planned is taking place in favor of the locally determined, not just within the federation, but within each state, county, and school board.

In Snohomish County, Washington, rural landowners seek to break the country free from "big-city bureaucrats." Residents of Staten Island have considered seceding from New York City, and Long Island, Maine, from Portland. In Kansas, nine southwest counties want to form a new state called "West Kansas," complete with a constitutional convention and local control of taxes. Vermont celebrated its 200th anniversary with a debate on secession, after which 1,500 Vermonters voted two-to-one for independence. Although the vote was more tongue-in-cheek than serious, it is indicative of larger trends looming.

In California, proponents are planning to split up one of the nation's most powerful states. The rural north is fed up with laws imposed by the urbanites in the South. No sooner does the North adapt to some "unneeded" smog or zoning regulation than it turns around and finds that the majority of the voters (mostly in the South), want to take all their water away. Although Southern Californians view the secessionists as jokers, the voters are dead serious: over two dozen counties recently voted to secede, and plans are already in the works. If California breaks up, the movement will likely spread to other megastates beset with regional differences, such as Texas, Florida, South Carolina, and Massachusetts.

Even without formal devolution, de facto devolution has already come to the fore, with individual states acting more and more like independent countries, seeking to make "treaties" with foreign powers, offering tax concessions, and establishing foreign "embassies."

Every year, Oregon spends over $25 million ($25 per household) on wooing out-of-state businesses. North Carolina provides a corporate jet to shuttle business executives around the state. California dedicates a public relations firm to advertising and marketing surveys; the governor has promised "to spend time and effort in merchandising California as a place in which to do business."

Virginia, like many states, is luring Japanese-based globocorps to set up operations there; the state has a trade office in Tokyo, and the governor makes trips to Japan to court the decision makers. The investment has paid off: in five years, Japanese investment surged from a few tiny sales outlets to over sixty Japanese companies employing thousands of locals and investing $660 million in facilities. And the numbers keep growing.

States are also experimenting with business-government alliances to attract companies from other states. Ohio created nine technology centers to commingle the resources of government, industry, and universities. Pennsylvania's Industrial Resource Center Network has helped hundreds of companies compete in global markets. Oregon focuses on education and workforce training. The efforts of these state governments are analogous to what Japan's powerful MITI (Ministry of International Trade and Industry) performs at the national level.

MEDIEVAL CITY-STATES

EVEN *CITIES* MUST REACT to global trends to remain vibrant. Oakland, California, once the largest West Coast shipping port and key building block to nearby prosperous San Francisco, is battling to preserve its economy. The increased pace of Pacific Rim trade has spawned a new generation of megaships too big to enter Oakland's shallow harbor, forcing business to deep-harbor ports in Seattle, Long Beach,

Los Angeles, and elsewhere. Falling revenues have left the port authority in red ink, and shifts in environmental regulations make disposal of often-toxic sludge problematic.

Los Angeles is eager to pick up Oakland's slack. Despite citywide budget shortages, government officials spend over a million dollars a year in travel expenses for golf tournaments, conventions, worldwide seminars, and a business agent in Tokyo.

City officials for the Port Authority of New York and New Jersey are even more aggressive. Its seven-person Tokyo office promotes tourism and air cargo, recruits tenants for the World Trade Center, and even seeks investors for regional development projects.

Sometimes governments are so eager to attract or retain key employers that they pull out all the stops. When Northwest Airlines let the word out that it was looking at forty cities to relocate its hub, the state government of Minnesota provided nearly a *billion* dollars in subsidies to retain it—over $400,000 per job saved!

When McDonnell Douglas considered building aircraft outside California, nine cities offered packages worth up to half a billion dollars in subsidized loans, tax incentives, site improvement, and free employee training. Kansas City was so eager to attract new companies that it even offered to raise property taxes on existing residents to subsidize the added costs.

City officials are learning that placelessness thrusts each city into a highly competitive global arena, not unlike medieval city-states, or Hong Kong or Singapore today. In the Fourth Dimension, operating a city is like running an international business where initiatives must be seized if prosperity is to be won.

FRESH STARTS

EVERYWHERE IN THE WORLD, power is slipping from the center to the periphery. Though the dynamics appear to be different, in each case we have seen that fragmentation is caused by placelessness: communications dispels the myth of power, making possible a global awareness, and reinforcing tribal identity that transcends country borders. Global trade empowers small countries to access resources and enter markets on a par with their larger neighbors. Low-cost labor and widely available raw materials remove the need for military expansion, and the fluidity of terrorism removes the advantages of size.

Just as the factories of the Industrial Revolution legitimized the concept of governmental gigantism, the decentralization of business now under way is providing the intellectual justification for governmental downsizing as well. If the large nation-states wither, what will take their place? Are we moving toward a world where each nation becomes a state, an independent being? In a world of some 4,000 languages, would we need as many nations? If so, what is the minimum size of the future nation-state? Would the Amish community in Pennsylvania qualify? Or the aboriginal Ainu people on the tiny islands off northern Japan?

If large national structures collapse, how will subregional conflicts be resolved? Will the rich regions still subsidize the poor? And how does all this square with the opposite trend, where the world's economy is globalizing and becoming more integrated?

The emerging realities suggest that the Placeless Society will give currency to a new form of flexible federalism that will all but replace the hierarchical nation-state. Large nation-states like Russia, Canada, India, and China may survive the twenty-first century, but only if they take the concept of federalism to the limit: devolving full autonomy to smaller regions (for local business such as, say, building codes, education, and police) while retaining only minimum functions at the federal level (such as regional defense, currency, and uniform commercial codes). Under autonomous federalism, even obscure tribal minorities (like the Sorbs or Wends in Germany, or the Miskito Indians in Nicaragua) can have some autonomy, without any loss of order and economic cohesiveness—as long as their economic systems remain "plugged in" to the global economic web, and as long as they enjoy a regional security blanket.

In the twenty-first century, it is likely that some form of least common denominator will gain legitimacy as a model of governmental organization. For example, in large multidenominational regions like the United States or India, religion is more appropriately outside the state's jurisdiction, whereas in unidenominational regions like Ireland or Iran, it may more persuasively fall in the purview of the state. There is no single model of federalism for every region; each has to evolve freely in its own set of circumstances, and change as the social dynamics shift.

The concept of "least common denominator" holds special meaning in the Placeless Society. The concept of "state"—as we generally understand it—involves the public welfare in a specific geographic area, yet ideological tribal allegiances are less and less determined by place. In such a world, it is natural that the administrative boundaries between states in the twenty-first century will be optimally determined by the few factors that are still geographically bound: rural versus urban, resource rich versus resource poor, tax drain versus tax subsidy, ethnic versus ethnic, and so on. It is these dwindling physically based factors that will determine the natural administrative lines for microregions in the twenty-first century. The administrative trick will be to provide mechanisms that allow physical boundaries to shift with the underlying realities, while overlapping global structures flow with placeless tribal affiliations.

The twenty-first century will give rise to new types of federalism where jurisdictions overlap more as a matrix than a hierarchy. We already see this in nuclear storage: regulated by national or provincial laws at one level, and by overlapping transnational rules at another. We see it in the possibility that both the Republic of Ireland and England may oversee security in Northern Ireland. Look, too, at the Basque ETA separatists extracting a "revolutionary tax" from Basque businesses, or the PLO once collecting taxes through local Arab governments from Palestinians in Saudi Arabia, Kuwait, Jordan, and elsewhere. Just as in the world of commerce, there is no longer any compelling reason for government organization to be hierarchical, nor for it to be defined by contiguous landmass.

In such a matrix federalism, Kurdistan, for example, can function as a single unit at some levels of government, yet still be under the auspices of Iraq, Iran, and Turkey in other areas—as long as the degree of Kurdish autonomy is high. We might see the Arctic people of Canada being part of a Canadian Federation on certain matters, but also federated with the Arctic peoples of Greenland, Finland, Siberia, and elsewhere on others.

In this context, federalism in the twenty-first century will be a complex labyrinth of hybrid forms that will evolve as each situation dictates. The matrix form of political organization is most advantageous: it allows for political groupings in the Fourth Dimension when tribal affiliations have nothing to do with place; but when place is the core issue (as in regional defense, highways, or flood control), it allows geographically defined governmental structures to remain.

MICROSTATEHOOD

AS FOR THE CITIES and regional governments, placelessness will strip them of their protective umbrellas; no longer able to hide under their national governments, they will be thrust onto the world stage. The most dynamic ones will be the hypernimble city-states that send trade missions abroad and effect treaties with other city-states and autonomous regions, globocorps, or foreign governments. They will network with other city-states and federations seeking common answers to common problems. Together they will leverage strength against strength in a dynamic swirl of organizational bodies, whether they are defined by place or not.

But as power devolves to the most local of levels, many questions remain unanswered. Political scientists, sociologists, and economists have no theories or tools for solving the challenges posed by the Placeless Society. Still unknown is how conflicts will be resolved, or how—and if—the enormous wealth accumulated by the rich in one region will be redistributed to assuage the plight of the poor somewhere else. And if questions of income distribution are not resolved, does it not usher in an age of class warfare, unprecedented global immigration, and terrorism? And how will these tiny microstates solve the larger problems that not even today's nation-states can solve (global pollution, international drug flows, illicit arms shipments)?

Turning our attention to these areas, we now discover the ultimate paradox of the twenty-first century: while power is devolving, it is also consolidating. While the nation-state is breaking into smaller autonomous units, other powers are coalescing into large supranational blocks. Indeed, placelessness may bring ultimate sovereignty to the only level where conflicts can be resolved, one that offers both the promise of a warless world and the constraints of Big Brother; where the world's peoples are for once free, but the risk of global tyranny makes that freedom more uncertain.

We next unveil the elements falling into place that are already inching us inexorably toward global government.

13

GLOBAL GOVERNMENT

JOHN MELON DICTATED notes into his desk terminal before the videoconference was to begin. Chairman of a large oil company, he had adapted to one global change after another. Operations had been decentralized. Much of exploring, drilling, and refining had been outsourced; the rest was computerized and networked. With a few voice commands, he found out about anything he needed to know, and reacted immediately.

Yet John was perplexed about what to do next. The World Parliament had just imposed a hefty half percent value-added tax to all globocorps to finance its world-development projects and had again increased its surcharges for telecommunications and fossil fuels. These nascent taxes were of profound concern to John as he made plans to restructure his company again, in anticipation of increases over the next five years.

—

Daw Tu pulled the scrap of paper out of her shirt pocket and began to dial the number. She knew that the welts on her arms and back were abnormal, but when her two-year-old daughter died, she had to take action.

In a back alley behind dilapidated buildings, near the center of Rangoon, she and fifteen other women worked under slave conditions, keeping robotic assembly equipment supplied with chemicals, and making sure the feeder chutes didn't get jammed. One of her colleagues had lost her right thumb, two others were completely blind. As for Daw, she was sure that her welts and her daughter's death were due to the toxins she worked with every day. If she reported it to the Rangoon government, she would only get fired, and then where would she turn?

The toll-free number connected her anonymously to the World Labor Safety Organization hotline in Geneva: the WLSO would likely conduct a surprise plant inspection within a few days and help the plant upgrade to more modern chemicals and techniques without any closure. She hung up and hopped on the bus for her village.

———

Adegboyega Bamgbose was packing his rucksack in the bedroom he shared with his brothers. He had just finished secondary school deep in the Imo jungle of Nigeria and was looking forward to making his mark in the larger world. Since his father had been killed in intertribal warfare, his younger siblings would remain with his aging mother.

Adegboyega was off to join the World Militia and hoped to be assigned to the regiment that oversaw the security of equatorial Africa. Many of his friends were lured into nearby Lagos, but there were no jobs. By being in the Militia for a two-year tour of duty, he would do his part as a world citizen and perhaps prevent others from being slain as his father had been.

———

The new millennium will mark the devolution of power from the large nation-state to local administrations, and conversely, a shifting of other powers to supranational, even global, authorities.

In the twenty-first century, we will each retain our "indigenous" cultures, our unique blend of tribal affiliations, some acquired by birth, others chosen freely. Many of us will live in one place for most of our lives and take pride in the local region. Yet our passion for the large nation-state, for which our ancestors fought with their blood, will dwindle to the same emotional consequence of county or province today. A new spirit of global citizenship will evolve in its place, and with it, the ascendancy of global governance.

Placelessness is unleashing a new class of problems that can only be described as global in nature: Governmental bodies are decentralizing while the problems they are meant to grapple with are broader in scope and are more intractable than ever. How can this mismatch be reconciled?

The answer lies in the misunderstood concept of "decentralization." Unlike fragmentation, where everything flies to pieces, in decentralization the pieces are autonomous, but they act in concert with one another. Decentralization always occurs in a context.

Our economy, we have seen, is decentralizing, yet it is held together by an all-pervasive, omnipresent market economy (rules of contract, billing and banking, accepted standards, customs and conventions). This context allows individual pieces of the economy to act autonomously, even as the world economy is expanding.

Organizations, too, are decentralizing even as they are going global. Divisions and operating managers are given more autonomy than ever before. Yet even at IBM, the decentralization is occurring in a specific context of corporatewide objectives regarding profitability, with rules governing how divisions relate to one another, the use of the IBM logo, joint ventures, and the like.

In the political realm, our large nation-states will also yield heightened autonomy to their divergent regions, but only in the context of larger supranational blocks coalescing to govern activities that can no longer function at the nation-state level.

LE CLUB EUROPÉEN

NOWHERE IS THIS PROCESS more visible today than in Europe.

Even without regional nationalities demanding autonomy, no single country in Europe has an economy as large as the American or Japanese ones. By European standards, the United States seems to offer a tremendous structural advantage over Europe: this giant "customs union" of fifty states shares a common language, laws, and currency, and goods move effortlessly across its internal borders. As for Japan, it has mastered world markets by building an export juggernaut unrivaled in Europe. As the Japanese gain world market share each year and the Americans hold their own, Europe is sinking ever deeper. Unemployment, no longer seen in strictly cyclical terms, is now so embedded as to become institutionalized.

Europe has no less technology than the United States and Japan (in many cases, they have invented things that the other two later commercialized). The problem is that each country has acted on its own, with its own national airlines, its own automakers or steel mills. The British drive on the left using miles, while the French drive on the right in kilometers; Milan speaks Italian, Munich speaks German; here it's English Law, there it's the Napoleonic Code. Even consumer tastes are different: the French like top-loading washing machines, the English like front-loading; Germans like electric ranges, Italians prefer gas.

While the rest of the First World has already moved toward the Age of Everything-Everywhere, Europe is trapped in its own balkanized world. Its economy was cursed not by the number of individual countries but by the barriers between them.

The solution, as seen by many Europeans, is to knock down those barriers within the European Union, creating a single vast market like the United States, where goods and people could travel freely from the Mediterranean to the Arctic, with one currency and uniform laws and regulations.

What was considered impossible fifty years ago is becoming a reality. The attraction of a regional trading block is so strong that Germany and France—erstwhile enemies—have joined hands at the core of a new Europe. Portugal, Spain, and Greece are moving their economies up on a parity with northern Europe. Trade within Europe is growing. Students from overcrowded lecture halls in Germany go to Britain, as British pensioners retire in the sunny south of France.

In Brussels, a European parliament has been established, along

with a European Court, and the early foundations to a common currency called the ECU will soon replace the Deutsche mark and the
French franc. The European Union is already sending delegates to
the United Nations and elsewhere, who will soon eclipse those of its
member countries.

Although the road to unity is paved with many obstacles, for every
step back, it takes two forward. While member countries chafe at
each new rule, or seek the best perks, none wants to leave the Union,
and many more are clamoring to get in. What started with two countries, then became six, then sixteen, currently has a prospective waiting list of over a dozen more.

The growth has been so fast that what will likely emerge in the early
twenty-first century is not a monolithic Europe, but a transcontinental block of "Europeaness" with some countries more "European"
than others. The most likely scenario will be a central group, perhaps
the integrated economies of France and Germany as the backbone,
with arms and legs extending to Britain, Spain, and Italy, and fingers
stretching out to grasp Poland, Romania, and other central European
states. The result may be less an area that can be circled on a map
than a "concept" of unity seeking to expand, with more and more flexible boundaries.

Ironically, the people who want the European Union the most are
the keenest for local autonomy—the Scots, the Basques, the Corsicans, the Catholic Northern Irish, and others. The Union provides
potential autonomous regions the umbrella they need to seek independence within a context of integration. The larger "community" allows each region to be itself, while outsourcing economic stabiliza-
tion, regional defense, and commercial codes to a more collective
level. The changes sweeping Europe are a microcosm of the world,
where each group seeks to be autonomous while reaching for supranational membership.

THE COWBOY CLUB

THE NORTH AMERICANS, fearful of being locked out of a united Europe, and needing to react to a global Japan, have formed their own regional trade block in the North American Free Trade Agreement—NAFTA. Through it, the United States, Canada, and Mexico have each yielded some of their sovereignty in exchange for a union expected to increase the standards of living for all.

Under NAFTA, the three largest North American countries have set up a rudimentary "supergovernment," empowered to resolve disputes among the club members. Cut out of the process are the congresses, court systems, and constitutions of the member countries. In a very real sense, NAFTA is a sovereign government reigning over nearly 400 million people and an economy equivalent to nearly a third of the world's output. Its rules dictate that disputes be submitted to an arbitration panel whose findings supersede the domestic laws of each member nation. For the first time, US, Canadian, and Mexican courts will be bound to enforce the decisions of an international body against its own trade officials.

What each country has surrendered in autonomy, it has gained in wealth. In the first year of tariff reductions between the countries, trade skyrocketed, tens of thousands of jobs were created on all sides, and most important, each country has become wealthier and more globally competitive.

Free trade blocs generate wealth for the same reason that the Fourth Dimension spawns creativity and unleashes new wealth: ideas, technology, machines, people, markets, and motivation become interlinked in just the right proportion. In the Placeless Society, these factors become compressed into one point, creating a critical mass and an explosion of wealth. The magic of placeless technologies—high speed transportation, videoconferencing, computer networks—is in providing the necessary interlinkages.

In the absence of free-trade agreements, national borders block the process by building firewalls between the key ingredients. Customs officers delay shipments; immigration officials eject foreigners who might provide the critical talent, skills, or muscle. Even with trade agreements, however, currency-exchange risks turn a "sure thing" into a possible loss, and differences in language, legal systems, and culture add further layers of uncertainty. But in time, even these elements converge.

Tearing down borders allows the elements in each economy to be combined in novel ways. Crops that grow only in Mexico can be processed in California and shipped to Norway. Mining technology from Canada can be exploited in Mexico for shipping minerals to Brazil. Canadian timber can be processed into furniture in Minneapolis and sold to Japan. In a larger trading context, the critical mass of the combined available resources is expanded, more wealth and jobs are created, and more exports to outside the trading block are possible than when each country acts alone.

THE CHOPSTICK CLUB

THESE POWERFUL DYNAMICS have not escaped the attention of the economically forward players in Asia. Japan has demonstrated extraordinary strength in technology and organizational skills, and has provided an anchor for the rest of the continent. Taiwan, South Korea, Singapore, and Hong Kong are among the fastest growing economies in the world. And today's China—with its 1.2 billion people—will undoubtedly dwarf all the rest as technology penetrates its vastness in the twenty-first century.

The missing ingredient is connectedness. More so than Europe, each Asian culture is distinct in language, culture, and often, alphabet. Asians remain shy of a once-imperialistic Japan and resentful of rich local Chinese. The cultures of Southern and Eastern Asia evolved in relative isolation from one another, spread out over thousands of miles along the South China Sea, and beyond to Indonesia, Australia, and New Zealand. Unlike in Europe, there is no common aristocratic class that once connected the dispersed cultures.

But placelessness is now reversing history. For the first time, Asians as a group are beginning to view themselves as a distinct people with common interests. Technology is providing the links by video images, by ship, and by air; the first hypersonic commercial aircraft of the twenty-first century will certainly ply the Pacific first. Hong Kong–based Star Television Network already provides pan-Asian entertainment, with well-known Thai or Japanese singers animating the top songs of Guangdong. In Vietnam, Thailand, and Japan, children follow the cartoon exploits of a gang of Asian children and their robot playmate in "Foramen."

The dynamic growth of the Asian economies is giving the region a new self-confidence. No longer does Asia catch a cold when America sneezes. It has displaced America as Japan's most important economic partner. The Asian development models, based on the Japanese formula of corporate pooling and a strong government industrial policy, is gaining recognition as *the* way to develop Asian economies.

Unlike Europe with its EU, or North America with its NAFTA, the future structure of the Asian Club is still evolving. Seven countries have come together in ASEAN (Association of Southeast Asian Nations): Singapore, Thailand, Indonesia, the Philippines, Malaysia, Vietnam, and Brunei. They are joined by a dozen more in APEC (Asia Pacific Economic Cooperation): Japan, China, Taiwan, South Korea, Australia, and others. Many of the countries believe they need more time to adjust domestic markets before opening their doors fully to the outside world. China's internal markets are not fully decentralized, and other countries have national industries they wish to protect. Even powerful Japan, the supposed leader of the pack, feels a need to hold on to its unique culture, incestuous *zaibatsu*, subsidized agriculture, and archaic distribution systems.

But everywhere, each country recognizes that its entry into an everything-everywhere world cannot long be forestalled; national borders are slowly dissolving. China, South Korea, and Indonesia are sitting down at the same table discussing free trade, and even Cambodia and Laos may soon join Vietnam in ASEAN—ideas just not conceivable a decade ago. China, Taiwan, and Hong Kong, once scarcely on speaking terms, are now poised to link their dynamic economies. Over a dozen countries have agreed to start bringing down the internal firewalls erected among them: the developed economies of Japan, New Zealand, and Australia by 2010; the "middle-tier" countries by 2015; and the laggards—including China—by 2020.

The result would match the technology and financing of Japan with the labor pool of China, the drive of Korea and Taiwan, the transshipment expertise of Singapore and Hong Kong, and the cultural diversity of Australia, Indonesia, and the Philippines to create a single market of some 2 billion people in the fastest growing economy in the world.

The effect is astounding. From an economic point of view, *Tokyo and China would be one and the same.* Nissan and Panasonic could set up shop in Guangdong Province as if it were part of Japan; Australia and New Zealand could invest freely in Indonesia and the Philippines; China, Taiwan, and the Chinese diaspora throughout the South China Sea would be reunited more tightly. Asia would be interlinked, forming a mass of talent and capital, technology and markets, and opportunities unseen since the discovery of the New World, half a millennium ago.

OTHER BLOCS

WHILE THE COUNTRIES OF Europe, North America, and Asia coalesce into a powerful triumvirate, they are not the only ones. A swift transformation is overtaking Latin America as well. Scarcely two decades ago, Latin American countries were highly nationalistic, suspicious of their neighbors, and highly addicted to state intervention. Today, the diffusion of knowledge has displaced dictators; the market economy has triumphed over state intervention. With these changes, the economies of Latin America have been untethered from their confining national borders and are beginning to merge.

Mercosur has linked Latin America's most powerful countries, Brazil and Argentina, and absorbed Uruguay and Paraguay. Comprising two-thirds of the South American population and landmass (stretch-ing over 4,000 miles from the Amazon to the Antarctic) and three-fourths of its economy, Mercosur is gradually reducing internal tariffs to zero and easing the movement of labor and capital.

Not to be outdone, Venezuela, Colombia, Ecuador, Peru, and Bolivia have formed the Andean Group, while another five countries (Guatemala, El Salvador, Honduras, Nicaragua, and Costa Rica) are part of the Central American Common Market.

Even Africa, despite its deep tribal divisions, is merging the colonial-era nation-states into economic trade blocs. In the wake of lifting sanctions against the former apartheid regime in South Africa, the tip of the continent is again bristling with activity. The Southern African Customs Union links five countries (South Africa, Botswana, Lesotho, Namibia, and Swaziland); a would-be "Common Market for Eastern and Southern Africa" links twenty-two; in time Kenya, Uganda, and Tanzania will certainly coalesce in the East African Com-munity; Nigeria will likely expand its economic sphere over West Africa; and in Central Africa, Zaïre, Burundi, and Rwanda will surely become more interlinked. The result is an Africa as a single dynamic placeless bloc, rather than so many cubbyholes of backward isolation-ism. Africa still has a long way to go in building its internal transport and communication infrastructure, but the unmistakable shift toward integration has begun.

Elsewhere, now-independent regions of the former Soviet Union are reconsolidating as an economic alliance under the Commonwealth of Independent States (CIS); Turkey and the republics of central Asia are contemplating a union; and even Israel and its Arab neighbors are considering joining economic forces.

INTERGALACTIC MARRIAGES

AS EACH BLOC FORMS, regional trade heightens and the need for a common currency, uniform product labeling, and commercial regula-tions rises. In each case, we are experimenting with new ways to link countries, to yield sovereignty in exchange for something more than what is lost.

Just as Europe developed the original model for the nation-state at the dawn of the Industrial Age, it is now showing us the next step as we enter what some call the Postindustrial Age. Of all the recent blocs, the European Union stands out as the boldest experiment in giving birth to a new concept of government.

It is perhaps the first multilingual, multiethnic empire assembled voluntarily, even democratically, without external force. It is meant to accommodate rich and poor, big and small countries, and to meld federalist political philosophies (France and Germany) and nationalist ones (Britain and Denmark). Its economic system is predicated on the early tools of placelessness (communications networks, low-cost air cargo, high-speed trains) and downward-spiraling computer costs. What happens in Europe will very much be the model for world consolidation in the twenty-first century, not just economically, but politically and socially as well.

As nation-states coalesce into trade blocs, conflicts with a curious twist are developing between them. For most of us in our everyday lives, commercial disputes involve *high* prices, whether for gasoline, eggs, or housing. We would never complain too loudly if a merchant put in our sack three apples for the price of two, or if the gasoline pump gave us too much gasoline for our dollars.

Yet, in the battles of global commerce, that is exactly what *countries* are doing. Technology is giving once-backward countries the means to produce more for less. Europeans complain that American wheat is too cheap; the Japanese claim that US rice is priced too low; Americans and Europeans each complain that the others' aircraft are too inexpensive; Japanese steel is too cheap, as are their televisions and VCRs. As technology reduces manufacturing costs closer to zero, labor is displaced, and the testy debates turn to allegations of "dumping" (selling below cost) and "subsidies" (government payments to companies that artificially increase profits).

Economic and political "experts" tell us that the world will eventually consolidate in three blocs—Europe, North America, and Asia;

each will act as a center of gravity spinning ever more countries into its orbit, until the world consolidates into three galaxies of power like the Eurasia, Oceania, and Eastasia of George Orwell's *1984.*

Journalists are fond of turning these blocs into combative trade blocs: they talk of "fortress Europe" or "trade wars." Journalists and politicians prod pep rallies about which regional blocs will "win" in the twenty-first century, and which will "lose." But they fail to see that in the Age of Everything-Everywhere, power will no longer be defined strictly in terms of regional empires etched on two-dimensional maps. While old-world politicians meet to form trading blocs, placelessness is already linking each bloc to the others in complex ways.

None of the blocs is a monolith. Asian tensions are heightened by attempts to link Confucian, Hindu, and Japanese sensibilities. North America is cleaved by three languages and cultures—English, Spanish, and French—and Europe by nine or more. The cultural diversity within blocs weakens them, while at the same time, it forms the basis for links to other blocs.

Britain, as a result, has a closer affiliation in many ways to the United States and Canada across the Atlantic—and to Australia diametrically across the globe—than to continental Europe just a "Chunnel" away. Spain has a special link to Latin America, as does Portugal to Brazil. Many small countries in Asia want to redefine "Asian" to mean "Pacific," thus pulling in the United States as a counterweight to powerful Japan and potentially explosive China.

We are beginning to learn that in the Placeless Society, trade blocs need not even be contiguous landmasses. We have a new class of "hyperblocs" entirely in the Fourth Dimension, as globocorps continue to grow their webs completely blind to place. The effect is an invisible shuttle flying between blocs, tightening the warp and weft into a single fabric. The United States and Canada are part of NAFTA in North America, but also key members of APEC in the Pacific Rim. Mexico, too, is in NAFTA, but also part of the free-trade Group of Three linking it with Colombia and Venezuela. Chile would "logically" fall in with the Andean Group or Mercosur, but may first join

NAFTA centered some 5,000 miles to the north. Brazil, already the anchor for Mercosur, is being courted by both NAFTA, for its American credentials, and the European Union, for its Portuguese and Spanish connections.

Each piece seems awfully complex, and that is precisely the point. The lines are blurring and liaisons that depend strictly on place become irrelevant. Just as nation-states are already rendered obsolete by global trade, so too are regional trade blocs. The politicians cloistered in meeting rooms may draw the map of the world however they want, but in reality, Asia and North America are inexorably linked, as are both with Europe and the rest of the world.

Historians looking back on us today will view regional blocs as a mere stepping-stone toward the *world* as a trading bloc, perhaps one political unit. In the EU, NAFTA, and elsewhere, countries are now learning to yield sovereignty to supranational bodies, to trade a bit of autonomy (some say in a Faustian bargain) for a higher standard of living and greater regional security. It will only be a matter of time before these blocs, in turn, merge into a whole.

THE WORLD CLUB

THE FORMALIZED CONSOLIDATION may be already at hand.

The collapse of the centralized economies of the communist camp have left the world with one model for the engine of economic wealth: capitalism. Economists the world over now understand that in the long term, free trade (even with its temporary displacements of workers) raises general living standards in rich and poor countries alike, and that international trade, when properly done, is a win-win game in which all participating countries benefit (usually through the twin benefits of lower domestic prices and increased export opportunities).

In response, countries are already positioning for the next step: the world as a single trade bloc. The foundations to such a reordering have already been laid in the pathbreaking World Trade Organization.

The WTO is a worldwide trade bloc linking 124 nations. Effective in 1995, it was built on the foundations of its predecessor, GATT, to bring it up to date with the new realities of world trade. The eight-year "Uruguay Round" to update GATT demonstrated the need for more than a one-time trading agreement; what was needed was a *mechanism* to update the agreement on an ongoing basis. The earlier agreement, GATT, had no teeth: countries were flaunting the rules with impunity, "freeloader" countries were taking but not giving; disputes were often never resolved.

The WTO changed all that by effectively setting up a limited world government with sovereignty over world trade. It has replaced an arcane trading system with a new one regulated by the uniform rule of law, where the mighty nation-states and the tiny ones are treated equally. Under the rules of the WTO, each country has one vote. St. Kitts or Fiji has the same vote as the United States or Japan. Whenever three-quarters of the countries agree, the decision becomes binding on every member of the group, and noncompliance elicits stiff fines, sanctions, or expulsion.

The WTO is the most expansive free-trade agreement in the world's history, reducing tariffs everywhere on the globe to almost zero, bringing the Age of Everything-Everywhere to the institutional level. It limits government subsidies for basic research, agriculture, and other industries, and provides for much swifter settlement of disputes between members, an overwhelming advantage in reducing regulatory risks of trade.

These notions are far-reaching, but the most significant aspect of the WTO is that member governments have voluntarily yielded sovereignty over domestic laws governing the environment, food, safety, and way of life. Under the new agreement, one country can challenge any *domestic* law of another as a restraint on trade. If a three-person WTO tribunal of "experts" agrees, their decision becomes international law, unless the country can somehow convince the hundred or so others to vote against it within sixty days.

Ultimately, what constitutes an "unfair trading practice" is at the sole discretion of the WTO. Social policies achieved in the twentieth century may be unraveled in the twenty-first. No international law, for example, requires a minimum wage, and therefore products made with sweat-shop labor could not be kept out. So too with products that destroy rain forests or are made with polluting processes. A Geneva-based panel already ruled that the US government can no longer restrict tuna caught with methods that kill dolphins.

Each country is also losing its sovereignty to protect its citizens from imports that may infringe on public safety. Prior to the WTO, the United States could restrict imports of foods carrying traces of dangerous pesticides. Since many countries use these same pesticides widely, is not the American restriction an unfair trade barrier? The Europeans already complain that the US smog-control regulations restrict European auto imports.

By coaxing the nations of the world to surrender sovereignty freely in exchange for a more regulated marketplace, the World Trade Organization is raised to a level that supersedes the constitutions of each member country. In many ways, its ascendancy represents the triumph of the globocorp over nation-states that are still steeped in a regionalized world. In a very real way, the power vacuum created in the Fourth Dimension has been filled by commercial interests, leaving the politicians behind in its wake.

Some fear that the WTO will usurp the rights of individual nations to determine their own environmental rules, health, and labor standards. Local, state, and national democratic institutions are jeopardized by faceless bureaucrats more concerned with increasing trade for its own sake than adapting to human and cultural idiosyncrasies.

The organization is devoid of the checks and balances normal to a modern democracy. When panels on agribusiness meet to discuss pesticides, the interests of commerce, trading companies, and chemical companies will be heavily represented; environmentalists and consumer-safety advocates will likely be shut out as being "ignorant" of the lofty notions of world trade. Meetings behind closed doors will be inaccessible to public review.

In a very real sense, the WTO is a tyranny of commercialism. The laws at the nation-state level are mature ecosystems that have evolved over centuries. The sudden rise of placelessness, with sovereignty over laws now subject to world bodies, has left us naked. We do not yet have robust international equivalents of national antitrust, consumer protection, air and water pollution, corporate accounting, and minimum wage and labor laws. The WTO, as much as it is needed for trade, has exposed new imbalances in power.

THE DISUNITED NATIONS

AS WE SEEK SOLUTIONS, we naturally look toward our existing institutions for answers. At the close of World War I, the world established the League of Nations in the hope that it would end all wars by peaceful conflict resolution. But the League unraveled during the Great Depression. In time, its impotence invited Japan's incursion into China, Italy's into Ethiopia, and Germany's rising militarism.

The victors of war sought to reestablish the old product with a new label, the "United Nations," to collect all nations under one roof and resolve conflicts before they could erupt into war. Its primary mission was global security.

Today the reach of the United Nations is vast. With a $5 billion budget and a professional staff of some 20,000 employees, it is the umbrella over an alphabet soup of agencies: WTO, IMF, IBRD, FAO, IAEA, IDA, IFC, ICAO, IFAD, ILO, IMO, ITU, USESCO, UNICEF, UPU, WHO, WIPO, WMO, and numerous others. It is the UN that seeks to impose sanctions on errant South Africas, Haitis, and Serbias, that rekindles democracies in Cambodia and El Salvador, that moves armies in Korea and Iraq.

It has been instrumental in helping keep the Yugoslav crisis from spilling into Macedonia. In Haiti, UN sanctions helped cause the dictators to fold. In Iraq, it is dismantling, piece by piece, a military machine with potential nuclear and biological weapons. It feeds the hungry throughout Africa and brokers power sharing to limit bloodshed.

Its successes include the birth of the new nation Namibia. In Cambodia, El Salvador, Mozambique, and South Africa, it has actively promoted democracy.

The UN's International Monetary Fund (IMF) is acting behind the scenes in India to free up one of the world's most regulated economies. The World Bank, also in the UN family, is hoping to direct the establishment of market economies in Eastern Europe, Africa, Asia, and Latin America. It has organized global conferences on the environment in Rio, human rights in Vienna, social issues in Copenhagen, women's rights in Beijing, and others elsewhere. It is the only world agency equipped to help refugees, isolate and reverse modern plagues, respond to natural disasters, mediate international disputes, resolve civil wars, and arrange impartial elections.

On the surface, the United Nations seems best equipped to provide global governance into the twenty-first century, but the problems ahead are daunting: the gap between rich and poor is widening; refugees abound; ethnic tensions in the former Eastern bloc are mounting; Africa and parts of Asia are feeling population pressures; the arms trade is booming; and drugs, genocide, plagues, hunger, pollution, terrorism abound. The UN is overwhelmed, just as its once-rich patrons are suffering from "compassion fatigue."

As the world grows smaller, the UN, for all its accomplishments, is ill-equipped to deal with our passage into the twenty-first century. Indeed, it was designed by its very structure *not* to work.

Despite its lofty charter and seemingly global membership, the United Nations is an anachronism today. The only body that can enforce its resolutions is the elite Security Council of scarcely more than a dozen countries. Most of these rotate in and out: Zimbabwe this year, Malta the next. But for half a century, the inner circle has been the victors of World War II: Britain, France, the United States, the Soviet Union (now Russia), and China. If *one* of these "permanent members" vetoed an important resolution, it was dead. Locked in the capitalistic-socialistic struggle, East and West sought to block each other at every turn, paralyzing the organization virtually since its founding.

True, the Security Council may be reformed with the probable addition of Germany and Japan, but the problems remain. How can half a dozen or so countries decide the fate of 200? Where is the moral legitimacy of so few countries governing the many?

The absence of an army is also weakening the effectiveness of the UN. The secretary-general is theoretically a commanding general over armies of thirty different countries, each seeking to keep its autonomy. Since the end of the Cold War, the Security Council has passed many resolutions, but they have been only selectively enforced, based on the whims of the large countries with powerful armies. Even the Gulf War was a transparent effort of the United States and Western Europe to hand oil from one Arab state to another. In UN enforcement where the powers have little strategic interest, one or two dead soldiers sends the whole lot whimpering home. How can the world community take it seriously?

The most global thing about the United Nations is its General Assembly, with delegates from each country. But even that is little more than a discussion group, a place where heads of state can pound their shoes on the table, verbally abuse each other, or lament poverty in the Second World. Mostly, the General Assembly allows each party to tell the others what they already know: the group has no budget, no ability to pass meaningful laws, and no power.

When the victors of World War II dreamed up the structure of the General Assembly, they were perhaps inspired by William Penn, who wrote over 300 years ago, "Let the people think they govern and they will be governed." But in the Placeless Society, people are not so easily swayed.

Like the General Assembly the World Court is absolutely powerless. It has no jurisdiction over anything except those parties that agree to be adjudicated by it. And even if the court imposes a verdict, there is no way to enforce it.

The manager of all this is the secretary-general, chosen unanimously by the victors of World War II. Careful to protect their own power, they have always picked candidates from politically weak countries. Up until today, reformers have not been welcome.

And reform is long overdue.

The UN building in New York is stuffed from the basement to the thirty-eighth floor with deadwood: lifetime civil servants, political appointees chosen by home country rather than by expertise. Its structure is rife with unclear mandates, lack of direction, overlapping and duplicate responsibilities. More than thirty top bosses report directly to the secretary-general, a structure that would sink any organization. Turf wars are so widespread that even publishing its internal telephone directory creates extraordinary difficulties.

The question is not why the UN fails, but how it gets anything done at all.

DO WE NEED LAWS?

IS THE UNITED NATIONS impotent because, even as we slip into a global age, we are not yet sure we *need* a global government? The great powers that control the veto levers for the whole structure are happy with the status quo; the Second World gets free advice and an occasional loan that it hopes not to pay back; and many feel that, even as 14 million children die indirectly from hunger each year, it is enough to send off a few planeloads of rice and stop at that.

For many, the prospect of giving more power to a global government is frightening. Would not global government trample our self-identities as Americans, as Frenchmen, as Koreans? Would it not homogenize humanity? What of our national sovereignty? If a tyrant took power, how would he be stopped, where would we go? Even if these problems could be solved, we look at our bloated city, provincial, and national governments and decry yet another layer on top of that. Or we pull data from the Orwellian conspiracy tabloids full of power-grabbing theories of a fringe "elite"—the Trilateral Commission, the Bilderberg Group, the Council for Foreign Relations, the Royal Institute for International Affairs, World Socialism, the Communist Party, the Illuminati. The world, we are told by others, is going global only because of a handful of conspirators equipped with antigravity machines and the "hoax" of ozone depletion.

We have twice tried to organize the world in the twentieth century, each time following major global catastrophes. Both the League of Nations and the United Nations fell short of their lofty promises of a warless utopia. Is there any wonder then that in a *Time* survey, Americans believe that the twenty-first century is more likely to bring us a visitor from another planet than a world government?

But it is a moot issue. We no longer have the choice of retaining our national sovereignty; forces much larger than any of us have already stripped nations of any ability to go it alone.

Whether or not we *want* to surrender our sovereignty to supranational institutions, sovereignty is already slipping away. Our capital, ideas, and corporations are already global, as are our migrants, terrorists, and pollution. Our frontiers have become more imaginary than real, and the problems more real than imaginary. Each step toward placelessness blurs the distinction between domestic and international, between mine and someone else's problem; we are just too intertwined.

For all the criticism we heap on the UN—its impotence, inefficiency, corruption—the returns are great compared to the cost. The United States, the largest contributor to the UN budget, spends just a fraction of 1 percent of its budget on it, and gets back global security and coordination significantly greater than its investment. Sharing costs and resources across borders increases effectiveness. For instance, it is much cheaper to stop boats from leaving Cuba than it is to blockade the open sea. Cocaine might better be controlled where coca leaves are grown than after it is sent into distribution. Cooperation becomes a force multiplier: the price of the solution declines.

Indeed, this concept is at the core of government, trade associations, and organizations. It explains why we have governments at all, why we have a United Nations, and why its role is destined to expand.

We need global governance because we need widely developed and accepted laws. It is no longer tenable that the kids with the biggest stick or house set the rules. Such is the formula for war, terrorism, and discord. In the Placeless Society, individuals no longer acquiesce blindly to top-down hierarchy, but instead come to terms only through broad consensus.

We need a broad body of international law because our current system is a mismatch of national laws that stop at borders and don't represent the realities of our world. Most of us agree, for instance, that terrorism and murder are wrong. But if a master terrorist operates from, say, Libya, and Libya chooses not to prosecute him, does the destructiveness to society go unpunished? We have seen how careless pollution in Leningrad affects fishermen in Finland, or how dams in the Sudan could parch farms in Egypt. How are these disputes among neighbors to be resolved if not by the objective application of international law?

The nature of our commercial organizations in the Placeless Society creates fresh challenges. When an individual is convicted of a crime, it is foolish to ask which cluster of cells was responsible: was it the hand? the brain? the penis? the biceps? Crime is holistic, not piecemeal. In the emerging Amoeba Form of organization, the different parts can each be legal in their own jurisdictions (banking in Switzerland, growing cocaine in Peru, training terrorists in Sudan, processing plutonium in North Korea, freedom of association in America, freedom of passage on the seas), but when the organism is put together, its effect can be globally sinister. The holes and loopholes in parochial national laws in the Placeless Society create a world where we are all at risk. Only by stepping back on an omninational platform can the placeless beasts be tamed.

In a society where everything is everywhere, we are confronted with the "problem of the commons." Nature's gift to us is bountiful, but only to a point. We learned hundreds of years ago that each villager could improve his wealth by bringing a sheep to the village commons to get fattened, but there reached a saturation point beyond which the village was worse off: the sheep were too many, the grass too short, the water fouled, and disease rampant. At that point, more becomes less. To maximize the wealth of the village, access to the commons has to be regulated somehow at the villagewide level. This reality is accepted by economists of every persuasion.

As placelessness shrinks the whole planet into one village, the problem of the commons again haunts us. The West built its wealth largely by burning fossil fuels, and now China is powering itself into the twenty-first century on the strength of its vast coal reserves. Just as carbon dioxide emissions are poised to explode, equatorial jungles are being axed to the ground. Additionally, increased ultraviolet radiation may be degrading our phytoplankton. Without the jungles and the plankton, where will our oxygen come from? And where will our carbon dioxide go? Has not the atmosphere become our commons in the global village?

So, too, with the fish in the seas. As maritime nations fish the global seas, each seeking to outfish the other, the total catches have been declining. Technology such as school-tracking sonar, better understanding of migration patterns, and mile-long nets have made us *too* efficient at fish harvesting. The no-longer-boundless sea has also become our commons, where more is less.

To whom do the sky and the seas belong? What right has one state to diminish their value for the next? And even if some states cooperate to protect the commons, what of those who don't? In the Placeless Society, the commons has expanded, but we have no village elders to adjudicate the common good. Who owns the seafloor? Or Antarctica, migrating birds, endangered species? Who owns the precious few equatorial geosynchronous orbit slots or even space? Who owns this megahertz band, and do global communications webs have an owner? What of Internet and international telephone service? And to whom does the human genome belong? These items are only beginning to be pressing issues because our exploitation of them has only begun. But they will become major turf battles in the coming decades and will pose fresh challenges for international governance.

As our global consciousness rises and the once-sacred barriers of state sovereignty erode, we are beginning to apply village ethics in the global arena. In the village, if we see our neighbor beating his children, at what point do we intervene? In the post–Cold War world, the

United Nations is for the first time looking past the national borders toward the rights of the individual, even where the abuse has no bearing on the security of neighboring countries.

Today we *care* how prisoners are handled in China, how Kurds are treated in Iraq. We see them on television, we see their leaders interviewed in New York and Paris. Slowly, we are moving toward a world where the Universal Declaration of Human Rights will have a meaning beyond mere words, where international norms will justify the rescue of "the neighbor's children." There will no longer be an arbitrary distinction between domestic affairs and international affairs. Both are *human* affairs.

The UN of the past was a timid sort. It sought to cajole, coax, argue, bluster, and beg its way toward international order, but each house was its own master. As problems from one country spill over into the next, the twenty-first century will find global governance less respectful of national sovereignty. The notion of a global body intervening in the domestic affairs of one of its members will no longer seem abhorrent.

THE THIRD TRY

THE QUESTION FOR most people is not whether we need international governance, but to what extent and how the power is to be distributed. If we have laws, who shall make them? The United States? Japan? The rich countries? The poor ones? And if we set up a broad-based legal body, what form should it take? If the League of Nations and the United Nations failed, will we get it right the third time? And how should it be different?

As the decentralizing forces of placelessness move each country toward democracy, ironically the UN itself is far from democratic. Many members feel alienated, victims of a Security Council controlled by the victors of a long-ago war. Yet one-country-one-vote, as in the World Trade Organization or the General Assembly, doesn't work either, since it gives São Tomé or Vanuatu the same power as China or the United States. It is likely the world will eventually move toward some middle ground.

The primary challenge is enfranchising those now excluded without upsetting the existing world's balance. How do we prevent rich countries from getting overrun by poor ones? And although big countries like China and India need a stronger vote than microstates, the latter need protection as well. A workable system also calls for protections for religious and ethnic minorities.

Many will look for solutions in the same form as our current democracies, where power is balanced by requiring new laws to pass multiple hurdles. Great Britain has a two-house parliament, one for the aristocracy and one for the "commoners" (an anachronism to be sure); the United States has one chamber (the Senate) to balance large states against small ones, and another (the House of Representatives) to yield power based on population. Even then, prospective laws have to pass committees, the risk of veto, and judicial review to become law.

A corresponding world body would have to have similar checks and balances to weigh the diverse world interests of, at the very minimum, population and wealth—the festering gap of the North-South schism.

Whatever structure evolves will work only if no single country can ever hold the world hostage—whether through the veto of Russia, the atomic bombs of North Korea, the terrorism of Libya, the wealth of Japan, or the military of the United States.

The power of full enfranchisement in promoting world unity cannot be overstated. A world dominated by the great powers will increasingly be viewed as not having legitimacy on many issues when viewed from the standpoint of the disenfranchised. Many will ask, for example, by what right do the Americans tell North Koreans that they cannot make an atomic bomb, when they can point to a United States that has thousands and dropped two that killed hundreds of thousands of innocent civilians? Others will question by what right the First World tells Brazil that it cannot clear its forests, or China that it cannot burn its coal or build its refrigerators, when the West has done precisely that, and continues to expand its highways to boot? The technologically powerful can no longer dictate rules for the rest to follow; the placeless world must be one of consensus.

It is likely that the judiciary will be reformed with affirmative jurisdiction over disputes. As in Western democracies, it would act as a check on potential excesses of the World Parliament over local autonomy, and protect ethnic, religious, and individual rights. The decentralized aspect of placelessness may enable individuals to bring suits *directly* before the World Court, even bypassing their own governments. The court would have mandatory jurisdiction over war crimes, violations of international humanitarian law, global terrorism, and any laws falling within the purview of the World Parliament.

Laws require enforcement, too. Since the end of the Cold War, most UN efforts have collapsed largely because donated armies do not work. The ragtag military collections from several countries invariably take months to organize, and miscommunication and disorganization abound. In the past, UN forces have been known to arrive on relief missions so disorganized that a commanding officer once fed his troops only with the help of his Visa card. In another instance, radio communication between troops of two different countries got so mixed up that one group could find the other only by following the sound of gunfire through the winding streets.

Perhaps what is needed is a world police force with special training and equipment usually not found in armies designed to seize and hold territory. Any global force is likely to need language skills in the areas under patrol. They will need special equipment, transport for refugees, tent cities, prefabricated buildings, generators, mass food-preparation, water-filtration equipment . . . and guns.

Peacekeepers have to be a combination of social worker, policeman, riot police, and Rambo-style SWAT commandos. Commanders need to be half diplomat, half city mayor, as well as military strategist. Fighting is as likely to be hand-to-hand with back-alley knives and fist-sized stones as with AK-47 assault rifles. Learning how to use handcuffs will be as important as training with hand grenades. These traits, not found in national armies more prepared for conquering territory than rehabilitating people, are desperately needed in the twenty-first century.

Because all of this takes money, the present financing system of the United Nations is inadequate. A few countries overpay, many underpay, and too many are in arrears. Financing UN operations has been compared to financial bungee jumping: bold resolutions are passed without the resources to enforce them.

Global taxes will likely come into being in areas that depend on the maintenance of peace: taxes concerning Antarctica and seafloor mining, fishing, and transport; long-distance aircraft, air freight, and passengers. Look, too, for pollution taxes, particularly on carbon dioxide, fluorocarbons, and other global pollutants. Atomic energy may be taxed, as may be trade in armaments, satellite launchings, orbit slots, microwave bands, telecommunications and global television, and globocorps.

Diversifying the income stream makes it impractical for one country to sway the world body merely by withholding dues. Global taxation will also match tax receipts to those people or countries most likely to benefit from peaceful global development.

Global taxation has one other important benefit. As many of us are being thrust into the Fourth Dimension with its new wealth-generating capacities, the majority of humankind is being left behind. A billion people live on less than a dollar a day, and they will propel the major thrust of world population growth in the twenty-first century. The rich countries can say it is "their" problem, but in the Placeless Society it becomes "ours." The East-West confrontation of the Cold War era has given way to a North-South split over wealth. It is bringing unwanted migrants into rich countries, global discord, new strains of antibiotic-resistant diseases, global terrorism, urban malaise, and crime.

Taxing the tools of placelessness would dampen the trajectory of the First World but would provide the means to bring the Second World up to speed. The rich world grumbles at taxation, but it may be the only way to keep the delicate fabric of humanity from shattering in the twenty-first century. The rich may own the world, but will it be a world worth owning?

THE UNRESOLVED CHALLENGES

WITH PROBLEMS SO COMPLEX, and with so many competing interests, it would be naive to suppose that any future architecture could be determined in advance. But we do know some things: constitutions, parliaments, armies, and tax systems have adapted before. Perhaps the continuing evolution of the multicultural European Union will give us further insight into structures to imitate and structures to avoid.

The greater challenge is in *organizing* large-scale institutions. Our governments are top-heavy; bureaucracies, laws, and tax codes are easier to legislate than to "unlegislate"; money is easier to spend than to collect; corruption, cronyism, even nepotism, is more a rule than an exception.

The need for a world government is clear, but about how to organize its day-to-day details, we do not have a clue. How are task forces formed and objectives defined? How is duplication eliminated? Or should it be? These are important questions because the United Nations of the past has scored low and the needs of the future are high.

The global government of the twenty-first century is unlikely to be a "World Government" in the Orwellian sense that many of us today visualize. It will not be a singular, monolithic structure hierarchically "superior" to states. We do not need world govern*ment;* we need world govern*ance*—the result, not the institution.

It is more likely to be interglobal than global, an amalgam of agencies, some international, some governmental, nonprofit organizations and volunteers. It will consist of coalitions of the willing, each responsible for its own efficiency and trimming of bureaucratic waste, yet each with power and roles calibrated like lenses in a well-crafted telescope, to zero in on common objectives. The very structure of a decentralized interglobal government renders impossible a would-be tyrant seeking to defy the democratic will.

In the past, the global bodies that worked the best have been those decentralized from outside interference, with a clear mandate and objectives. This was the case in Operation Desert Shield, as well as with the World Meterological Organization, the International Telecommunication Union, the International Atomic Energy Agency. UNICEF has been clever at raising money for children and UNHCR has made snap decisions to help refugees. All these organizations have successfully supplied the world with badly needed services. In other cases, over a thousand nongovernmental or nonprofit agencies have been indirectly woven into the fabric of international governance: Amnesty International, the International Red Cross, Greenpeace, various religious and medical organizations, and others.

There is no question that the extraordinary effectiveness of these groups is the direct result of their independence from a larger hierarchy. In addition to their autonomy, they have effectively used modern communications to coordinate their operations.

A successful global governance will have its foundations firmly in the Fourth Dimension, connecting banking regulators in Bonn with Washington and Tokyo, refugee workers in Africa with embassies in Helsinki and Brasília. It will link the World Bank with its projects in China and Eastern Europe. During regional disasters or wars, the public will be kept informed of global rescue missions via broadcasts by television and radio; parties the world over will coordinate a focused solution. Access to satellite surveillance will also be needed to watch for shifts in crops and land use, and to forecast likely regions of famine.

Communications empowers decentralization, resulting in an odd structure where neither the nation-state nor the interglobal structures are entirely sovereign. Each party will have a role and responsibilities to the other, and each problem will be solved at the appropriate level with a maximum of efficiency and a minimum of duplication.

How do we get there from here? To some extent, we are already there. We already have a degree of world governance through the General Assembly, the Security Council, the World Court, the World Trade Organization, the International Monetary Fund, the World Bank, the Universal Postal Union, the International Civil Aviation Organization, the International Labor Organization, the High Commissioner for Refugees, the World Health Organization, and on and on—enough to fill a telephone directory. In "big science," where research into atomic fusion, cyclotrons, space exploration, AIDS, and the human genome project is ongoing, the cost is so huge and the benefit so universal that all the peoples of the world are beginning to put their resources into a common pot to reap a common reward.

We know that global governance will grow because we are increasingly intertwined and need to seek common solutions to common problems. But is the United Nations the right vehicle?

A French diplomat once described the plight of the UN: "You cannot repair a car while you are driving it at 120 miles per hour." It is possible that the United Nations *cannot* be fixed, having grown too large and ossified, and that power needs to shift to new structures. Perhaps the new World Trade Organization, with its finger on domestic laws and its potential to tax commerce, will be the rising core of a world parliament. Perhaps some outside threat will unite the world: a riotous stampede of humanity from Africa to Europe, a new Great Depression, a rising sea covering Florida and Bangladesh, fundamentalist terrorism, the horrors of nuclear diplomacy, or a new biological warfare agent. Perhaps it will be something else, some unforeseen combination of factors; we don't know precisely. But we do know that the *pace* of world change makes certain catastrophes inevitable.

As world globalization looms, some will hold tightly to a known past rather than yield to an unknown future. Indeed, the twenty-first century is likely to see a rise in terrorism, citizen activism, and clandestine militia as the displaced and the nostalgic seek to fight against powerful currents carrying them downstream. Many of the saboteurs of global governance are glued to road maps drawn in the nineteenth and twentieth centuries. Yet others foresee a growing global bureaucracy, excessive world taxes, intrusive policies, and the prospect of world tyranny. And some of them might be right.

But the alternative of *not* having world governance may be far worse. Jawaharlal Nehru, the first prime minister of India, appropriately stated, "Democracy is good. I say this because other systems are worse." We may also say that global governance is superior to any other alternative, for in its absence, the Fourth Dimension will render the world ungovernable. We do not know how the cards will play out, nor can it be known; the only certainty is that we will not be governed in the twenty-first century as we were in the twentieth.

We should not be surprised that in the decades just ahead the nature of government and rules of wealth will be transformed beyond what we've known until now. "Elbows" in history—dramatic changes in how we are organized—have happened before, and never has the confluence of technological change been so rapid as today.

It is comforting that through all our social changes, the fundamental structure of the traditional family has remained largely the same. Yet, as unveiled in the next chapter, this is only because it has never before been subjected to the tearing forces of placelessness. . . .

Part Seven

YOU AND ME

14

THE PLACELESS FAMILY

ADELAIDE MARSHALL HAD JUST laid out her towel on the warm sand of Cannes. It was winter in New Zealand and she'd come for some summer warmth.

She looked at the sea of bare-fleshed bodies carpeting the beach. Off in the distance was a sight she had seen before in Colombia, Puerto Rico, and the United States. Equipped with ammunition belts and submachine guns, a pair of men dressed in camouflage military fatigues meandered through the sand. From the opposite direction, two more were approaching.

Adelaide remembered reading about them in the guide book. A decade earlier, the beach patrols had started to reduce the flow of migration streaming over the sea by boat from northern Africa. They became so effective, even at reducing domestic crime, that the hotels started to pay for the patrols to provide a secure haven for tourists.

—

It was Enrique Matadora's first night out with "Los Tiburones," and he was so proud to have been accepted by the group. On this moonless night, the only light came from Los Angeles in the valley below. Griffith Park had always been a favorite with young lovers.

They walked boldly but silently up the road, in a fixed formation. Around the bend, a lone sports car parked between two trees caught their attention. Each of the five Tiburones pulled out spray paint cans and began to methodically tag the windows of the car to the horror of the two faces inside. Pepe gripped a boulder from the hillside and pounded the hood in, as the others were scraping the body with screwdrivers fished from their pockets. It was then that Pepe made his trademark move.

Waltzing around the side of the car, he hurled the stone through the side window, smashing it. He quickly reached in through the opening and flung the door open, exposing the driver. Enrique knew that now was his turn.

He pulled a shiny blue Colt 45 from his jacket and ordered the guy to resume kissing his girlfriend or he'd kill him. They started kissing, and Enrique fired a round that sliced through both their necks, spattering blood on the opposite window.

The Tiburones let go a raucous roar of laughter just as Pepe spied another car that had just pulled up to the next bend.

———

Jimmy Tomba, age fourteen, went around the side of the house and let himself in through the kitchen door. After downing three bowls of cereal, he went up to his room, jumped onto his bed, and grabbed for the remote in a single motion. He skimmed the stations: here a car going fast, there a couple arguing on a couch, an ad for tomato sauce, a preacher, a cartoon, a "limited offer" auction for a bunch of zirconium rings.

It was the pornography channel that Jimmy liked the best. He slipped off his shoes, and got under the sheets. He wondered when he would be able to do what the guy on the screen was doing. He didn't understand all the chains, but he thought the two girls were shapely.

By the time Jimmy's stepmother got home, he was engrossed in a western. He ate an apple and went to bed. He didn't have time to do his homework, but maybe tomorrow on the bus, on his way to school.

———

The forces of the Placeless Society will tear apart the existing social order. Individuals seeking to maintain community will establish new concepts of civic morality. An abundance of low-cost consumer products will dazzle us; a plethora of personal-service companies will specialize in satisfying our whims, leaving us more autonomous. We will "know" many people scattered over wide areas, but will remain ignorant of our next-door neighbors and our own family members.

Family structures as we know them are being redefined. In many cases, the nuclear family, the grounding point of humanity for millennia, will disintegrate. New structures will take its place.

The reordering of society will strain the established moral order. It will give way to new ethics based on the primacy of the individual, while the placelessness of world cultures will contribute to a "moral relativism" that challenges traditional notions of right and wrong. Organized religion will also be transformed in the twenty-first century, spawning fresh philosophies and attitudes in a world thirsty for spiritual answers.

THE MILLENNIUM GENERATION

JUST AS THE WORLD MIGHT look toward the European Union for insights into future forms of governance, we can look at America for clues of where ethics and morality are headed in a placeless age, for it is here that placelessness is the most advanced. It has the highest number per capita of telephones, home and office computers and computer networks, air miles, cars, overnight packages, and so on. Its technology has also helped it become one of the most affluent and consumer-oriented cultures, with more gadgets, devices, and gizmos than anywhere else on the planet.

But for all its technical and material advances, the American ethical culture shows evidence of a breakdown, of gaping tears in its social fabric. Among the rich countries of the world, the United States stands out as having the highest per capita homicide rate, assaults, rapes, drug use, prison population, divorce, single parenthood, teen-age pregnancy, and on and on.

As we enter the new millennium, we find the ripples of the 1960s still lapping at our shores. But today, it is the *children* of the Now Generation who are unleashed in a world changed yet again, this time by the forces of placelessness and access to a new technological revo-lution. Like their parents before them, these children—the "Millen-nium Generation"—are destined to forge a new revolution in social values.

To understand how this emerging generation will be different, we need to first look at their parents.

The sexual revolution of the 1960s forever altered the relationship between men and women: for the first time, sex was decoupled from procreation. Today, we are progressing far beyond birth control. Within a decade, scientists will have perfected fertility "vaccinations" to turn fertility on and off. We now have sex without children, and children without sex. In all this, the institution of marriage is dimin-ished.

Economic bonds in the family have disappeared too. The break-through of women in the job market, together with the rise of in-dividuality in the 1960s, animated feminism. Women sought their rightful place as engineers, mechanics, professors, and pilots. For the past half century, they have each year, in each profession, increased their ranks. Although the revolution is far from complete, wage and training differences between men and women are narrowing, and gender is becoming less relevant in the job market. The twenty-first century's rich and democratic regions are likely to see the sexes equal in every area.

The income equality on the job translates to equality at home and a collapse of family hierarchy. With equal incomes—or with the woman outranking her partner—women are no longer dependent on mar-riage in order to survive. The university diploma has replaced the marriage certificate as the path to security.

LOST IN PLACE

ALONG WITH A GENERAL CULTURAL shift empowering the individual over the collective comes independent thinking in the family. Although marriage in the United States is honored as a lifetime commitment, in reality it is becoming a temporary arrangement. While this may be the triumph of freedom and individualism over an imperfect union, the effects on the children—the Millennium Generation—are profound. Parents everywhere love their children, but unstable familial relationships are unwittingly reducing many of them to commodities to be stored, packaged, sorted, or shipped, as needed.

Many children from the Millennium Generation barely know their parents, just as the parents themselves often don't know each other. American parents now spend *half* as much time with their children as twenty years ago, and future prospects look bleak. Each travels in a separate orbit, to work, to stores, to the gym, to school, to the hairdresser. At home, each is on the phone or the Internet, or watching television or playing Nintendo, effectively transported somewhere else through placelessness.

Placelessness allows dispersed people to work together in business, and it also holds physically dispersed families together through faxes, phone calls, and bank transfers. However, it may tear apart families desperately seeking to be under one roof. The most potent culprit is television, which acts as an antisocializing force, transporting everyone watching it to another place, creating a passive trance. Nobody's talking.

Even worse, the American household often has numerous television sets: one in the living room, one in the parents' bedroom, another one for the kids. Equipped with a VCR, often connected to a cable carrying 40—soon 400—channels, television gives everyone the opportunity to seek his or her own interests.

But where is the family culture, the community life? What is the reason to exist as a family? Does placelessness account in part for the US divorce rate, the highest in the world?

THE NEW INSTRUCTORS

THE EROSION OF FAMILY is no trivial event in human development.

Throughout history, countries and empires have split and united, wars have been fought, economic and tax systems changed. But *family*—perhaps with its vegetable plot and cobbler shop—has been a universal constant. The family unit has been the most elemental, indivisible social structure upon which all others were built.

Now, placelessness has revealed a particle even more fundamental than the family: *the individual*, who in turn is forming new constellations of relationships to replace the old.

We already witness new familial structures with gay and lesbian unions, complex stepfamilies, roommate arrangements and communes, as well as single living. Children are raised by immigrant nannies and boarding schools, parents are sent to geriatric homes. These novel structures existed in the past, to be sure, but never have they become so mainstream and commonplace as in the Age of Everything-Everywhere.

The Service Age is also displacing the traditional family structure and neighborhoods defined by place. Not long ago, everyone in the village would help raise the new barn, each helping the other when his turn came up. Today, each person has been reduced to a commodity, a line in the yellow pages where, for a price, one is as good as another.

The Placeless Society has given us a world where we teleconference to any point on the globe, speed in our cars, fly in our commercial jets, interact and trade with people all over the planet, yet we do not know our next-door neighbors. The individual is decoupled from place. *Near* and *far* become one and the same; that which is near is no longer closer to the heart.

More than any other social institution, the family has been the transmitter of social knowledge from one generation to the next. In the crucible of the family, the newly born human learns the peculiarities of his species, how to speak, how to eat properly, how to fold a blanket—the million and one complex and subtle things that no encyclopedia could ever attempt to detail. We unwittingly learn important lessons on resolving conflicts, about empathy and compassion, revenge and jealousy, sharing. It is in the family that character is forged.

Traditions are formed by the repetition of tasks as well. Parents impose the rule of law, ethics, and a way of looking at the universe. In the past, this and more has been learned in the family. It has given society its equilibrium, acted as the guarantor of ethics, civility, and a sense of commitment.

Lost for the Millennium Generation is that sense of commitment. Many more children see parents who easily marry and divorce, dads who forget their progeny from one marriage to the next. The average American family changes households and jobs every few years. The millennial child learns cultural cues from television, which allows easy "zapping" and "channel surfing." In Nintendo and other video games, the characters are easily shot and disposed of; even the cartridge is replaceable. People, places, and things are all commodities, objects of convenience. There is no permanence in relationships, no culture of commitment.

The average American child spends four hours per day watching television, far more than talking to parents, reading, or playing. The new reality, therefore, is that television has become the de facto teacher, the exemplar supreme of modern life.

That might be fine, except for what television conveys. The inventors of the early television systems foresaw it as a possible window to the world, to educate and inform, to raise humanity to a higher level. Instead, the bulk of programming has fallen to the basest level of commercialism. By the time an average student has finished grade school, he or she has witnessed 8,000 murders and 100,000 acts of violence. Sitcoms are replete with sexual innuendoes every four minutes, or an "entertaining" world of drug dealings, people thrown off bridges, machine guns, fast cars, knife duels. Even cartoons are full of gratuitous violence that glorifies mean and nasty behavior. We end up with children who are incapable of drawing moral distinctions.

The system has so evolved because, unlike the traditional family vested in the long term, television is driven by the need to sell advertising. Producers argue that the moral content of their programming is irrelevant. It's not their job, they say, to indoctrinate people on how to live. Besides, they are only "reporting" what goes on in real life.

Maybe so. But at the same time, they are magnifying, glorifying, and distorting. And they are dismissing their very real moral and social responsibility to society.

As virtual reality increases in realism and the incentives of its creators are commercial, not moral, the Age of Everything-Everywhere is bringing us a world that panders to our most primitive senses. The distinctions between imagination and reality are blurred. If one has practiced a thousand times the drive-by shooting in the arcade game, why not try an actual window on an actual sidewalk? What's the difference? In the real situation, the adrenaline rush takes the gamesman to a higher "high."

The dumb repetition of the bizarre has numbed many to the cause-and-effect implications of their actions. By magnifying reality, we have unwittingly altered it, debased and cheapened it. Could it explain the epidemic of American kids shooting their parents or killing themselves, of gangs slashing others for sport?

"FAMILY" REDEFINED

ALTHOUGH THE NUCLEAR FAMILY has declined and technologies have risen, we won't all be plugged into a television monitor, virtual-reality headset, or arcade game in the twenty-first century. These are only the pastimes of some of us. We'll still need to form human affiliations; we are, after all, a gregarious lot.

What is changing in our placeless age is the freedom to associate.

The sedentary village of old had its main street and town square. Each individual was a member of a family clan, with a rigid structure of grandparents, aunts and uncles, siblings and cousins. We established social intercourse with the baker, the cobbler, the grocer. The constellations of sociability were fixed and, for the most part, immutable. Association was determined by place.

In the Fourth Dimension, association is no longer determined by the lottery of place or blood, but by *choice*. The traditional family is giving way to new associations: roommates, homosexual marriages, stepfamilies, third-time marriages, marital "swinging," latchkey children, one-person households. Displaced and alone, children seeking other "families" for company and fulfillment join gangs; the aged enter retirement communities; businesspeople look to their fraternal luncheons and others their environmental or church groups.

In a very real sense, placelessness is redefining the family. Old bonds are broken and new ones are forming. Each new "tribe" develops its own unique set of ethical standards and values. And they are all different.

For the urban gangs, it's perfectly all right, even meritorious, to kill some perfect stranger for sport, but to kiss someone else's girlfriend is a capital crime. For many gays and lesbians, homosexuality embodies love and commitment; for a number of church groups, it is a "sin." Businesspeople often value profits over the environment; for the environmentalists, it is the other way around.

In the new moral relativism, diverse notions of right and wrong have evolved. Each "family" or tribe has its own ethical point of view. To many cynics, moral relativism lacks a single set of accepted social standards. It has the potential to convey a smorgasbord morality, where almost any action can be justified.

We see it as politicians "justify" ways to bypass election finance rules, or to exempt themselves from taxes. A lack of broad-based ethical standards allows a gang member to shoot another in a rival camp, or businesses to knowingly pollute streams. "Insiders" trade and manipulate stocks for profit. Bankers lend money to themselves at a discount. It is a triumph of iniquity over altruism and courtesy.

Self-serving actions have always existed; the difference today is that placelessness has connected people of like mind as never before. We no longer have one central morality, with occasional deviations, but scores of ethical tracks that never meet.

The United States is not alone in the Placeless Society. As affluence, technology, and communications envelop the First World, the same patterns are repeated over and over in the world. In much of Europe, the institution of marriage is giving way to cohabitation; having children out of wedlock is more and more the norm, along with a rise in single-parent and one-person households. Even in Japan, the traditional three-generation families are becoming rare, and the traditional nuclear family is losing ground. Everywhere, individuality is asserting itself over the collective.

It is as if each region were entering its own life cycle, triggered by its entry into the realm of placelessness. Polycentrism is rising, authority is questioned, and hierarchy is tumbling. As society restructures, a Millennium Generation caught in its grips will struggle to maintain its all-essential civic morality.

In the United States, morals have already slipped. According to surveys, the percentage of people who would keep a lost wallet or not correct a waiter who undercharged them has doubled over the past seven years. Two-thirds of American high-school students acknowledge they would cheat if it helped them pass an important exam.

THE PRICE OF MADNESS

THE NEED FOR MINIMUM ethical standards is no mere prudish request: they are desperately needed in the Fourth Dimension. Technology has so leveraged the actions of individuals that ethical breaches matter more than ever before. Small actions can have devastating effects.

The Chernobyl "accident," for example, was no accident. The nuclear meltdown in the Ukraine was, in fact, caused by two very bright electrical engineers who had passed the rigorous academic standards of the former Soviet Union. On April 26, 1986, they chose to do an unauthorized experiment to see how long the generator flywheel would continue to spin if the steam jets were shut down. To do so, they had to shut down the reactor, override multiple safety systems, and physically block open automatic shutoff valves.

For Chernobyl to blow up, ethical standards had to shut down first. Operating rules based on fundamental principles of physics were disregarded. As a result, the worst disaster imaginable occurred: a reactor breach spewed tons of radiation over half the world, fueling the premature death of thousands, and (arguably) accelerating the collapse of the Soviet government.

The *Exxon Valdez* disaster, which spilled 11 million gallons of crude oil from a giant supertanker, simply could not have happened a hundred years ago, no matter how drunk the ship captain. Today, cities of millions of individuals rely on water supplies controlled by a few. Jumbo airliners packed with 450 passengers are turned over to pilots, and hydraulic systems are serviced by lone mechanics. Once understood, the human genome further creates the potential for a lone madman to wreak yet unknown havoc, even to threaten the survival of humankind.

Technology has acted as an "ethical multiplier" where the effect of one ethical breach, even a small one, is multiplied a thousand million times. Society needs a common ethical ground as never before. Bertrand Russell said it best: "Without civic morality communities perish; without personal morality their survival has no value."

It should be noted that civil laws are no substitute for ethics. Laws are mechanical and bureaucratic, and their application often has little to do with justice, whereas ethics delves into the subtleties of integrity, intent, duty, and reputation. Ethics acts even when unseen, laws only when seen. Commerce, for example, cannot be run by laws alone, but operates best in a field of commonly shared ethics.

This principle is particularly relevant in face of the Amoeba Form in the twenty-first century. In the extreme, it allows individuals to act alone or in groups scattered around the world. Unlike the more bureaucratic Corporate Form where employees' actions are easy to monitor, the Amoeba Form puts a greater reliance on individual ethics. Thus, cultures devoid of strong ethical standards will be at a severe economic handicap in forming reliable organizations able to react to a changing economy. Those without ethics will be shunned from global alliances, not unlike physical banishment from societies of old.

CHALLENGING FAITH

IF PLACELESSNESS EXERTS centrifugal forces that tend to pull the nuclear family apart, it is only natural to look toward spiritual values as a source of ethical inspiration. Human beings have always sought to understand the universe, to go beyond what is knowable with the five senses, and to create profound and complex philosophies transcending everyday existence. Thus, ethics and morality have evolved and intertwined with transcendental thought.

In many traditional cultures individuals experience birth and death in the same village, if not the same dwelling. Intermarriage is usually among the near-at-hand, with people of common culture. This stability gives rise to common beliefs in morality and ethics, buttressed by the same spiritual understanding of the universe.

With the advance of the Fourth Dimension, these once-confined moral systems are set loose on the world stage. Europeans and Americans travel to India to take up the dharmic teachings of Buddha, and American cities like Chicago now have more Hindus than Episcopalians, more Buddhists than Hindus, more Muslims than Jews. We are no longer monocultural but polycentric, attempting to balance complex dogmas and beliefs.

The problem is that many of these are mutually exclusive. In 1993 the Parliament of the World's Religions met in Chicago for the first time since 1893, with some 7,000 representatives of religious sects from all over the globe. Many assumed that if any group could find the universal essence of morality, surely it would be these leaders. Hopes were high that they would set the foundation for a universal ethic common to all religions.

What they produced fell far short: a brief proclamation denouncing environmental degradation, violence against women, and hate crimes. Totally absent was any consensus on anything else. So diverse are religious beliefs that the joint statement of world religions made no mention of "God": Buddhists believe in spirituality without god, Hindus believe in multiple gods, and at least one protester outside decried, "What about goddesses?" The commonality between religions is so sparse that any attempt to combine them to be all-inclusive satisfies no one.

The polycentric culture that inevitably issues from placelessness puts tremendous strains on ethical and moral guidelines. Some fundamentalists (both Christian and Islamic) are enthusiastic for the death penalty; other groups view the *executioner* as the sinner. Protestant fundamentalists in Northern Ireland claim that God wants them to control the Catholics, while the Catholic minority says it is *they* who have divine claims. Warring Sikhs and Hindus each assert that God is on their side. If a polycentric culture cannot even agree on something as egregious as death and murder, how can it even *begin* to provide any guidance on everyday ethics and morality?

Even if this abyss could somehow be bridged, placelessness presents yet another challenge to faith, this time to many mainstream religions. Traditionally, the office of the priest was to make sacrificial offerings, observe rites or interpret the beyond, to act as an intermediary between an individual and the divine or supernatural. But everywhere, placelessness is removing the need for intermediaries, "middlemen." The culture of disintermediation will spread into the realm of theology, affecting the day-to-day organization of large institutional religious groups and tearing into the role of the clergy.

In the Placeless Society, many will begin to question the traditional role of the clergy. The twenty-first century will see a resurgence of individual self-empowerment at the spiritual level. The clergy will still play a role, but it will be as a guide, not as a conduit.

THE COMING RENAISSANCE

THROUGHOUT HISTORY, religion has proven remarkably resilient and adaptable. It will survive, even as newer beliefs evolve alongside established creeds. But many religions in the United States can no longer rely on family bonds for membership, with the second generation automatically following the parents in tow. In reaction, some groups are aggressively marketing themselves like business ventures.

These new churches use niche-marketing techniques right out of Harvard Business School. They survey communities to calculate what services are needed (day care, geriatric care, counseling); they bring flashy music, skits, even comedians; schedules are made out with production-line efficiency.

Others use the tools of the Fourth Dimension: ministries are conducted over television, turning each living room into a "church." There's no need to step out of the house to be with a "fellowship" of thousands. Toll-free numbers flash; video and audiotapes are offered at a price, and donations are accepted on Visa cards.

The methods change, but the need for spirituality remains. The human fiber *wants* to be ethical. We each have a social sense, perhaps honed over millions of years, to enhance our survival as a species. It required the individual to yield to the group, for the parent to give up his or her life for the child, for the one to die for the many.

Our primitive selves are perhaps illustrated in wild animals. Chimpanzees often risk their lives to save others, or admonish one another to establish rules of appropriate behavior. Even birds in the wild scream warnings to others at their own peril. There seems to exist an innate sense of empathy, of altruism even at the risk of death, of universal order and ethics.

Religion will not die in the twenty-first century. In the impoverished Second World, it will provide an alternate path to dignity for people who have no chance of catching up with the First World, and a protective shield against the cultural shifts of placelessness. The hierarchical religions—Islam in Africa and Central Asia, Roman Catholi-

cism in Latin America, and perhaps Russian Orthodoxy in Russia—
are likely to survive in areas where authoritarian hierarchy still holds
sway.

In the rich First World, religion will surge in places, but for other
reasons. Many will join a congregation to form personal long-term
bonds in an otherwise impersonal and temporary world. To many, religion will provide a link to the known and traditional against a background of uncertainty and change.

Surprisingly perhaps, there is hope for future common ethics in the
Placeless Society. The experience of the Internet serves a good lesson. As we have seen, the Internet consists of millions of individuals
connected electronically in the Fourth Dimension. They are anonymous to one another, often only identified by a faceless code number
or a self-selected nickname. The Internet has been described as organized chaos of the first order because of its absence of hierarchy, police, or formalized "rules."

Yet, surprisingly, what has evolved is a highly organized social ethic
and sense of civil morality. Though a few individuals terrorize the network with headline-grabbing computer viruses, or seek to disrupt the
"conversations" of others, they are the exception to the rule. Deviants
are frowned on and shunned, or admonished by others. Specific customs have evolved regarding appropriate punctuation and capitaliza-
tion (all capitalized words are akin to shouting rudely and are to be
avoided). People go to great pains to spare others' feelings; one will
defend another against a third. Participants often type detailed three-
page answers to queries posed by perfect strangers. We may see in
these actions altruism and an innate need for social order.

No, ethics and morality will not perish in the Fourth Dimension; if
anything, they will grow stronger. There will be a revival of morality
based more on reflections of the individual from within, and less on
the blind force of tradition without. As a result, convictions will be
deeper as each person confronts competing ideas and rethinks his or
her spirituality and the reasons for choosing a particular path.

The polycentric culture of the Placeless Society will also force us to
be more tolerant of other beliefs, for a society that cannot be all inclu-

sive in the twenty-first century will surely explode.

Much of the adaptation to a polycentric culture will take place in the schools. Those not already doing so will introduce instruction in morality and ethics (altruism, civility, integrity, respect) based on a common-sense approach, perhaps modeled on a revival of the French *Leçon de Morale* and *Intruction Civique*.

But schools in the United States are already under siege to provide training in hygiene, school lunches, medical attention, sex education—all traditionally undertaken by the nuclear family. The addition of ethics and morality may distract further from core learning: reading, writing, science, mathematics, and other subjects.

Many argue that American schools need more resources, more years of language, national standards for the sciences, better teachers. But as we see next, this may not be enough. What is needed in the Placeless Society is a complete rethinking of this thing called school. . . .

15

PILOTS OF THE
TWENTY-FIRST CENTURY

EIGHT-YEAR-OLD MELISSA GROSSENKOPF was engrossed in the Trojan War. All around her were soldiers dressed in exotic armor, on a chaotic battlefield. She heard a sound from behind and turned quickly to "feel" a spear graze her ear.

Spying the citadel of Troy, Melissa pointed with her finger and sailed like a bird to its tower. As a baritone voice read from Homer's *Iliad,* she saw life as it was in 1200 BCE: the finely crafted stone walls, the houses crowded together, the storage jars beneath the floor boards. Upon reaching to examine a shiny pot, she was transported to a copper smelting operation, and educated on the fabrication of bronze and its influence on the progress of humanity. Through the eyes of Heinrich Schliemann, she learned archeology and how lost histories are unearthed.

Satisfied, she returned to Troy to enter the beguiling Trojan Horse, to see the city finally sacked and burned, its women carried away. Through Odysseus she learned about duty and patience, through Agamemnon, strategy and valor.

Melissa pealed off her virtual-reality headgear and ran outside to play soccer.

━━

Joel Altman, age twelve, set up the tripod with care. Every detail had been planned out the day before; last-minute changes were made through a conference call after they'd all gone home.

Joel learned that making a documentary film was not easy. His team of classmates roamed databases all over the world looking for tidbits of information, like in a galactic Easter-egg hunt. From a class in Nome, Alaska, they gathered data on migratory birds. An English class in Germany got to review and critique the screenplay. Another class would do the editing and titles. Yet another would produce a theme song with their school orchestra and choir.

The project taught Joel teamwork and cooperation, communication, schedules, duty, commitment. Proud to be part of a dynamic global team, he couldn't wait to get the film into distribution and show it on the new Video Internet to his E-mail pen pals in Tokyo and Helsinki.

━━

The most fundamental, and perhaps most critically important change in the twenty-first century will be in our schools. Our global citizens will be divided into two worldwide camps: those who can soar in the Fourth Dimension and those still enmeshed in the Second and Third. With the advance of technology, computers, robotics, and artificial intelligence, those who have relied on routine tasks to make a living will be displaced by low-cost mechanization, or held hostage to wages forever depressed. Unskilled people in Bangladesh or inner-city Chicago will share the same lot.

The other group will have made the leap into the new millennium in highly competitive jobs. Those who know how to combine diverse building blocks of knowledge and resources will be in great demand and will receive high salaries and royalties. The global market will leverage superior skills; those with average talent will make a living, but will never become rich.

Here is the challenge for government in the twenty-first century. If a country is a *physical place* defined by the people who live in it, then its standard of living is set by the collective income of its people. Everything else—corporations, banks, stock exchanges—exist only in the Fourth Dimension, and have little to do with notions of country (except for the people working in them).

In such a world, if a government can have only one function, *education* should be the one. Nothing else a government provides—roads, tax laws, regulations, defense, police—comes even close in importance. If education is in place, helping people earn a high standard of living and compete in the global marketplace will follow naturally. Without education, in time, the economy collapses, tax revenues plummet, ethics and morality turn to chaos, drugs and violence rule, technology and defense deteriorate, democracy degrades, the infrastructure rots—all is for naught.

Our schools are frighteningly ill-equipped for the challenges ahead. Except for the overhead projector and colored chalk, they are identical to medieval ones. Thirty or so desks are facing an overwhelmed teacher lecturing about this or that, while students look out the window. Then comes the "test," the bell rings, and off they go to the next lecture.

The school system of the past was well-suited to the Industrial Age just ended. Our current schools mimic the bureaucratic, hierarchical factory system, with everyone in one place from the beginning to the end of the shift, at which point students can go home. Too often, the instructor spills forth doctrines not to be questioned, and the students blindly carry out instructions. For some, this assembly line is too easy, leading to boredom and unmet potential. For others, the line is too hard, leading to humiliation and rejection. Either way, society loses for not marshaling all its human resources.

SCHOOLROOMS WITHOUT WALLS

THE COUNTRIES THAT THRIVE in the twenty-first century will be those adapting their educational systems to the Placeless Society.

People will need not only to solve problems but also to define the problems to be solved. They will be self-motivated, adapt easily to teamwork, combine knowledge from multiple disciplines, and be conversant with electronic media as a source and medium of knowledge.

But how can this be translated in our schools?

To adapt to the Fourth Dimension, schools will need to use its very tools: interactive multimedia systems and computer technology, combined with heightened sensory stimulation (3-D sound and wraparound vision). Unlike books, in which knowledge is presented linearly page after page, the new systems will allow knowledge to be freely "navigated" by the student. Such systems can be distributed to all students—in the suburbs, in the inner cities, in rural areas—and provide an equal access to knowledge. They would incorporate the views of the leading specialists in the field under study and the best pedagogues. Students would progress at their own pace.

Education redesigned in this way mimics reality: the senses are simultaneously used, knowledge can be "touched" and "felt," and the student is free to pause and explore. Especially for children, multimedia education can be infinitely more interesting than the printed book; learning can be made fun without compromising educational integrity. All the while, the student searches out new tools and resources in diverse electronic databases; networks with other students by E-mail, telephone, or videoconferencing; and masters all the skills needed in the economy of the future.

Knowledge becomes interdisciplinary. Even something as seemingly frivolous as organizing a go-cart race can become an anchor tying together profound thought on research in a variety of areas: students could study Newtonian physics, examine common hand tools, or perhaps program robotic machine tools. Then they could research historic competitions, write rules of play employing principals of ethics, design a system of governance and judging, calculate costs, and maybe even translate their results into other languages. In the twenty-first century, the most sought-after employees will be experts at integrating multiple disciplines.

The role of libraries will also change. As our body of knowledge keeps expanding, libraries based on books will be displaced by electronic media (in France the traditional *bibliothèque* has given way to the *médiathèque*). Electronic dictionaries, for example, offer faster access to data and rapid cross-referencing. Electronic encyclopedias already outsell printed versions. In the electronic format, magazine articles and books are instantly scanned and sorted. New graphic displays will be as clear, readable, and portable as a book. The Millennium Generation growing up with these media will—by the time they are adults—view cellulose books more as dust-collecting relics than sources of knowledge or enlightenment. It is not that the *information* in the books will be displaced, but the *medium* of conveying that information will radically shift.

Perhaps even more important, the students themselves will become a database. By linking terminals electronically, students can exchange ideas with peers around the world. Exploring hobbies together and working on common projects develops vital give-and-take communication skills and an empathy for other cultures. The universe becomes a single classroom without walls.

In the midst of these changes, the teacher's traditional role will be redefined. A new breed of "celebrity instructors" will evolve whose skills are reproduced a million times through electronic media. Behind the scenes, an industry of programmers, multimedia specialists, and educators will produce interactive scripts designed to stimulate and develop all minds to the maximum of their potentials.

Classroom teachers will still exist, since even in the Placeless Society there is no substitute for the human touch. But they will act more as facilitators, making sure the student is working on the right material, and that progress is being made. They will challenge, guide, and bring students to their full potential as human beings, as individuals.

In the twenty-first century, the school diploma will disappear. Employers will be more interested in what a student knows *right now*, than what he *once* knew. Because of the advancement of knowledge, learning will become not a one-time event like a vaccination, but rather an ongoing process for life. We will find learning systems in factories and companies, even small ones.

Universities will not resemble today's institution. They will continue to educate the youth, but they will also offer lifelong education to individuals of all ages. And with multimedia learning systems, it makes no sense for Nobel laureate professors to deliver the same lecture each semester to 300 or 1,000 students. Better to record good lectures once for wide distribution and allow professors to spend time in small groups on individual concerns.

Universities will refit their sprawling campuses. They will partition lecture halls into smaller meeting rooms fitted with videoconferencing terminals, E-mail systems, and database access. Basic laboratory work will be simulated electronically, allowing students to do chemical experiments, design aircraft wings, or dissect bodies, without the cost of expensive laboratories. The laboratories will then be freed up for truly experimental, cutting-edge work.

With these changes, there will be more learning done at less cost, because once the basic infrastructure is in place, expensive resources can be shared across universities, instruction can be semiautomated, and the cost of adding an additional student with a terminal at home is near zero.

WHAT DO I DO WITH ALEX?

PARENTS OF THE Millennium Generation are concerned about their children's standing as we collide with the future.

For many, the first step toward quality education will be to control television at home by selecting programming and limiting viewing. They will also train their children in the use of home computers, which will be equipped with software offering the appropriate balance between entertainment and education. Systems are getting more sophisticated every year as glitzy programmers are being nudged aside by serious educators.

More parents are using the global computer networks, such as the Internet and Prodigy, to steer their youngsters to the appropriate forums or databases, harnessing the power of the network for their schoolwork and hobbies. They encourage the use of E-mail forums where kids can exchange ideas with their peers, whether they are in Asia, Europe, North America, or elsewhere.

Most importantly, parents will recognize that the new electronic gadgets are only tools for the future. There is no substitute for spending time with one's children, and sharing ideas and problems. The family then becomes a grounding point, a source of inspiration, interweaving the lessons at school with those at home to make a seamless whole.

Finally, we must provide high moral and ethical standards. In a polycentric culture, the details will remain personal, but the universal values so important for civil discourse will hold true. In the Placeless Society, each child of the Millennium Generation will span the globe, and your reputation and skills will be the key to whether you are invited into the game.

As we grip the handrails and accelerate into the third millennium, we see unfamiliar structures ahead, and our peripheral vision begins to blur. We need fresh eyes to guide us, and had damn well better prepare our youth.

16

DESTINY REVEALED

WE HAVE TAKEN a long journey, you and I.

We started at the campfire of our ancestors, as a "dot culture," where our social world was the people sitting around the fire with us. In time, we entered the First Dimension, where we started growing crops and trading with the other dots, until soon, the lines became connected in trade. In the Second Dimension, geographical areas matured into empires that spanned rivers and mountains, and later the seas. The Third Dimension gave us flight and the ascent into space.

With each dimensional shift, our political, social, and economic structures changed dramatically. With the accelerative thrust of technology, we are now propelled into the Fourth, and perhaps final, Dimension—where distance ceases to exist.

Through these changes, ours has become a global world. Every facet of our lives is pulling us there: our trade, television and news, fashions and consumer goods, food sources, pollution, immigration, computers, banking, terrorists and illicit drugs, systems of governance, jobs, and for a growing percentage of us, our families.

But while our world is global, we are individuals, and social structures depend on each of us interacting with one another in a human context: here as an employer, there as a customer, again as an educator, a parent, a friend. All political and economic organizations throughout all time have this constant reality. We are social animals.

In many ways, traditional social constellations can be viewed as rigid crystalline structures, with individuals as the atoms that comprise its matrix. Until now, these social structures depended on the primacy of place; we interacted chiefly with the near at hand, we formed households, factories, offices, villages, and nations whose existence were so obviously dependent on place that we did not even discuss its significance. Processes in the crystalline lattice were easy to see and understand. And so social pathways were set.

In the Placeless Society, the pathways are more fluid, less visible. We are moving into a realm where each "atom" can interact with another, regardless of where they are physically. When viewed through the lens of the traditional Third Dimension, the emerging society will seem bizarre and disjointed. It will appear that individuals are in some kind of inexplicable Brownian motion by themselves and without clear purpose.

Yet, when viewed through the lens of the Fourth Dimension, the emerging realities come into sharper focus: an insurance adjuster in Los Angeles, a data-entry person in Manila, a bank teller in New York, an accountant in Chicago, a government regulator in Washington, DC, an aircraft safety expert in Toulouse, a stranded traveler in Vancouver, an airline executive in Bogotá, a foreign ambassador in Berlin, a terrorism investigator in Paris. . . . These individuals and hundreds like them scattered all over the world can be perfect strangers to one another at one moment, but can be brought together quickly to form an effective reaction force responding to a sudden human need—for example, within minutes of an airline crash somewhere over the Atlantic.

All of society is affected by the coming realignments. In these pages we have seen how the classical rules of wealth are being rewritten, organizations restructured, and government reconstituted. In all of this we see that rigid command-and-control hierarchies are crumbling, and as power slips from the center to the once-remote periphery, autonomy and self-realization are being enhanced. At the same time, we are moving inexorably into a common global context, where the reach of each of our activities extends to the furthest points on the globe.

The world of the next few decades presents us with fresh opportunities, but problems too. The Fourth Dimension will undoubtedly soar, but under its wings are enigmas yet unsolved: population growth, hunger, migration, terrorism.

Perhaps one of our greatest organizational challenges over the next two decades will stem from the various speeds at which the forces of the Fourth Dimension are changing society—with each element lurching forward at a different clip. The world's economy is accelerating faster than our political structures. Some industries, some companies, some jobs, are becoming placeless at a quicker pace than others. Individuals are adapting unequally as well; perhaps the Millennium Generation—our current youth in their rooms with their Nintendo cartridges and Internet access codes—will surpass their parents. Or perhaps not.

As each portion of society accelerates forward at its own pace, it creates cracks in our delicate social façade; these may soon expand into gaping chasms of dimensional inequality.

What about those who might be left behind? What about those trapped in the Second World with no path to the First? The topic is too broad to cover here—and might best be covered in another book—but this much can be said now: the plight of the disenfranchised must be solved—for all of us. In the highly structured, place-oriented world of yesterday the poor could be contained, segregated, controlled, . . . and forgotten. But in the placeless realm, old concepts must be left behind, and new paradigms embraced.

We now live in a world where, whether we like it or not, we approach each other face-to-face as naked individuals. Hierarchies are tumbling, knowledge is widespread, the individual is empowered. Any attempt to maintain a two-class society of the enfranchised and the disenfranchised, the haves and the have-nots, is doomed to failure.

We have seen how placeless technology favors the terrorist; technologies of public terror are just too widespread, and the social fabric is too fragile, too vulnerable, to ignore.

We will certainly adapt to all the other shock waves caused by our collision with the future, but the rift between those propelled into the future, and those left behind is growing too great, and the consequences too dangerous. Placelessness brings the First World and the Second face to face in urban centers in every country on the globe. Technology is yielding a universe where the First World no longer needs the Second. This holds a time bomb set to explode sometime during the twenty-first century. Perhaps in a placeless society it will not be World War III so much as Chaos I. We just don't know. As with earthquakes, we don't know when or precisely where the tremors will occur—but left unchecked these growing cracks in humanity are the ones that leave us most exposed to social anarchy.

Chaos may be an apt metaphor.

We are now learning about the complexity of the world through our study of chaos theory. Computer simulations of weather patterns tell us that even the gentle flutter of a butterfly's wings on one side of the Earth can, through a complex chain of cause and effect, lead to a powerful typhoon on the opposite side of the Earth fifty years later. We have seen how the actions of a Christ, a Mohammed, an Einstein— even a Marx or a Hitler—can be magnified through the lens of history, to completely restructure the world fifty years or two millennia hence.

Our future will depend greatly on seemingly unrelated events: the economic success of the European Union, tyranny in Russia, a succession crisis in China, population growth and migration from Africa, environmental decay, the mapping of the human genome, a chance mutation of HIV. But we cannot predict the future when historians cannot even agree on the past, let alone the present.

We may enter a world of autocratic rule and tyranny, or one of democratic utopia. Our civil liberties may be endangered by one person developing a biological strain so horrible it would require placeless intrusion on each of us to protect all of us. Yet we may, as a people, develop an early allergy to concentrated power and not allow it to take root.

While the forces blowing a leaf are easy enough to measure, the path and destination of the leaf are far from certain. All of us must be vigilant about where we are headed. Although we cannot stop progress, we can all lean together to steer its course.

As society changes, it is comforting that much of what happens will be determined by us all. Placelessness favors democracy in that each person has access to information. The means exist to have one's opinion registered, thus, we hope, preempting tyranny. The collapse of organizational hierarchy empowers the individual, and distributes decision-making power to the people at large.

Yet the decisions we face just ahead are numerous, and perhaps we should be a little afraid. It was fear, after all, that kept our ancestors alive in the Zero Dimension; those who were not afraid tended to die. Fear is a healthy reaction to the unknown, and we need it now more than ever. It is fear that causes us to lose sleep, to think, to plan, to prepare.

Yes, we have come a long way. . . . Or have we?

Looking back over our shoulders, our new world—with near equals far the defining paradigm—seems completely different from much of human history. Yet on closer inspection, it is much the same. In some cosmic paradox, the Fourth Dimension has transported us back to where we started: a single dot in space.

A Bold New World.

NOTES AND
AUTHORITIES

IN THE COURSE of researching *Bold New World*, we began with a blank sheet of paper and a blind eye to ideology. We combed through approximately 8,000 bibliographic references, and present here the most salient 1,036, spread out over 119 journals and scores of reference books.

With no initial thesis, but only raw data and an appetite to sort out the puzzle of the twenty-first century, we found that the universe is complex and our minds are simple. Each effect has multiple causes; each cause has multiple effects. How can the data be translated into *our* terms? Can we simply distill the knowledge?

Seeking order in the data to extract its essence, we endeavored to understand the future, not merely trace its trends. We compared diverse logical arguments from various sources and found the common denominator to the knowledge in the sources below. Quite simply, "near equals far" is the defining paradigm of the twenty-first century, the common thread that weaves through the bibliographic authorities listed below, the spine to which all pages connect.

Key:
[AA] *Advertising Age* • [AAE] *The Academic American Encyclopedia,* online edition (Danbury, Conn.: Grolier Electronic Publishing,

1995) • [AB] *Across the Board* • [ACC] *American City & Country* • [ACW] *Air Cargo World* • [ALT] *Alternatives* • [AMM] *American Metal Market* • [ATW] *Air Transport World* • [AW] *Aviation Week & Space Technology* • [BAS] *Bulletin of the Atomic Scientists* • [BH] *Business Horizons* • [BIO] *Bioscience* • [BNJ] *Business Journal of New Jersey* • [BR] *Barron's* • [BW] *Business Week* • [BY] *Byte* • [BZ] *BUZZWORM* • [CC] *Common Cause Magazine* • [CD] *Chilton's Distribution* • [CH] *Challenge* • [CHT] *Chatelaine* • [CM] *Commentary* • [CMW] *Commonwealth* • [CR] *Current* • [CSM] *Christian Science Monitor* • [CT] *Christianity Today* • [CTD] *Children Today* • [CW] *Computerworld* • [DD] *Daedalus* • [DM] *Datamation* • [DS] *Discover* • [DSD] *US Department of State Dispatch* • [EB] *Encyclopedia Britannica* (15th ed.) • [EF] *Executive Female* • [EL] *Electronics* • [ENV] *Environment* • [FA] *Foreign Affairs* • [FB] *Forbes* • [FC] *Family Circle* • [FR] *Fortune* • [FRB] *Federal Reserve Bulletin* • [FW] *Financial World* • [GH] *Good Housekeeping* • [HBR] *Harvard Business Review* • [HDF] *HDF: The Weekly Home Furnishings Newspaper* • [HIT] *Health Industry Today* • [HM] *Humanist* • [HOC] *Home Office Computing* • [HSUS] *Historical Statistics of the United States: Colonial Times to 1970,* 2 vol. (US Department of Commerce) • [IC] *Inc.* • [ISN] *Insight on the News* • [IW] *Industry Week* • [LAT] *Los Angeles Times* • [LATM] *Los Angeles Times Magazine* • [LF] *Life* • [LHJ] *Ladies' Home Journal* • [LJ] *Library Journal* • [MC] *Maclean's* • [MGT] *Management Today* • [MLR] *Monthly Labor Review* • [MN] *Money* • [MR] *Monthly Review* • [NB] *Nation's Business* • [NCR] *National Catholic Reporter* • [NPQ] *New Perspectives Quarterly* • [NR] *National Review* • [NS] *New Scientist* • [NSS] *New Statesman & Society* • [NW] *Newsweek* • [NYT] *New York Times* • [OM] *Omni* • [OOQ] *Occupational Outlook Quarterly* • [PB] *Playboy* • [PM] *Popular Mechanics* • [PRM] *Parents' Magazine* • [PS] *Popular Science* • [PSY] *Psychology* • [PT] *Psychology Today* • [PW] *People Weekly* • [RA] *Railway Age* • [RB] *Redbook* • [RD] *R&D* • [RL] *Release 1.0* • [RS] *Rolling Stone* • [SA] *Scientific*

American • [SAUS] *Statistical Abstract of the United States* (1992), US Department of Commerce • [SC] *Science* • [SF] *Sea Frontiers* • [SI] *Sports Illustrated* • [SK] *Skiing* • [SL] *Soviet Life* • [SMM] *Sales & Marketing Management* • [SMS] *Smithsonian* • [SN] *Science News* • [SPH] *Sulphur* • [SR] *Sierra* • [SU] *Scholastic Update* • [SY] *Society* • [TA] *The Atlantic* • [TCC] *The Christian Century* • [TCM] *Town & Country Monthly* • [TE] *The Economist* • [TEU] *The European* • [TF] *The Futurist* • [TH] *The Humanist* • [TLS] *Times Literary Supplement* • [TM] *Time* • [TN] *The Nation* • [TNR] *The New Republic* • [TNY] *The New Yorker* • [TP] *The Progressive* • [TR] *Technology Review* • [UN] *UNESCO Courier* • [USA] *USA Today* (Magazine) • [USN] *US News & World Report* • [VS] *Vital Speeches* • [WA] *The World Almanac and Book of Facts, 1992* (New York: Pharos Books) • [WER] *Whole Earth Review* • [WH] *World Health* • [WPR] *World Press Review* • [WSJ] *Wall Street Journal* • [WW] *Working Woman* • [WWD] *WWD*

CHAPTER 1: FROM WHERE WE CAME

First Dimension: *"From India, the Arabs . . . "*: Will Durant, *Our Oriental Heritage* (New York: Simon and Schuster, 1935), pp. 934–37.

Second Dimension: *"Within a span of only . . . "*: James Dale Davidson and Lord William Rees-Mogg, *The Great Reckoning* (New York: Summit Books, 1991), pp. 60–61, 141.

Third Dimension: *"By 1950 about 20 . . . "*: [SAUS], p. 622.

CHAPTER 2: THE GATEWAY TO PLACELESSNESS

Introduction: *"When we finally take . . . "*: Michael Antonoff, "Real Estate is Cheap Here . . . ," [PS], June 1993, p. 124; and Shawn Carlson, "Virtual Mars?" [HM], March–April 1991, pp. 43–45. • *"Medical researchers, too . . . "*: Sharyn Rosenbaum, "Robotics, Virtual Worlds Need Medicine," [HIT], November 1992, pp. 1ff; and "Invisible Mending," [TE], 10 April 1993, p. 93.

The New Phones: *"To solve this, over . . . "*: Joan M. Feldman, "Bane of Business Travel?" [ATW], September 1993, pp. 44ff; and Susan Antilla, "What's on TV? Our 10 AM Meeting," [WW], February 1992, pp. 42ff.

Free Connections: *"It is said that . . . "*: "The Fruitful, Tangled Trees of Knowledge," [TE], 20 June 1992, p. 87. • *"In the one second . . . "*: Scott Cunningham and Alan L. Porter, "Communication Networks: A Dozen Ways They'll Change Our Lives," [TF], January–February 1992, p. 19; and Robert Wrubel, "Data Highways," [FW], 19 January 1993, p. 43. • "*While the cost of . . .*": Peter Fuhrman, "An Unlikely Trustbuster," [FB], 18 February 1991, pp. 100–101. • "*In 1993 alone . . .*": Gary Stix, "Domesticating Cyberspace," [SA], August 1993, p. 102.

Electronic Neighborhoods: "*The Effectiveness of electronic . . .*": "The Fruitful, Tangled Trees of Knowledge," [TE], 20 June 1992, p. 87. • "*By mid-1995 . . .*": David Kirkpatrick, "Hot New PC Services," [FR], 2 November 1992, pp. 108–109; and "Action on the Boards," [USN], 18 November 1991, p. 96.

Where Scientists Chat: "*But unexpectedly, this . . .*": Daniel P. Dern, "Under Construction: Information Superhighway," [HOC], August 1993, p. 36; John Teresko and William H. Miller, "Tripping Down the Information Highway," [IW], 2 August 1993, pp. 32ff; and "News from Cyberspace," [RS], 15 April 1993, p. 36.

Knowledge Amplifiers: "*Ubiquitous communication acts . . .*": Linda Marsa, "Interview: Robert E. Kahn," [OM], December 1992, p. 84.

The Nation Race: "*The island-nation . . .*": Reese Erlich, "Singapore's Computer-Connected Future Worries Government Critics," [CSM], 13 August 1993, p. 9; "Pacific Watch: Singapore," [LAT], 6 April 1992, p. D-3; and Robert Wrubel, "Data Highways," [FW], 19 January 1993, pp. 43, 101ff. • "*The Japanese plan . . .*": "Knit Your Own Superhighway," [TE], 16 October 1993, pp. 101ff; and John Teresko and William H. Miller, "Tripping Down the Information Highway," [IW], 2 August 1993, pp. 32ff. • "*Not to be outdone . . .*": Robert Wrubel, "Data Highways," [FW], 19 January 1993, p. 43; and "The Fruitful, Tangled Trees of Knowledge," [TE], 20 June 1992, p. 87. • "*In France the ground . . .*": Michel Feneyrol, "Telecommunications—A Sector of Excellence in French Technology," [SA], March 1993, p. FR-24. Minitel examples paraphrased from Mimi Tompkins, "A Second French Revolution," [USN], 7 May 1990, p. 56. • "*Although American leadership . . .*": Alan Joch, "Is America Losing Its Edge?" [BY], September 1991, p. 234; and Gary Stix, "Domesticating Cyberspace," [SA], August 1993, p. 102. • "*As the networks . . .*": "The Fruitful, Tangled Trees of Knowledge," [TE], 20 June 1992, p. 87; and "Knit Your Own Superhighway," [TE], 16 October 1993, pp. 101ff.

Crystals and Pebbles: "*Until now, processing . . .*": Raymond Kurzweil, "The Paradigms and Paradoxes of Intelligence: Building a Brain," [LJ], 15 November 1992, pp. 53–54. • "*The first large-scale . . .*": Rory Donaldson, "An Incomplete History of Microcomputing," [WER], Spring 1987, pp. 116ff. • "*The same power . . .*": Samuel E. Bleecker, "The Information Age Office," [TF], January–February 1991, p. 19. • "*Computers will be further . . .*": Will Hively, "Incredible Shrinking Optical Act," [DS], February 1993, pp. 22–23. • "*Their prices are plummeting . . .*": Malcolm Brown, "The March of the Mighty Chip," [MGT], 9 October 1991, pp. 26ff; and Bob Ryan, "Downsizing: Bane or Boon?" [BY], September 1991, p. 228.

Alice in Wonderland: *"But that is largely . . . ":* "Minds With Mobility," [DS], November 1992, p. 104. • *"We can fly airplanes . . . ":* Frank Lidz, "It's the Real Thing, Virtually," [SI], 7 October 1991, pp. 8–9; Bob Berger, "Fairway to Heaven," [OM], November 1991, p. 33; Josh Lerman, "Virtue Not to Ski?" [SK], February 1993, p. 20; and Michael Antonoff, "Living in a Virtual World," [PS], June 1993, pp. 85–86. • *"Those who crack sophomoric . . . ":* Walter Lowe, Jr., "Virtual Sex," [PB], April 1992, p. 164. • *"One system providing . . . ":* Joan O'C. Hamilton et al., "Virtual Reality," [BW], 5 October 1992, p. 99; and Michael Antonoff, "Living in a Virtual World," [PS], June 1993, p. 86. • *"Within a decade . . . ":* Doug Stewart, "Interview: Jaron Lanier," [OM], January 1991, pp. 46, 113–14; Michael Antonoff, "Living in a Virtual World," [PS], June 1993, pp. 86, 124; and David Gale, "Meeting in a Virtual World," [NS], 13 March 1993, p. 24.

Silicon Brains: *"Benchmarks have been . . . ":* Ivars Peterson, "Voices in Command," [SN], 3 April 1993, p. 93; and Gene Bylinsky, "At Last! Computers You Can Talk To," [FR], 3 May 1993, p. 89. • *"Computers are even piercing . . . ":* "Computer Translators," [PS], January 1992, p. 50. • *"Besides speech, computers . . . ":* "Talking About Thinking," [DS], November 1992, p. 100. • *"Such a computer . . . ":* Paul Wallich, "Silicon Babies," [SA], December 1991, pp. 132, 134; "The Burden of Knowledge," [TE], 14 March 1992, p. s-13; and Lloyd Chrein, "Where's Hal?" [OM], September 1991, p. 16; "Cyc-ed Up," [CW], 10 May 1993, pp. 104–105; and Esther Dyson, "Cyc: A Context for Newton," [RL], 15 June 1992, pp. 4ff. • *"Cyc and his brothers . . . ":* Linda Marsa, "Interview: Robert E. Kahn," [OM], December 1992, p. 84. • *"Roger Traub . . . ":* "Model of the Origin of Rhythmic Population Oscillations in the Hippocampal Slice," [SC], 10 March 1989, pp. 1319ff. • *"Wall Street gurus . . . ":* Evan I. Schwartz, "Where Neural Networks Are Already at Work," [BW], 2 November 1992, pp. 136–37.

Air, Land, and Water: *"One major change . . . ":* Richard Monastersky, "The Supersonic Question," [SN], 26 October 1991, pp. 270–71.; Edwin M. Reingold, "Supersonic Boom," [TM], 30 September 1991, p. 48; and "The Next SST," [PS], February 1991, p. 58. • *"Japan's powerful MITI . . . ":* Michael A. Dornheim, "Japan Leads Team Effort to Test Mach 5 Powerplant," [AW], 17 August 1992, pp. 48, 51, and 55; and Michael A. Dornheim, "JAL Business Routes Require Longer Range than Offered by Current SST Plans," [AW], 17 August 1992, p. 57. • *"Germany's Deutsche . . . ":* Edwin M. Reingold, "Supersonic Boom," [TM], 30 September 1991, pp. 48–49. • *"Already, from 1970 . . . ":* [SAUS], p. 625 and [WA], p. 670. • *"We already see . . . ":* Pierre Sparaco, "TGV Rail Link Key to De Gaulle Growth," [AW], 29 March 1993, p. 39; Tom Peterson and Stan Kaderbeck, "High-Speed Rail," [ACC], October 1992, pp. 56ff; and "Faster than a Speeding Bullet," [TE], 4 March 1992, pp. 87–88. • *"The reason for . . . ":* "Learning to Fly All Over Again," [TE], 12 June 1993, p. s-8; and "Planes, Trains and Automobiles," [TE], 12 September 1992, pp. 73–74; Tom Peterson and Stan Kaderbeck, "High-Speed Rail," [ACC], October 1992, pp. 56ff. • *"Though their countries . . . ":* [WA], pp. 734–821. • *"But American transportation . . . ":* Christopher O'Maaley, "Rapid Rails," [PS], June 1992, pp. 74ff; Tom Peterson and Stan Kaderbeck, "High-Speed Rail," [ACC], October 1992, pp. 56ff. • *"Pennsylvania . . . ":* "Supertrains for Us," [TF], July–August 1992, p. 54; and William D. Middleton, "High Speed Rail and the Freight Railroads," [RA], August 1993, pp. 113ff.

The Sum of the Parts: *"Tacoma, Washington . . . ":* Joseph Asher, "Dockside Yards Spur Tacoma Growth," [RA], April 1993, pp. 47ff. • *"Authorities at Charles . . . ":* Pierre Sparaco, "TGV Rail Link Key to De Gaulle Growth," [AW], 29 March 1993, pp. 39–40; and Christopher O'Maaley, "Rapid Rails," [PS], June 1992, pp. 74ff. • *"Perhaps among the best . . . ":* "All Strung Up: Federal Express," [TE], 17 April 1993, p. 70.

Investor Beware: *"The fervor for cabling . . . ":* John Teresko and William H. Miller, "Tripping Down the Information Highway," [IW], 2 August 1993, p. 32.

Using Robots and Jets: *"The intimate linkage . . . ":* Julie Candler, "Just-in-Time Deliveries," [NB], April 1993, pp. 64ff. • *"Motorola's pager . . . ":* John H. Sheridan, "America's Best Plants: IW Salutes 12 Facilities that Have Achieved True Manufacturing Excellence," [IW], 15 October 1990, pp. 27ff. • *"The interconnectedness of . . . ":* Dawn Barreto, "Getting Auto Parts Shipping into High Gear . . . ," [ACW], January 1993, pp. 9ff; and Deborah Catalano Ruriani, "In the Outsourcing Driver's Seat," [CD], May 1990, pp. 110ff.

The Effective Employee: *"In one company . . . ":* John R. Wilke, "Computer Links Erode Hierarchical Nature of Workplace Culture," [WSJ], 9 December 1993, p. 1.

CHAPTER 3: FOOTLOOSE HUMANITY

Introduction: *"For the 70,000 . . . ":* David Holley, "The Maids of Hong Kong: A Journey of Loneliness, Humiliation," [LAT], 1 October 1991, p. H-2. • *"He looked up . . . ":* inspired by Nancy Wride, "Season of Hope: A Look at the Future through La Quinta's Students," [LAT], 20 June 1994, p. E-1.

A Xenophobic Siege: *"With its massive . . . ":* John Dillin, "Migration to US Expected to Break Record in '90s," [CSM], 21 November 1991, p. 8; and Katie Monagle, "America's Changing Population," [SU], 11 January 1991, p. 4. • *"With 2,000 mosques . . . ":* Rone Tempest, "A Place for Islam in Europe," [LAT], 8 February 1992, p. A-1; William D. Montalbano, "A Global Pursuit of Happiness," [LAT], 1 October 1991, p. H-1; and Alan Riding, "France Sees Integration as Answer to View of Immigrants as 'Taking Over,' " [NYT], 24 March 1991, p. 3. • *"Asia's England . . . ":* Bob Drogin, "For Australia, Migrants Mostly a Gain, Not a Drain," [LAT], 1 October 1991, p. H-3. • *"National lines are . . . ":* William Montalbano, "A Global Pursuit of Happiness," [LAT], 1 October 1991, p. H-7; and "Africa," [LAT], 1 October 1991, p. H-5.

Push and Pull: *"The mounting population . . . ":* Warren Zimmermann, "Addressing the Needs of Refugees: A High Priority in the Post–Cold War Era," [DSD], 12 July 1993, pp. 502ff; "Voting with their Feet, Their Trabants and Their Oars," [TE], 23 December 1989, pp. 17–19; Douglas Waller, "A World Awash in Refugees," [NW],

9 October 1989, p. 44; and [WA], p. 824. • *"In most warring . . . "*: [WA], pp. 734–821. • *"Moreover, the erosion . . . "*: "Environmental Refugees," [TF], May–June 1989, p. 54. • *"As population growth . . . "*: James Dale Davidson and Lord William Rees-Mogg, *The Great Reckoning* (New York: Summit, 1991), p. 207; and Crissy Gonzalez, "Cheese? Swiss Make Good Bread Too," [LAT], 11 February 1992, p. D-1.

Porous Borders and Travel Agents: *"Thousands of Albanians . . . "*: Simon Freeman, Carol Reed, and Dalbert Hallenstein, "Open Sesame," [TEU], 16 August 1991, p. 9; and Naomi Marks and Carol Reed, "Albania Opens Refugee Floodgates," [TEU], 16 August 1991, p. 1. • *"The United States's 2,000 . . . "*: Scott Armstrong, "Growth in Illegal Immigration Causes Stir over Sanctions," [CSM], 23 April 1991, p. 1; and Lindsey Grant, "Facing the Consequences of Illegal Immigration," [USA], January 1991, p. 10. • *"The idea of fining . . . "*: Josh Meyer, "Fake Green Card Ring Was Largest in US," [LAT], 28 September 1991, p. B-1; Scott Armstrong, "Growth in Illegal Immigration . . . ," [CSM], 23 April 1991, p. 1; and "Justice Plans to Beef Up Border Security," [CSM], 11 February 1992, p. 6. • *"Chinese crime . . . "*: Ann Scott Tyson, "US Senate Delegation Takes Aim at Chinese Crime Syndicates," [CSM], 24 December 1991, p. 4. • *"The yakuza . . . "*: Abby Tan, "The Labor Brokers: For a Price, There's a Job Abroad—Maybe," [LAT], 1 October 1991, p. H-5. • *"In Poland the . . . "*: Paraphrased from Bruce W. Nelan, "Europe Slams the Door," [TM], 19 July 1993, pp. 38ff.

Street Sweepers and Valedictorians: *"As a result, our . . . "*: Louis S. Richman, "The Coming World Labor Shortage," [FR], 9 April 1990, pp. 70ff; David Kilburn, "The Sun Sets on Japan's Lifers," [MGT], September 1993, pp. 44ff; John Teresko, "Hello, Dollies!" [IW], 7 September 1992, pp. 39ff; "The Missing Children," [TE], 3 August 1991, pp. 43ff; Hana Hermanova, "The Clock Can't Be Stopped," [WH], November–December 1991, pp. 12ff; and S. Jay Olshansky et al., "The Aging of the Human Species," [SA], April 1993, p. 46. • *"With so many economically . . . "*: Jean-Claude Chasteland, "The Greying of the Planet," [UN], January 1992, pp. 40ff. • *"Many economic studies . . . "*: Ben J. Wattenberg and Karl Zinsmeister, "The Case for More Immigration," [CM], April 1990, p. 20; L. Gordon Crovitz, "Come One, Come All," [BR], 26 February 1990, p. 9; Stephen Moore, "Who Should America Welcome?" [SY], July–August 1990, p. 58; Mortimer B. Zuckerman, "Give Us Your Brainpower," [USN], 29 October 1990, p. 108; Stephen Moore, "Mixed Blessings," [AB], March 1991, p. 46; Julian Simon, "Lots More Immigration Would Be a Windfall," [FR], 26 March 1990, p. 154; and "Brooklyn-on-Volga," [TE], 9 June 1990, p. 25. • *"Their countries of birth . . . "*: "Waiting for the Next Wave," [TE], 16 March 1991, p. 42. • *"Nearly half the Soviet . . . "*: Jon D. Hull, "A Tide of Hope," [TM], 14 January 1991, p. 23. • *"American science . . . "*: Jonathan Weber, "Around the World and Back at the Speed of Light," [LAT], 1 October 1991, p. H-6; and Stephen Moore, "Mixed Blessings," [AB], March 1991, pp. 46, 49.

The New Detached Labor: *"When US customers . . . "*: Jonathan Weber, "Around the World . . . ," [LAT], 1 October 1991, p. H-6. • *"Cartons of data . . . "*: James

Fallows, "Entangling Alliances: How the Third World Shapes Our Lives," review of *How the Third World Shapes Our Lives,* by John Maxwell Hamilton, [TA], July 1990, pp. 97ff; Richard J. Barnet et al., "Creating a Level Playing Field," [TR], May–June 1994, pp. 46ff; and George White, "Cheap—and Smart—Labor," [LAT], 3 June 1991, p. D-1. • *"California-based Sun . . . ":* Jonathan Weber, "Around the World . . . ," [LAT], 1 October 1991, p. H-6; Susan Moffat, "Sun Microsystems Taps Russians for Computing Talent," [LAT], 4 March 1992, p. D-1; "Child of Nippon: Malaysia's Proton Car," [TE], 11 May 1991, pp. 68ff.

Where Are the Workers?: *"A gigantic, self . . . ":* Donald Woutat, "The Carrot Kings: Bakersfield Triumvirate Is Tops in the Field," [LAT], 15 August 1993, pp. D-1ff; and [SAUS], p. 664. • *"Today fewer than . . . ":* Richard Crawford, *In the Era of Human Capital* (New York: Harper Business, 1991), p. 47; [SAUS], p. 396; and Todd M. Godbout, "Employment Change and Sectorial Distribution in 10 Countries, 1970–1990," [MLR], October 1993, pp. 3ff. • *"By 2025 . . . ":* Projections based in part on [SAUS], pp. 8, 396. • *"At GM's Pontiac . . . ":* Neal E. Boudette, "GM: Computers in Symphony," [IW], 18 June 1990, pp. 59ff. • *"Each truck is . . . ":* "Back to the Future," [TE], 17 October 1992, pp. S-7ff.

Information Workers at Risk: *"For instance, sophisticated . . . ":* John H. Sheridan, "Toward the CIM Solution," [IW], 16 October 1989, pp. 35ff; and "IBAS Explained," [IW], 7 September 1992, pp. 42ff. • *"A customer will . . . ":* "Back to the Future," [TE], 17 October 1992, pp. S-7ff. • *"Information workers such . . . ":* Howard Goldner, "Pharmaceutical Labs Benefit from a Healthy Dose of Robotics," [RD], May 1994, pp. 21ff. • *"New ideas spread . . . ":* "Bodybuilding without Tears," [TE], 21 April 1990, pp. 94ff.

The Coming Disunion: *"Yet, since World . . . ":* Steve Hulett, "Don't Blame Unions for Industry's Demise," 3 November 1991, p. D-3; [WA], p. 180; and Donald Thompson, "New Role for Labor Unions," [IW], 9 February 1987, pp. 30ff. • *"The unions have simply . . . ":* Michael A. Verespej, "No One's a Winner at Caterpillar," [IW], 5 April 1993, pp. 20ff; and Robert S. Eckley, "Caterpillar's Ordeal," [BH], March–April 1989, pp. 80ff. • *"Unions will thrive . . . ":* Tamara Jones, "German Strikes Threaten to Paralyze Air, Freight Traffic," [LAT], 4 May 1992, p. A-29.

And My Career?: *"Since the end of World . . . ":* Arthur B. Shostak, "The Nature of Work in the Twenty-First Century," [BH], November–December 1993, pp. 30ff. • *"In many industries . . . ":* Bruce Wallace, "Reward or Sacrifice: Europeans Clash Over Proposals to Introduce a Four-Day Week," [MC], 14 March 1994, pp. 38ff; John Daly, "The Four-Day Week," [MC], 14 March 1994, pp. 36ff; and Charles A. Cerami, "No Help Wanted," [PB], May 1994, pp. 78ff. • *"In twenty years . . . ":* Arthur B. Shostak, "The Nature of Work . . . ," [BH], November–December 1993, pp. 30ff. • *"The trick will . . . ":* Paraphrased from Michele Morris, "15 Fast-Track Careers," [MN], June 1990, pp. 108ff. • *"The third growth . . . ":* Liesel Brand, "Occupational Staffing Patterns within Industries through the Year 2000," [OOQ], Summer 1990, pp. 40ff; and "Jobs for the Year 2000," [USN], 20 January 1990, p. 62.

CHAPTER 4: SYMBOLIC CAPITAL

Introduction: *"Welcome to the . . . ":* Robert Lenzner et al., "The Age of Digital Capitalism," [FB], 29 March 1993, pp. 62ff. • *"Capital is what . . . ":* Paraphrased from investment banker Felix Rohatyn as reported in Ed Magnuson, "The Crash," [TM], 2 November 1987, p. 36.

Capital, Capital Everywhere: *"More currency moves . . . ":* Austin H. Kiplinger and Knight A. Kiplinger, *America in the Global '90s,* (Washington, DC: Kiplinger Books, 1989), p. 52; and "Trading Posts," [TE], 21 July 1990, p. S-7; and Jeremy Main, "How to Go Global—and Why," [FR], 28 August 1989, p. 76. • *"Cross-border stock . . . ":* "The Surprising Emergence of Distant Shares," [TE], 16 November 1991, p. 93; Robert F. Black et al., "Danger and the Dollar," [USN], 28 September 1992, pp. 60ff; and William Tucker, "Investing Overseas: A Passport to Riches?" [ISN], 11 April 1994, pp. 16ff. • *"The shift to international . . . ":* "The Lure and the Let-Down of Other People's Markets," [TE], 14 September 1991, p. 91; and Shirley Skeel, "City Under Siege," [MGT], March 1991, pp. 62ff. • *"And investment opportunities . . . ":* Lawrence Malkin, "Fishing in Foreign Waters," [TCM], December 1993, pp. 52ff; and James Flanigan, "New Trends in Global Investment Pose Challenge for US," [LAT], 10 June 1992, p. D-1. • *"As their economies . . . ":* Cecily Patterson, "Going Global: The Investment Strategy for the 1990s," [FB], 19 October 1992, pp. S-1ff.

Frictionless Pipelines: *"Each of the top five . . . ":* [WA], pp. 734–821; and "The World's 100 Biggest Commercial Banks," [FR], 30 July 1990, pp. 269–278, 325–26. • *"With 2,200 . . . ":* Thomas McCarroll, "Citicorp Fights to Rise Again," [TM], 30 July 1990, p. 50. • *"Today any terminal . . . ":* Steven Golob, "Sell Abroad; You Can Collect," [NB], November 1987, pp. 44ff; "Rushing Your Cash Back Home," [IC], November 1993, p. 137; Jeremy Main, "How to Go Global—and Why," [FR], 28 August 1989, p. 76; and Rahul Jacob, "Capturing the Global Consumer," [FR], 13 December 1993, pp. 166ff. • *"Citi's 2,000 . . . ":* Thomas McCarroll, "Citicorp Fights to Rise Again," [TM], 30 July 1990, p. 50; Judith Graham, "Cirrus, Plus ATM Net Launch Overseas Battle," [AA], 11 September 1989, p. 100. • *"They will soon share . . . ":* Gary Hector et al., "Why US Banks Are in Retreat," [FR], 7 May 1990, pp. 95ff; and "How It Happened," [TE], 19 September 1992, pp. S-9ff.

Redefining Wall Street: *"The future belongs . . . ":* Victor F. Zonana, "NASDAQ Inaugurates Early Trading Session," [LAT], 21 January 1992, pp. D-1ff. • *"Yet other avenues . . . ":* Paraphrased from "The Next Hundred Years," [TE], 9 May 1992, pp. 97ff. Also Guy Halverson, "Global Shops on Wall Street," [CSM], 1 April 1991, p. 7; Victor F. Zonana, "Big Board Blues," [LAT], 9 February 1992, p. D-1; and Shirley Skeel, "City Under Siege," [MGT], March 1991, pp. 62ff. • *"The automation of global . . . ":* "Why London?" [TE], 4 May 1991, p. 15. • *"Eager to keep . . . ":* "Screen Wars," [TE], 21 July 1990, p. S-12. • *"Using computers . . . ":* Steve H. Hanke et al., "Easy Money," [FB], 31 January 1994, p. 141; Robert Lenzner et al., "The Age of Digital Capitalism," [FB], 29 March 1993, pp. 62ff; "Tips from the Master," [TM], 9 November 1992, pp. 23ff; and Stephen Taub et al.,

"The $650 Million Man," [FW], 6 July 1993, pp. 38ff. • *"The computer revolution has utterly . . . "*: Robert Lenzner et al., "The Age of Digital Capitalism," [FB], 29 March 1993, pp. 62ff; paraphrased from [TE] as quoted in "Screen Wars," [TE], 21 July 1990, p. s-12.

Nations out of Control: *"Today when the American . . . "*: Horst Brand, "The End of Keynesianism," [MLR], December 1992, pp. 42ff; "The Diminished Fed," [TE], 4 May 1991, pp. 17ff; "Talking about the Dollar, Worrying about the Economy," [TE], 27 April 1991, pp. 79ff; and Peter F. Drucker, *Post-Capitalist Society* (New York: Harper Business, 1993), p. 143. • *"The fluidity of digital . . . "*: "Brady's Fading Plan," [TE], 12 August 1989, p. 16; Robert B. Reich, "Who Is Them?" [HBR], March–April 1991, p. 85; "Stability Concerns Spark China Capital Flight," [LAT], 16 December 1991, p. D-7; and Thomas Sowell, "What Capital Shortage?" [FB], 19 August 1991, p. 79.

Business with No Money Down: *"Entrepreneurs without capital . . . "*: Kenneth R. Sheets, "Firms Now Lease Everything But Time," [USN], 14 August 1989, pp. 45ff; David S. Glick, "The Leasing Generation," [FB], 19 February 1990, pp. A-1ff; and Harvey Shapiro, "Equipment Leasing: Stronger Than Ever," [FB], 3 October 1988, pp. A-1ff.

Where Do I Invest?: *"Today, however, the smart . . . "*: Cecily Patterson, "Going Global," [FB], 19 October 1992, pp. s-1ff. • *"Transfers through the physical . . . "*: William Tucker, "Investing Overseas," [ISN], 11 April 1994, pp. 16ff. • *"Many investors in the . . . "*: Kerry Hannon, "Live Here, Invest Abroad," [USN], 4 April 1994, p. 65; and Robert H. Stovall, "The What, How and Why of ADRs," [FW], 7 December 1993, p. 102. • *"International mutual funds . . . "*: Cecily Patterson, "Going Global," [FB], 19 October 1992, pp. s-1ff; and Guy Halverson, "Foreign Stocks Attract US Buyers," [CSM], 11 February 1992, p. 8.

CHAPTER 5: UBIQUITOUS RESOURCES

Introduction: *"Todd's car had . . . "*: Inspired by Karen Wright et al., "The Shape of Things to Go," [SA], May 1990, pp. 92ff; Thomas McCarroll, "Solid as Steel, Light as a Cushion," [TM], 26 November 1990, pp. 94ff; Thomas M. Rohan, "Materials Battle Heats Up," [IW], 2 October 1989, pp. 70ff; and Jason Zweig, "Déjà Vu—Yet Again," [FB], 16 November 1987, pp. 282ff.

Kansas Crude and Maine Cane: *"GM's Saturn plant . . . "*: John Teresko, "Project Saturn," [IW], 19 November 1990, pp. 32ff; and Robert R. Rehder, "Japanese Transplants," [BH], January–February 1990, pp. 87ff. • *"A mere dollar . . . "*: "On Course for Firmer Rates?" [SPH], November–December 1991, p. 18; and "War Risk Pushes Freight Rates Up," [SPH], March–April 1991, p. 17.

Golden Dirt: *"On the exhaustion . . . "*: Sheldon Richman, "Forget the Myth of Overpopulation," [ISN], 20 December 1993, pp. 20ff; Ronald Bailey, "Captain Planet for Veep," [NR], 14 September 1992, pp. 40ff; and Ray Percival, "Malthus and His Ghost," [NR], 18 August 1989, pp. 30ff. See also Julian L. Simon, *The Ulti-*

mate Resource (Princeton: Princeton University Press, 1981). • *"In 1800, for example . . . ":* Sheldon Richman, "Forget the Myth of Overpopulation," [ISN], 20 December 1993, pp. 20ff; Tsukasa Furukawa, "Remote Sensing Flies Down Under," [AMM], 20 July 1992, p. 7; and David Bjerklie, "The Electronic Transformation of Maps," [TR] April 1989, pp. 54ff. • *"Another excellent example . . . ":* Author interviews: Lanny R. Ream, 21 September 1994; and Frank L. Ludeman, 1 October 1994. • *"Sulfur-eating bacteria . . . ":* William J. Cook, "The Little Bugs that Dig for Gold," [USN], 17 April 1989, p. 62; "Some Like It Hot," [TE], 25 June 1988, p. 88; and Al Senia, "Gold Rush!" [FB], 14 July 1986, pp. 60ff; and Elizabeth Dougherty, "Bio-Derived Materials," [RD], June 1990, pp. 58ff.

Diamonds from Peanut Butter: *"Our most useful . . . ":* Eric D. Larson, "Beyond the Era of Materials," [SA], June 1986, pp. 34ff. • *"In 1950 an average . . . ":* Ian Steele, "Materials Technology and the Third World," [TR], January 1988, pp. 8ff. • *"We are leaving . . . ":* Alexander Kouznetsov of the UN, per Ian Steele, "Materials Technology and the Third World," [TR], January 1988, pp. 8ff. • *"Scientists have even . . . ":* William T. Allman, "The Stuff of Dreams," [USN], 26 November 1990, pp. 60ff. • *"Yet others are . . . ":* Elizabeth Dougherty, "Bio-Derived Materials," [RD], June 1990, pp. 58ff.

Hot Jets and Floating Trains: *"For example, a California . . . ":* "First All-Composite Auto Bridge Planned," [SN], 15 May 1993, p. 319; and "The Right Stuff," [TE], 24 November 1990, pp. 95ff. • *"Researchers in Texas . . . ":* William T. Allman, "The Stuff of Dreams," [USN], 26 November 1990, pp. 60ff. • *"Aircraft manufacturers may . . . ":* "The Right Stuff," [TE], 24 November 1990, pp. 95ff; and Gary Stix, "Running Hot," [SA], December 1992, pp. 46ff. • *"Even more revolutionary . . . ":* Ivan Amato, "New Superconductors," [SC], 15 January 1993, pp. 306ff; and Tim Studt, "Materials," [RD], 28 September 1992, pp. 90ff.

CHAPTER 6: THE POLLUTION ROADBLOCK

A Car in Every Garage: *"A thousand years ago . . . ":* Nafis Sakik, "World Population Continues to Rise," [TF], March–April 1991, pp. 9ff; [WA], p. 822; and "Population," [EB], vol. 14, p. 816. • *"During most of history . . . ":* Sheldon Richman, "Forget the Myth of Overpopulation," [ISN], 20 December 1993, pp. 20ff; S. Jay Olshansky, "The Aging of the Human Species," [SA], April 1993, pp. 46ff; Nancy Wells, "Killer Illnesses of History," [USN], 12 January 1987, p. 69. • *"A critical factor . . . ":* Denis-Clair Lambert, "Does Wealth Equal Health?" [UN], August 1987, pp. 9ff; Stephen Budiansky, "10 Billion for Dinner, Please," [USN], 12 September 1994, pp. 57–62; and Sheldon Richman, "Forget the Myth of Overpopulation," [ISN], 20 December 1993, pp. 20ff. • *"Most demographers believe . . . ":* Charles C. Mann, "How Many Is Too Many?" [TA], February 1993, pp. 47ff. • *"In the last fifty . . . ":* Paraphrased from Alan Durning, "How Much Is Enough?" [TR], May–June 1991, pp. 56ff.

Swimming in Sewage: *"Today's refuse sites . . . ":* William Rathje et al., "Five Major Myths about Garbage," [SMS], July 1992, pp. 113ff; and George J. Church, "Garbage, Garbage, Everywhere," [TM], 5 September 1988, pp. 81ff. • *"While the quantity . . . ":* John Langone, "Waste: A Stinking Mess," [TM], 2 January 1989, pp. 44ff. • *"The soil under our feet . . . ":* "Nuclear Grunge," [TE], 21 August 1993, p. A-23; Helen Ingram et al., "Managing Transboundary Resources," [ENV], May 1994, pp. 6ff; and Janusz Kindler, "An Action Plan to Clean up the Baltic," [ENV], October 1993, pp. 6ff. • *"The deleterious effects . . . ":* Paraphrased from "Air Pollution in the World's Megacities," [ENV], March 1994, pp. 4ff. • *"In Mexico City . . . ":* Lester Brown, "A Planet in Jeopardy," [TF], May–June 1992, pp. 10ff; "Private Cars Banned from Athens to Fight Pollution," Reuters America, Inc., 28 September 1994.

Radioactive Milk: *"Just look at Chernobyl . . . ":* Grigori Medvedev, *The Truth about Chernobyl* (New York: Basic Books, 1989), pp. 66–98, 264; and Natalya Buldyk, "Children of Chernobyl," [SL], April 1991, pp. 51–57. • *"Thousands of tons . . . ":* Daniel Egger, "West Germany Pours Hot Milk," [TN], 28 March 1987, pp. 392ff; Eliot Marshall, "Recalculating the Cost of Chernobyl," [SC], 8 May 1987, pp. 658ff; Charles Knox, "Chernobyl Health Effects May Never Be Seen," [SN], 17 December 1988, p. 391; and John Greenwald, "Deadly Meltdown," [TM], 12 May 1986, pp. 38ff. • *"Pesticides—a byproduct . . . ":* David Pimentel et al., "Environmental and Economic Costs of Pesticide Use," [BIO], November 1992, pp. 750ff. • *"Where do all . . . ":* Al Meyerhoff, "We Must Get Rid of Pesticides in the Food Supply," [USA], November 1993, pp. 51ff. • *"The most toxic ones . . . ":* Paraphrased from Michael Satchell, "A Vicious 'Circle of Poison,'" [USN], 10 June 1991, pp. 31ff; David Pimentel et al., "Environmental and Economic Costs of Pesticide Use," [BIO], November 1992, pp. 750ff.

The New Air: *"In Australia, the . . . ":* Tasha Diamant, "Sexy in Bronze?" [MC], 25 May 1992, p. 41; and Leon Jaroff, "The Dark Side of Worshiping the Sun," [TM], 23 July 1990, pp. 68ff. • *"So global temperature . . . ":* Larry B. Stammer, "Geopolitical Effects of Global Heating Gauged," [LAT], 10 February 1992, pp. A-1ff; Robert M. White, "The Great Climate Debate," [SA], July 1990, pp. 36ff.

Limits to Power: *"The quantity of . . . ":* Philip C. Cruver, "Lighting the 21st Century," [TF], January–February 1989, pp. 29ff; and Dan Charles, "New Ideas about an Old Fuel," [WPR], May 1993, pp. 22ff. • *"We also create . . . ":* Phillip Bayne, "Now, More than Ever, America Needs Nuclear Energy," [USA], November 1993, pp. 48ff; Wolf Hafele, "Energy from Nuclear Power," [SA], September 1990, pp. 136ff; and "The Fusion Thing," [TE], 8 February 1992, pp. 85ff.

Rising Eco-Limits: *"With environmental laws . . . ":* Laura M. Litvan, "The Growing Ranks of Enviro-Cops," [NB], June 1994, pp. 39ff; and Patricia A. Parker, "Crime and Punishment," [BZ], March–April 1992, pp. 34ff. • *"The reach of pollution . . . ":* Tim Beardsley, "Waste Not," [SA], April 1992, pp. 143ff; "Where Bankers Fear to Tread," [TE], 21 May 1994, pp. 85ff; Daniel Sitomer et al., "The Catch in the Zipper," [ACC], November 1993, pp. 54ff; and Leslie Fuller Secrest, "Seep No Evil," [ACC], May 1993, pp. 34ff. • *"A new class . . . ":* Jeffrey Salmon, "Greenhouse Anxiety," [CM], July 1993, pp. 25ff; Rudy Abramson, "Greenhouse Gas Curbs Costly, US Study Finds," [LAT], 6 December 1991, p. A-30; and Joel

Havemann, "EC Plans Energy Tax to Curb Emissions," [LAT], 14 December 1991, p. A-16. • *"Sweden already . . . "*: Paraphrased from "Making Polluters Pay," [TE], 2 September 1989, pp. S-6ff; and [SAUS], p. 845, table no. 1398. • *"A long list . . . "*: The World Almanac and Book of Facts, 1995 (Mahwah, N.J.: Funk and Wagnalls, 1994), p. 188. • *"In already impoverished . . . "*: "All That Gas," [TE], 18 June 1994, pp. E-14ff.

Life Without Pollution?: *"Germany, which has . . . "*: Daniel Sitomer et al., "The Catch in the Zipper," [ACC], November 1993, pp. 54ff; Christopher Boerner et al., "Making Recycling More Cost-Effective," [USA], May 1994, pp. 78ff; and "Virgin No More," [FW], 1 March 1994, pp. 34ff. • *"The results already . . . "*: Paraphrased from "Making Polluters Pay," [TE], 2 September 1989, pp. S-6ff.

CHAPTER 7: SERVICE, PLEASE

Vacuumed and Ready to Go: *"We are now learning . . . "*: Many of the examples in this chapter are from Ronald Henkoff, "Service Is Everybody's Business," [FR], 27 June 1994, pp. 48ff; and Patricia Sellers, "Companies that Serve You Best," [FR], 31 May 1993, pp. 74ff.

Death to the Checkout Line: *"With revenues fast . . . "*: Examples in this section are paraphrased from Gretchen Morgenson, "The Fall of the Mall," [FB], 24 May 1993, pp. 106ff; Amy Feldman, "That's Show Biz," [FB], 6 July 1992, p. 44; and M. Daniel Rosen, "Expanding Your Sales Operation?" [SMM], July 1990, pp. 82ff.

The New Intimacy: *"The A. C. Nielsen . . . "*: Pamela Young, "The Numbers Game; A New Technology Shakes up the TV Ratings," [MC], 29 January 1990, pp. 64ff; and William J. Hawkins, "TV Views Viewers," [PS], February 1990, pp. 74ff. • *"Citicorp even . . . "*: Martin Mayer, "Scanning the Future," [FB], 15 October 1990, pp. 114ff. • *"The salesman will . . . "*: Gary Stix, "Call and Tell," [SA], April 1991, pp. 152ff. • *"Perhaps the quintessential . . . "*: Jagannath Dubashi, "Customer Service," [FW], 29 September 1992, p. 58; and M. Daniel Rosen, "Expanding Your Sales Operation?" [SMM], July 1990, pp. 82ff.

Tort Attorneys and Movie Stars: *"Over the past century . . . "*: [HSUS], Series A-7, D-127, and K-174; [SAUS], no. 2 and no. 632; Ronald Henkoff, "Service Is Everybody's Business," [FR], 27 June 1994, pp. 48ff; and Todd M. Godbout, "Employment Change and Sectorial Distribution in 10 Countries, 1970–1990," [MLR], October 1993, pp. 3ff.

Bond . . . James Bond: *"While over two-thirds . . . "*: Marc Tanzer, "The Spying Game," [SMM], June 1993, pp. 60ff; Shari Caudron, "I Spy, You Spy," [IW], 3 October 1994, pp. 35ff. • *"The undetectable . . . "*: Timothy Middleton, "Spies Among Us," [BNJ], June 1993, pp. 36ff. • US department stores: Ingrid Eisenstadter, "The James Bond School of Business," [EF], March–April 1991, pp. 20ff. • *" 'Info-brokers' will . . . "*: Timothy Middleton, "Spies Among Us," [BNJ], June 1993, pp. 36ff; and Christopher Palmieri, "Dumpster Diving," [FB], 26 September 1994, pp. 94ff; Shari Caudron, "I Spy, You Spy," [IW], 3 October 1994, pp. 35ff;

and Thomas McCarroll, "Next for the CIA: Business Spying?" [TM], 22 February 1993, pp. 60ff. • *"National spy apparatuses . . . ":* Thomas McCarroll, "Next for the CIA: Business Spying?" [TM], 22 February 1993, pp. 60ff; and James Fox, "Security," [FB], 9 May 1994, pp. s-12ff. • *"But most companies . . . ":* Shari Caudron, "I Spy, You Spy," [IW], 3 October 1994, pp. 35ff.

"Info-Censors": *"Corporations will monitor . . . ":* Marc Tanzer, "The Spying Game," [SMM], June 1993, pp. 60ff; Shari Caudron, "I Spy, You Spy," [IW], 3 October 1994, pp. 35ff; Patrice Duggan et al., "The New Face of Japanese Espionage," [FB], 12 November 1990, p. 96.

Counting Beans: *"Today's bean-counter . . . ":* Ronald Henkoff, "Service Is Everybody's Business," [FR], 27 June 1994, pp. 48ff.

CHAPTER 8: THE CORPORATE TENTACLES

Economic Promiscuity: *"World trade accounts . . . ":* Jay Branegan, "Put Up or Shut Up," [TM], 20 December 1993, p. 46; [SAUS] (1994), table 1323; [HSUS], Series U-201 and U-202; and "To Protect or Not to Protect," [FW], 23 June 1992, pp. 50ff. • *"The average country . . . ":* [WA], pp. 734–821. • *"The average worldwide . . . ":* "Fact Sheet," [DSD], 9 August 1993, pp. s-17ff.

Globocorps: *"They cross national . . . ":* *The International Corporate 1000* (New York: Monitor Publishing Company, 1990); and [WA], p. 147. • *"These and 37,000 . . . ":* "The Discreet Charm of the Multicultural Multinational," [TE], 30 July 1994, pp. 57ff; Diane Francis, "The New Love Affair with Transnationals," [MC], 20 December 1993, p. 9; "The World's Biggest Industrial Corporations," [FR], 30 July 1990, pp. 269–292; and a statistical analysis of [WA], pp. 734–821; Herman Kahn, *The Future of the Corporation* (New York: Mason & Lipscomb, 1974), p. 37; *Ward's Business Directory,* vol. 1 (Belmont, Calif.: Information Access Company, 1988), p. 5; "The Forbes Foreign Rankings," [FB], 20 July 1992, pp. 241–282; and Gerard Piel, "Globalopolies," [TN], 18 May 1992, pp. 652ff. • *"Rather than be intimidated . . . ":* Diane Francis, "The New Love Affair with Transnationals," [MC], 20 December 1993, p. 9. • *"They take the best . . . ":* Jeremy Main, "How to Go Global—and Why," [FR], 28 August 1989, p. 70.

The New Quest: *"These patterns largely continued . . . ":* Constantinos C. Markides and Norman Berg, "Manufacturing Offshore Is Bad Business, [HBR], September–October 1988, p. 115; and "Asian Promise," [TE], 12 June 1993, pp. 74ff. • *"The results are open . . . ":* Joseph LaDou, "Deadly Migration," [TR], July 1991, pp. 46ff; Bruce Selcraig, "Border Patrol," [SR], May–June 1994, pp. 58ff; and Linda Robinson, "A Tale of Two Troubled Cities," [USN], 1 March 1993, p. 46. • *"This practice is demonstrated . . . ":* Maria Shao, "For Levi's, a Flattering Fit Overseas," [BW], 5 November 1990, p. 76. • *"Sometimes the geographical . . . ":* Murray Weidenbaum, "Success Isn't Guaranteed in the Global Marketplace," [LAT], 5 May 1991, p. D-2. • *"Take the pharmaceutical . . . ":* Jeremy Main, "How to Go Global—and Why," [FR], 28 August 1989, p. 70; and Robert Heller, "Global Embrace," [MGT], March 1994, p. 81.

Coca-Colonization: *"Thanks to their dispersed . . . ":* Constantinos C. Markides and Norman Berg, "Manufacturing Offshore Is Bad Business," [HBR], September–October 1988, pp. 114, 117. • *"Every three years . . . ":* [WA], pp. 734–822. • *"We in the First . . . ":* Paraphrased from Herman Kahn, *The Future of the Corporation* (New York: Mason & Lipscomb, 1974), p. 198. • *"As the poorer two-thirds . . . ":* "Pamper Them," [TE], 16 February 1991, pp. 56–57; Jerry Flint, "Will the Maginot Line Hold?" [FB], 8 July 1991, p. 58; Jack Egan, "Business without Borders," [USN], 16 July 1990, p. 29; and Gerard Piel, "Globalopolies," [TN], 18 May 1992, pp. 652ff. • *"It is no accident . . . ":* Chi-Fai Chan et al., "Whose Empire Is This, Anyway?" [BH], July–August 1994, pp. 51ff; and "The Discreet Charm of the Multicultural Multinational," [TE], 30 July 1994, pp. 57ff.

Tickets to Globalness: *"Ogilvy & Mather's . . . ":* Interview with Cynthia Wohler, 21 October 1992. • *"The very company that . . . ":* Robert W. Stewart, "NASA's New Endeavor Faces Challenging, Potentially Dangerous Flight," [LAT], 6 May 1992, p. A-27. • *"One Silicon Valley . . . ":* Emile Geisenheimer and Peter Imperiale, "After the Fall: The New Venture Capitalist," [EL], August 1990, p. 120. Subsequently, Momenta proved not to have been successful, but it still serves as a powerful symbol of things to come. • *"In hundreds of industries . . . ":* Jeremy Main, "How to Go Global—and Why," [FR], 28 August 1989, pp. 71, 76. • *"In preparing for these . . . ":* Ibid., p. 71; Jack Egan, "Business without Borders," [USN], 16 July 1990, p. 30; *Philip Morris . . . ":* Eric S. Hardy, "Overseas Opportunities," [FB], 10 October 1994, p. 97; and "Not So Fast," [TE], 25 July 1992, p. 64.

Señor Mitsubishi, S'il Vous Plait: *"The recent head of General . . . ":* Refers to Claude Benchimol as described in Jeremy Main, "How to Go Global—and Why," [FR], 28 August 1989, pp. 71–72. • *"Britain's Imperial Chemical . . . ":* Ibid., p. 72; "The Discreet Charm of the Multicultural Multinational," [TE], 30 July 1994, pp. 57ff; and Robert B. Reich, "Who Is Them?" [HBR], March–April 1991, p. 81. • *"With competition like this . . . ":* Paraphrased from Robert Reich per David R. Francis, "Advice to Execs: 'Think Globally,'" [CSM], 11 Apr 1991, p. 9. • *"Globocorps are so supranational . . . ":* Robert B. Reich, "Who Is Them?" [HBR], March–April 1991, pp. 78–79. • *"Needless to say . . . ":* Mary Munter, "Cross-Cultural Communication for Managers," [BH], May–June 1993, pp. 69ff.

The Foreign Domestics: *"Consider IBM, the . . . ":* IBM's *1991 Annual Report*, p. 25 and back flap; and "(SEC) Form 10-K" (public disclosures), 31 Dec 1991, Exhibit II. • *"Even the national companies . . . ":* Paraphrased from Robert B. Reich, "Who Is Them?" [HBR], March–April 1991, p. 81. • *"Xerox is thought . . . ":* Paraphrased from Murray Weidenbaum, "Success Isn't Guaranteed in the Global Marketplace," [LAT], 5 May 1991, p. D-2. • *"When Sony bought . . . ":* "Hooked by Hollywood," [TE], 21 September 1991, p. 79. • *"Most Americans regard . . . ":* Daniel F. Burton et al., "Multinationals," [CH], September–October 1994, pp. 33ff. • Martha Groves, "The Workers' View," [LAT], 25 January 1992, p. D-1; and Charles R. Morris, "The Coming Global Boom," [TA], October 1989, p. 55 • *"The nationality of . . . ":* David R. Francis, "Advice to Execs," [CSM], 11 April

1991, p. 9; and paraphrased from Louis Sahagun, " 'Buy American' Plan May Face Practical Problems," [LAT], 25 February 1992, p. A-1. • *"When Japan's prime . . . ":* Ohmae's *The Borderless World,* per Robert Dore, "How Business Goes Global, [TLS], 26 July 1991, p. 9; and Jack Egan, "Business without Borders," [USN], 16 July 1990, p. 30.

Imperialism Comes Home: *"While international business . . . ":* Karlheinz Kaske, the Chief Executive of Siemens, as quoted in Jack Egan, "Business without Borders," [USN], 16 July 1990, p. 29. • *"Corporations can play off . . . ":* Paraphrased from Robert B. Reich, "Who Is Them?" [HBR], March–April 1991, p. 83. • *"Finland, Costa Rica . . . ":* Sven-Eric Nilsson, per Herman Kahn, *The Future of the Corporation* (New York: Mason & Lipscomb, 1974), p. 6.

The Mindanao Syndrome: *"The government of the Philippines . . . ":* Brad Miller, "Land-Grab in the Philippines," [TP], November 1989, pp. 30–32. • *"This 'Mindanao Syndrome' . . . ":* "Corporation—Multinational Corporations," [AAE]. • *"Globocorps routinely hire . . . ":* Jean Cobb, "Political Currency," [CC], January–February 1990, pp. 28–30.

What's the Score?: *"President Bush's . . . ":* Robert B. Reich, "Who Is Them?" [HBR], March–April 1991, p. 84. • *"Politicians and economists . . . ":* Paraphrased from Austin H. Kiplinger and Knight A. Kiplinger, *America in the Global '90s* (Washington, DC: Kiplinger Books, 1989) p. 51. • *"Governments should look . . . ":* Susan Dentzer, "Meet the New Economic Bogeymen," [USN], 18 October 1993, p. 67.

CHAPTER 9: THE COMING AMOEBAS

Collapsing Goliaths: *"When the war ended . . . ":* Thomas A. Stewart, "The Whiz Kids," [FR], 18 October 1993, p. 127. • *"They are too inbred . . . ":* John S. McClenahen, "Can You Manage in the New Economy?" [IW], 5 April 1993, pp. 24ff. • *"In 1977, when . . . ":* Robert A. Mamis et al., "The Apple tree," [IC], August 1993, pp. 72ff. • *"IBM realized that . . . ":* William E. Halal, "Let's Turn Organizations into Markets!" [TF], May–June 1994, pp. 8ff. • *"Well-run companies . . . ":* Robert Heller et al., "The Manager's Dilemma," [MGT], January 1994, pp. 42ff.

The Rise of McSpaghetti: *"When RJR Nabisco . . . ":* Robert B. Reich, "Who Is Them?" [HBR], March–April 1991, p. 80. • *"Switzerland's Asea . . . ":* William Taylor, "The Logic of Global Business: An Interview with ABB's Percy Barnevik," [HBR], March–April 1991, pp. 92, 105. • *"Companies in the . . . ":* Robert B. Reich, "Who Is Them?" [HBR], March–April 1991, p. 80. • *"In the 1980s, the world . . . ":* Robert Howard, "The Designer Organization: Italy's GFT Goes Global," [HBR], September–October 1991, p. 28; Jeremy Main, "How to Go Global—and Why," [FR], 28 August 1989, p. 76; Scott Pendleton, "Giving Golden Arches Global Span," [CSM], 21 May 1991, p. 8; "Like Japan, but Different," [TE], 3 November 1990, p. 76. • *"The Japanese refer . . . ":* Maria Shao, "For Levi's, a Flattering Fit Overseas," [BW], 5 November 1990, p. 76. • *"In most Japa-*

nese . . . ": Jeremy Main, "How to Go Global—and Why," [FR], 28 August 1989, p. 76; and Peter F. Drucker in Herman Kahn, *The Future of the Corporation* (New York: Mason & Lipscomb, 1974), p. 61.   •   *"Levi Strauss, the most . . . ":* Robert Howard, "The Designer Organization," [HBR], September–October 1991, p. 34; and Maria Shao, "For Levi's, a Flattering Fit Overseas," [BW], 5 November 1990, pp. 76–77.   •   *"United Technologies . . . ":* "Like Japan, but Different," [TE], 3 November 1990, pp. 76–77.   •   *"McDonald's, with 1994 . . . ":* Alvin Toffler, *Powershift* (New York: Bantam, 1990), p. 340; Scott Pendleton, "Giving Golden Arches Global Span," [CSM], 21 May 1991, p. 8; McDonald's Corporation, *Annual Report,* December 31, 1994; and "Big McMuttons," [FB], 17 July 1995, p. 18.

Golden Marriages: *"For instance, Ford . . . ":* Paraphrased from Jeremy Main, "How to Go Global—and Why," [FR], 28 August 1989, p. 73; and Charles R. Morris, "The Coming Global Boom," [TA], October 1989, p. 51, 53.   •   *"When Motorola . . . ":* Linda Grant, "Partners in Profit," [USN], 20 September 1993, pp. 65ff.

Corporate Découpage: *"Somewhere deep . . . ":* "Farming out the Farm," [TE], 5 March 1994, p. 79.   •   *"In contrast, Chrysler . . . ":* Shawn Tully, "You'll Never Guess Who Really Makes . . . " [FR], 3 October 1994, pp. 124ff.   •   *"Lewis Galoob Toys. . . ":* Joe Neubauer, "Sticking to Your Knitting," [VS], 1 September 1993, pp. 695ff.   •   *"Riding ahead of . . . ":* John Teresko, "Leave the Designing to Them," [IW], 15 August 1994, pp. 66ff; and "Farming out the Farm," [TE], 5 March 1994, p. 79.   •   *"Seattle-based Stratos . . . ":* John Teresko, "Leave the Designing to Them," [IW], 15 August 1994, pp. 66ff.   •   *"A typical corporation . . . ":* Joe Neubauer, "Sticking to Your Knitting," [VS], 1 September 1993, pp. 695ff.   •   *"In this system . . . ":* Paraphrased from Walter Kiechel, III, "How We Will Work in the Year 2000," [FR], 17 May 1993, pp. 38ff.

The Borderless Company: *"The next decade will . . . ":* Nick Sullivan, "Yesterday, Today, Tomorrow . . . the Evolution of the Home Office," [HOC], September 1993, pp. 45ff.   •   *"Innovative companies like Levi . . . ":* Michael Malone, "Virtual Corporation," [FB], 7 December 1992, pp. s-102ff.   •   *"The British supermarket . . . ":* "Tying the Knot," [TE], 14 May 1994, p. 73.   •   *"Placeless technologies, by . . . ":* Walter Kiechel, III, "How We Will Work in the Year 2000," [FR], 17 May 1993, pp. 38ff.   •   *"Stanley Baldwin . . . ":* Paraphrased from "Tying the Knot," [TE], 14 May 1994, p. 73.   •   *"For this reason . . . ":* William E. Halal, "Let's Turn Organizations into Markets!" [TF], May–June 1994, pp. 8ff.

The First to Everywhere: *"Shifting toward the Amoeba . . . ":* Paraphrased from David Davidow as quoted in John Huey, "Waking up to the New Economy," [FR], 27 June 1994, pp. 36ff.   •   *"In contrast, European . . . ":* Robert Heller et al., "The Manager's Dilemma," [MGT], January 1994, pp. 42ff; and Michael Malone, "Virtual Corporation," [FB], 7 December 1992, pp. s-102ff.

A Thousand Thousand Companies: *"Unquestionably the most . . . ":* "It Doesn't Have to Be Like This," [TE], 2 September 1989, p. 21; and Louis Kraar, "The Drug Trade," [FR], 20 June 1988, pp. 26ff; Gustavo A. Goriti, "How to Fight the Drug

War," [TA], July 1989, pp. 70ff. • *"So tightly choreographed . . . "*: Stan Yarbro, "Colombian Antidrug Effort Is Challenged by Political Resistance, Cartel Shift to Heroin," [CSM], 31 January 1992, p. 1; and Stan Yarbro, "Cocaine Traffickers Diversify with Heroin," [LAT], 3 November 1991, p. A-10.

Amoeba Management: *"The new leaders . . . "*: Paraphrased from John Huey, "The New Post-Heroic Leadership," [FR], 21 February 1994, pp. 42ff.

CHAPTER 10: THE GLOBAL TRIBES

National Identity: *"An early turning point . . . "*: Liah Greenfeld, "Transcending the Nation's Worth," [DD], Summer 1993, pp. 47ff. • *"With the American . . . "*: Hans Kohn, "Nationalism," [EB], vol. 12, pp. 851–53.

The Flame of Allah: *"When Salman Rushdie's . . . "*: Lance Morrow et al., "The Faces of Islam," [LF], March 1993, pp. 58ff. • *"Cassette tapes . . . "*: Henrik Bering-Jensen, "Islam," [ISN]," 6 September 1993, pp. 6ff; Janice Castro, "Tapes of Wrath," [TM], 15 June 1992, p. 15; Amos Perlmutter, "Islamic Threat is Clear and Present," [ISN], 15 February 1993, pp. 22ff. • *"Laced across this . . . "*: Bradford R. McGuinn, "Should We Fear Islamic Fundamentalists?" [USA], November 1993, pp. 34ff; Henrik Bering-Jensen, "Islam," [ISN], 6 September 1993, pp. 6ff. • *"The fuel that is . . . "*: Martin Kramer, "Arab Nationalism," [DD], Summer 1993, pp. 171ff; Henrik Bering-Jensen, "Islam," [ISN], 6 September 1993, pp. 6ff; Bradford R. McGuinn, "Should We Fear Islamic Fundamentalists?" [USA], November 1993, pp. 34ff. • *"At some point, we need to ask . . . "*: Nathan Gardels, "The Post-Atlantic Capitalist Order," [NPQ], Spring 1993, pp. 2ff. • *"What of the thousands . . . "*: Henrik Bering-Jensen, "Islam," [ISN], 6 September 1993, pp. 6ff. • *"The green banner . . . "*: Lance Morrow et al., "The Faces of Islam," [LF], March 1993, pp. 58ff; and Hassan al-Turabi, "The Islamic Awakening's New Wave," [NPQ], Summer 1993, pp. 42ff.

The Built-In Collapse: *"Islamic fundamentalism, in contrast . . . "*: Daniel Pipes, "Same Difference," [NR], 7 November 1994, pp. 61ff. • *"Part of the problem . . . "*: Tom Bethell, "The Mother of All Rights," *Reason*, April 1994, pp. 41ff.

The Children of Abraham: *"While Hebrew has . . . "*: Robert S. Wistrich, "Do the Jews Have a Future?" [CM], July 1994, pp. 23ff. • *"So it is not . . . "*: Seth Kulick, "The Evolution of Secular Judaism," [TH], March–April 1993, pp. 32ff. • *"If there is a common . . . "*: Robert S. Wistrich, "Do the Jews Have a Future?" [CM], July 1994, pp. 23ff; "Poor Relation," [TE], 29 January 1994, p. 44; and Martin Kramer, "The Jihad against the Jews," [CM], October 1994, pp. 38ff; and Jay P. Lefkowitz, "Jewish Voters and the Democrats," [CM], April 1993, pp. 38ff.

Countryless Countries: *"The idea of a . . . "*: Brian Duffy, "Who Pays Arafat?" [USN], 26 April 1993, pp. 46ff; and "Palestine Liberation Organization," [AAE]. • *"When Kuwait was . . . "*: Alexander Cockburn, "Beat the Devil," [TN], 22 October 1990, p. 442; Murray Weidenbaum, "Success Isn't Guaranteed in the Global Marketplace," [LAT], 5 May 1991, p. D-2.

The Ubiquitous Dragon: *"The effects of . . . ":* "The Overseas Chinese," [TE], 18 July 1992, pp. 21ff. • *"Ethnic Chinese now . . . ":* Paraphrased from Louis Kraar, "The Overseas Chinese," [FR], 31 October 1994, pp. 91ff; "China's Diaspora Turns Homeward," [TE], 27 November 1993, pp. 33ff; and "The Overseas Chinese," [TE], 18 July 1992, pp. 21ff. • *"For example, when Taiwan . . . ":* Paraphrased from ibid.; and Louis Kraar, "The Overseas Chinese," [FR], 31 October 1994, pp. 91ff.

Eco-Tribes: *"The current wave of . . . ":* Based on Priscilla Painton, "Greening from the Roots Up," [TM], 23 April 1990, pp. 76ff; Michael D. Lemonick, "The Rivers Ran Black," [TM], 7 November 1994, p. 68; Victoria Pope, "Poisoning of Russia's River of Plenty," [USN], 13 April 1992, pp. 39ff; and Steve Huntley et al., "Disaster Strikes Europe's Most Storied Stream," [USN], 24 November 1986, pp. 8ff. • *"Starting out small . . . ":* Priscilla Painton, "Greening from the Roots Up," [TM], 23 April 1990, pp. 76ff. • *"The National Wildlife . . . ":* Dean Kuipers, "Eco Warriors," [PB], April 1993, pp. 74ff. • *"Some of these organizations . . . ":* Ibid.; and Susan Reed, "Eco-Warrior Dave Foreman Will Do Whatever It Takes in His Fight to Save Mother Earth," [PW], 16 April 1990, pp. 113ff. • *"The Sea Shepherds . . . ":* Paraphrased from Dean Kuipers, "Eco Warriors," [PB], April 1993, pp. 74ff. • *"Greenpeace, the world's . . . ":* John DeMont, "Frontline Fighters," [MC], 16 December 1991, pp. 46ff; and Leslie Spencer, "The Not So Peaceful World of Greenpeace," [FB], 11 November 1991, pp. 174ff. • *"Greenpeace targeted . . . ":* Ibid.; Dean Kuipers, "Eco Warriors," [PB], April 1993, pp. 74ff. • *"Thanks to the technologies . . . ":* Kevin Ellis, "Canadian Groups Twinned with Ecuador and Eritrea," [ALT], November–December 1993, pp. 14ff; and "Nuclear Nuggets," [TE], 19 January 1991, p. 53. • *"They showed unity . . . ":* Ronnie Wacker, "Earth Summit Wrap-Up," [SF], October 1992, pp. 17ff.

Black, Gay, and Feminine: *"If 2,000 women . . . ":* "Feminism Arrives," [NR], 3 July 1987, p. 31.

CHAPTER 11: THE NEW WARFARE

Introduction: *"His colleague in Panama . . . ":* Details based on Dean Kuipers, "Eco Warriors," [PB], April 1993, pp. 74ff; and Steven Manning, "Life in the Balance," [SU], 16 April 1993, pp. 2ff. • *"Each water bottle contained . . . ":* Marvin J. Cetron, "The Future Face of Terrorism," [TF], November–December 1994, pp. 10ff.

Less Is More: *"This is what military . . . ":* Joseph S. Nye, Jr., "Against 'Declinism,' " [TNR], 15 October 1990, p. 12; James Flanigan, "War May Strengthen US Resolve on Economic Front," [LAT], 3 March 1991, p. D-1; and John Naisbitt et al., *Megatrends 2000* (New York: William Morrow, 1990), pp. 31–32. • *"In the new economic order . . . ":* Patrick Glynn, "Is Nationalism the Wave of the Future?" [CM], August 1994, pp. 42ff; and Henry Gurnwald, "The Year 2000," [TM], 30 March 1992, pp. 73ff.

Topsoil and Dead Rats: *"A drive down . . . ":* Robert D. Kaplan, "The Coming Anarchy," [TA], February 1994, pp. 44ff; and [WA], p. 764.   •   *"Within hours, television . . . ":* Paraphrased from Robin Wright, "LA Riots Called Symptom of Worldwide Urban Trend," [LAT], 25 May 1992, p. A-1.

War without Rules: *"The power of terrorism . . . ":* Andrew Phillips et al., "India's Danger," [MC], 3 June 1991, pp. 26ff.   •   *"Three thousand miles . . . ":* Wayne Biddle, "It Must be Simple and Reliable," [DS], June 1986, pp. 22ff.   •   *"The new reality is that . . . ":* Morris Greenspan, "War, Laws of," [EB], vol. 19, pp. 538–42.

Tools of Terror: *"The design of the atomic . . . ":* David Albright, "A Proliferation Primer, [BAS], June 1993, pp. 14ff; and Stephen Budiansky, "The Nuclear Epidemic," [USN], 16 March 1992, pp. 40ff; Wayne Biddle, "It Must Be Simple and Reliable," [DS], June 1986, pp. 22ff; Marvin J. Cetron, "The Growing Threat of Terrorism," [TF], July–August 1989, pp. 20ff; and "To Ban the Bomb," [TE], 27 August 1994, pp. 10ff;   •   *"If just a few grams . . . ":* Marvin J. Cetron, "The Future Face of Terrorism," [TF], November–December 1994, pp. 10ff.   •   *"The advent of genetic . . . ":* Wayne Biddle, "It Must Be Simple and Reliable," [DS], June 1986, pp. 22ff; and Marvin J. Cetron, "The Future Face of Terrorism," [TF], November–December 1994, pp. 10ff.   •   *"Bio-terrorism need . . . ":* Paraphrased from Robert S. Root-Bernstein, "Infectious Terrorism," [TA], May 1991, pp. 44ff.   •   *"Terrorists worldwide . . . ":* Marvin J. Cetron, "The Growing Threat of Terrorism," [TF], July–August 1989, pp. 20ff; Marvin J. Cetron, "The Future Face of Terrorism," [TF], November–December 1994, pp. 10ff; and Wayne Biddle, "It Must Be Simple and Reliable," [DS], June 1986, pp. 22ff.

Madison Avenue: *"The bombing of Pan . . . ":* George D. Moffett, III, "US Seeks Means to Justice in Bombing of Flight 103," [CSM], 18 November 1991, p. 4.   •   *"More important than . . . ":* Wayne Biddle, "It Must Be Simple and Reliable," [DS], June 1986, pp. 22ff; Marvin J. Cetron, "The Future Face of Terrorism," [TF], November–December 1994, pp. 10ff; and Marvin J. Cetron, "The Growing Threat of Terrorism," [TF], July–August 1989, pp. 20ff.

Kevlar Cars: *"Then what is to . . . ":* Marvin J. Cetron, "The Growing Threat of Terrorism," [TF], July–August 1989, pp. 20ff.   •   *"Researchers are already . . . ":* Wayne Biddle, "It Must Be Simple and Reliable," [DS], June 1986, pp. 22ff.

CHAPTER 12: THE END OF THE NATION-STATE

From Castles to Countries: *"Before the advent . . . ":* Paraphrased from Richard Bean as quoted in Nathan Rosenberg et al., *How the West Grew Rich* (New York: Basic Books, 1986), pp. 60–61, 64–65; Michael Lind, "In Defense of Liberal Nationalism," [FA], May–June 1994, pp. 87ff.   •   *"But in our century . . . ":* Max M. Kampelman, "Secession and Self-Determination," [CR], November 1993, pp. 35ff; and John A. Hall, "Nationalisms," [DD], Summer 1993, pp. 1ff.   •   *"One by one . . . ":* Paraphrased from Maurice Cranston, "Freedom and Nationhood," [MR], 18 January 1993, pp. 44ff.   •   *"The United Nations has expanded . . . ":* Michael Lind, "In Defense of Liberal Nationalism," [FA], May–June 1994, pp. 87ff.

David and Goliath: *"Nor, as we have seen . . . ":* [WA], pp. 734–821.

One World, One Mind: *"Global communications turn . . . ":* Kermit Lansner, "TV: Handle with Care," [FW], 8 February 1991, p. 72.

Imperial Bookkeeping: *"Washington, DC, holds . . . ":* [WA], pp. 651–654, 734–821. • *"As Germany's* Die Zeit *. . . ":* Rudolf Walter Leonhardt, "Regionalism Rising," *Die Zeit,* as republished in [WPR], December 1990, p. 18. • *"For these reasons . . . ":* Ibid.; and James Fergusson, "Armed Struggle Heads Rebel Agenda," [TEU], 16 August 1991, p. 6. • *"Political maps, with . . . ":* Robert D. Kaplan, "The Coming Anarchy," [TA], February 1994, pp. 44ff.

The Bear's Children: *"But, no sooner . . . ":* George J. Church, "Splinter, Splinter Little State," [TM], 6 July 1992, pp. 36ff; "Tomorrow's Empires," [TE], 21 September 1991, p. 15; Anna Husarska, "Crimea Scene," [TNR], 1 August 1994, pp. 12ff; Daniel Sneider, "The World from Moscow," [CSM], 26 November 1991, p. 3; Anna Husarska, "Rebel Mandrills," [TNR], 10 October 1994, pp. 18ff; Steven Manning, "Nationalism Rising," [SU], 20 November 1992, pp. 2ff; and Justin Burke, "Yeltsin Faces Nationalist Protest," [CSM], 23 April 1991, p. 6. • *"If Moscow has . . . ":* Alan Cooperman, "The Wages of War," [USN], 16 January 1995, pp. 41ff. • *"Were Chechnya to . . . ":* "How Many Other Chechnyas?" [TE], 14 January 1995, pp. 43ff. • *"As each day passes . . . ":* George J. Church, "Death Trap," [TM], 16 January 1995, pp. 42ff; Julie Corwin, "Tightening Up the Old Ties that Bind," [TM], 7 February 1994, pp. 42ff. • *"The collapse of . . . ":* "Albania," "Bulgaria," "Czechoslovakia," "Germany," "Hungary," "Poland," "Romania," and "Warsaw Treaty Organization," [AAE].

Euro-Fission: *"Ironically, the country . . . ":* "Belgium Fights the Demon," [TE], 17 April 1993, p. 51. • *"The situation in Scotland . . . ":* "For Auld Lang's Syne," [TE], 6 March 1993, p. 59; and "Scotland's Separatist Aims," [MC], 16 March 1992, pp. 26ff. • *"In Spain and France . . . ":* "Where is the Basque Gerry Adams?" [TE], 29 October 1994, p. 57; David Lawday, "ETA Struggles for a Homeland," [USN], 7 November 1988, pp. 48ff; Gabriel Jackson, "Basque Elections Loom," [TN], 15 November 1986, pp. 518ff; Richard Z. Chesnoff, "Terror in the Pyrenees," [USN], 25 August 1986, p. 28; and "Basques," [AAE]. • *"Spain with its Catalonians . . . ":* Fred Halliday, "Letter from Ajaccio," [NSS], 10 September 1993, p. 11; "Bang Boom," [TE] 22 August 1992, pp. 38ff; and Scott Steele, "The Desire to Go It Alone," [MC], 16 March 1992, p. 28. • *"In Italy, too . . . ":* Paraphrased from Michael Barone, "An Inquiry into the Health of Nations," [USN], 18 June 1990, p. 35; and Scott Steele, "The Desire to Go It Alone," [MC], 16 March 1992, p. 28.

The Population Time Bombs: *"Present-day India . . . ":* James Dale Davidson and Lord William Rees-Mogg, *The Great Reckoning* (New York: Summit, 1991), p. 209; and [WA], pp. 739, 767–768, 790–91. • *"Free-market policies . . . ":* Ross H. Munro and Joydeep Bhattacharya, "India's Dissolving Glue," [CSM], 4 June 1991, p. 18. • *"India displays the signs . . . ":* Mark Fineman, "Few Defy Sikhs to Vote in Punjab," [LAT], 20 February 1992, p. A-4; and "Baltics South," [TE], 9

February 1991, pp. 41–42. • *"As population pressures . . . ":* Robert D. Kaplan, "The Coming Anarchy," [TA], February 1994, pp. 44ff. • *"Africa is in the same . . . ":* John Prendergast, "Breakups Likely in Africa's Horn," [CSM], 19 June 1991, p. 19; "Falling Apart," [TE], 8 June 1991, p. 44; and Ali A. Mazrui, "The Bondage of Boundaries," [TE], 11 September 1993, pp. F-28ff.

The Middle Kingdom: *"The reformed southern . . . ":* James L. Tyson, "Deng Tour Sends Mixed Signals on Reform," [CSM], 3 February 1992, p. 6; and "A Great Leap Forward," [TE], 5 October 1991, p. 19. • *"The Chinese social . . . ":* Lincoln Kaye, "Who Will Follow Deng?" [WPR], October 1994, pp. 14ff; and Robert D. Kaplan, "The Coming Anarchy," [TA], February 1994, pp. 44ff. • *"As for Taiwan . . . ":* "End of a Fiction," [TE], 27 November 1993, p. 34.

French Bread and Igloos: *"Canada offers little . . . ":* John Cruickshank, "Canada's Search for Identity," [CSM], 26 February 1992, p. 19. • *"While the autonomy . . . ":* "Quebec's Road-Map," [TE], 10 December 1994, pp. 37ff. • *"The Inuit-dominated . . . ":* William Clairborne, "Canada Agrees to Create Huge Region for Eskimos," [LAT], 17 December 1991, p. A-1; and "Something New in Canada's Frozen North," [TE], 4 January 1992, pp. 33–34. • *"Whether Quebec secedes . . . ":* Mary Williams Walsh, "Quebec Liberals Vote to Join Push for Sovereignty," [LAT], 11 March 1991, p. A-1.

The Disunited States of America: *"But now that the Cold War . . . ":* Paraphrased in part from Bruce D. Porter, "Can American Democracy Survive?" [CM], November 1993, pp. 37ff; and Thomas H. Naylor, "Downsizing the United States of America," [CH], November–December 1994, pp. 55ff. • *"Further, the United States incorporated . . . ":* Bruce D. Porter, "Can American Democracy Survive?" [CM], November 1993, pp. 37ff; Robert D. Kaplan, "The Coming Anarchy," [TA], February 1994, pp. 44ff; and "When Countries Splinter," [TE], 13 June 1992, pp. 11ff. • *"Like the rest . . . ":* Gebe Martinez, "El Toro, Laguna Hills to Vote on Cityhood as Trend Grows Statewide," [LAT], 4 March 1991, p. A-3; and Alvin Toffler, *Powershift* (New York: Bantam, 1990), p. 247.

Devolution Has Begun: *"In Snohomish County . . . ":* "Vermont Libre," [TE] 28 April 1990, p. 27; and "Love It or Leave It," [TM], 19 March 1990, p. 25. • *"In California, proponents . . . ":* Paul Roberts, "The Goodbye Whirl," [TNR], 21 November 1994, pp. 11ff; Suneel Ratan, "Secession Fever," [FR], 24 August 1992, p. 14; and "A Fault-Line Shivers," [TE], 13 June 1992, pp. A-28ff. • *"If California breaks . . . ":* Thomas H. Naylor, "Downsizing the United States of America," [CH], November–December 1994, pp. 55ff. • *"Every year, Oregon . . . ":* Bradley Inman, "Why the State's Efforts at Marketing Itself Have Ground Down to a Halt," [LAT], 19 April 1992, p. D-2. • *"Virginia, like many . . . ":* Takashi Oka, "Virginia Lures Japanese Business," [CSM], 22 May 1991, p. 7. • *"States are also . . . ":* Brad Knickerbocker, "States, Business Build New Alliances," [CSM], 20 May 1991, p. 8; and Scott Pendleton, "Illinois County Is Model for Success," [CSM], 15 May 1991, p. 8.

Medieval City-States: *"Even cities must . . . ":* Daniel B. Wood, "Silt Is Obstructing Oakland Shipping Traffic," [CSM], 11 December 1991, p. 9. • *"Los Angeles*

is . . . ": Rich Connell, "Port Officials' Travel Costs Nearly Double in 6 Years,"
[LAT], 29 October 1991, p. A-1; and Rich Connell, "Port Agent's Spending Questioned by Auditors," [LAT], 29 November 1991, p. A-1. • *"City officials
for . . . "*: Ibid. • *"Sometimes governments are . . . "*: "Hubsidies," [TE], 4 January 1992, p. 27. • *"When McDonnell . . . "*: Ralph Vartabedian, "McDonnell
Pins Project's Hopes on Rich Partner," [LAT], 14 October 1991, p. D-1.

Fresh Starts: *"If the large nation . . . "*: Paraphrased from Bluntschli per Michael
Lind, "In Defense of Liberal Nationalism," [FA], May–June 1994, pp. 87ff. Also
Henry Gurnwald, "The Year 2000," [TM], 30 March 1992, pp. 73ff; and George J.
Church, "Splinter, Splinter Little State," [TM], 6 July 1992, pp. 36ff. • *"Under
autonomous federalism . . . "*: Michael Lind, "In Defense of Liberal Nationalism,"
[FA], May–June 1994, pp. 87ff; and Scott Wallace, "Miskito Coast," [TN], 27 De-
cember 1986, pp. 724ff.

CHAPTER 13: GLOBAL GOVERNMENT

Le Club Européen: *"Even consumer tastes . . . "*: Thomas A. Steward, "A Heartland
Industry Takes on the World," [FR], 12 March 1990, pp. 110ff. • *"Students
from overcrowded . . . "*: Paraphrased from "A Singular Market," [TE], 22 October
1994, pp. S-10ff. • *"Although the road . . . "*: "1996 and All That," [TE], 22 October 1994, pp. S-19–S-21.

The Cowboy Club: *"In a very real . . . "*: [WA], pp. 734–822. • *"Its rules dictate . . . "*: Paraphrased from Jeremy Rabkin, "Trading in Our Sovereignty?" [NR],
13 June 1994, pp. 34ff. • *"In the first year . . . "*: "Northern Rumblings," [TE],
14 January 1995, pp. A-26ff; and Michael J. Boskin, "Pass the GATT Now," [FR], 12
December 1994, pp. 137ff. • *"Free trade blocks . . . "*: Luigi Campiglio,
"Europe on the Mark," [DD], Spring 1994, pp. 107ff.

The Chopstick Club: *"But placelessness is now . . . "*: Yoichi Funabashi, "The Asian-
ization of Asia," [CR], February 1994, pp. 32ff. • *"The dynamic growth . . . "*:
"Saying No," [TE] 19 November 1994, p. 37. • *"Unlike Europe with . . . "*: "Fact
Sheet," [DSD], 22 February 1993, pp. 111ff. • *"But everywhere . . . "*: "The
Opening of Asia," [TE], 12 November 1994, pp. 23ff.

Other Blocks: *"Mercosur has linked . . . "*: [WA], pp. 734–821. • *"Not to be outdone . . . "*: "NAFTA is Not Alone," [TE], 18 June 1994, p. 47. • *"Even Africa . . . "*: "Neighborhood Watch in Southern Africa," [TE], 3 December 1994, pp.
51–52; and Ali A. Mazrui, "The Bondage of Boundaries," [TE], 11 September
1993, pp. F-28ff. • *"Elsewhere, now-independent . . . "*: Robert D. Hormats,
"Making Regionalism Safe," [FA], March–April 1994, pp. 97ff.

Intergalactic Marriages: *"Economic and political . . . "*: Michael Lind, "In Defense
of Liberal Nationalism," [FA], May–June 1994, pp. 87ff. • *"Journalists are
fond . . . "*: Susan Aaronson, "The Policy Battle Over Freer World Trade," [CH],
November–December 1994, pp. 48ff. • *"Many small countries . . . "*: "The
Opening of Asia," [TE], 12 November 1994, pp. 23ff. • *"Mexico, too, is . . . "*:
"NAFTA is Not Alone," [TE], 18 June 1994, p. 47.

The World Club: *"The earlier agreement . . . ":* "Fact Sheet," [DSD], July 1994, pp. 17ff. • *"The WTO changed . . . ":* Jeremy Rabkin, "Trading in Our Sovereignty?" [NR], 13 June 1994, pp. 34ff; William F. Buckley, "WTO Coming Up," [NR], 12 September 1994, p. 94; and William R. Hawkins, "GATT May Be More Trouble than Treaty," [ISN], 22 August 1994, pp. 20ff. • *"These notions are . . . ":* Kevin Kelly, "Paradoxes of Free Trade," [CMW], 14 January 1994, pp. 6ff; and Michael J. Boskin, "Pass the GATT Now," [FR], 12 December 1994, pp. 137ff. • *"Under the new agreement . . . ":* Gabriela Boyer et al., "GATTastrophe," [TN], 13 June 1994, p. 821. • *"By drawing the nations . . . ":* William R. Hawkins, "GATT May Be More Trouble Than Treaty," [ISN], 22 August 1994, pp. 20ff. • *"Some fear that the . . . ":* Susan Aaronson, "The Policy Battle Over Freer World Trade," [CH], November–December 1994, pp. 48ff. • *"The organization is devoid . . . ":* Gabriela Boyer et al., "GATTastrophe," [TN], 13 June 1994, p. 821. • *"We do not yet . . . ":* Paraphrased from "We the People Must Awaken to GATT's Pillage, Control," [NCR], 2 December 1994, p. 36.

The Disunited Nations: *"Today the reach . . . ":* Ambassador Madeleine K. Albright, "What You Need to Know about the United Nations," [VS], 1 June 1993, pp. 486ff; and [WA], pp. 828, 830. • *"It has been instrumental . . . ":* Paraphrased from John Isaacs, "Just Put It on Our Tab," [BAS], October 1993, pp. 7ff; and Ambassador Madeleine K. Albright, "The Future of the US-UN relationship," [DSD], 25 July 1994, pp. 493ff. • *"The UN's International . . . ":* Paraphrased from "New Ways to Run the World," [TE], 9 November 1991, pp. 11ff. • *"It has organized . . . ":* "The United Nations," [TE], 12 June 1993, pp. 21ff. • *"The UN is overwhelmed . . . ":* Paraphrased from John J. Broderick, "Beyond Borders," [NCR], 10 September 1993, p. 31. • *"Despite its lofty . . . ":* Madeleine K. Albright, "The Future of the US-UN relationship," [DSD], 25 July 1994, pp. 493ff. • *"The absence of . . . ":* John Isaacs, "Just Put It on Our Tab," [BAS], October 1993, pp. 7ff; and Jeff Trimble et al., "Into the Valleys of Death," [USN], 21 June 1993, pp. 45ff. • *"When the victors . . . ":* Penn wrote this in 1693 in *Some Fruits of Solitude,* per Rhoda Thomas Tripp, *The International Thesaurus of Quotations* (New York: Thomas Y. Crowell Company, 1970), p. 147. • *"The manager of all . . . ":* "Another Chance for the UN," [TE], 23 February 1991, pp. 19ff; and Ian Williams, "Letter from the United Nations," [NSS], 1 April 1994, p. 11. • *"The UN building in . . . ":* Madeleine K. Albright, "The Future of the US-UN relationship," [DSD], 25 July 1994, pp. 493ff; "Quickly, Quickly," [TE], 30 November 1991, p. 17; and paraphrased from "The United Nations," [TE], 12 June 1993, pp. 21ff.

Do We Need Laws?: *"The great powers . . . ":* "Loaves and Fishes," [TE], 12 December 1992, p. 53. • *"For many, the . . . ":* Vicky Hutchings, "If They Ruled the World," [NSS], 15 January 1993, pp. 12ff. • *"Is there any wonder . . . ":* "The Future Poll," [TM], Fall 1992, pp. 12ff. • *"Each step toward . . . ":* Boutros Boutros-Ghali, "Empowering the United Nations," [FA], Winter 1992, pp. 89ff; Harlan Cleveland, "Rethinking International Governance," [TF], May–June 1991, pp. 20ff. • *"For all the criticism . . . ":* Madeleine K. Albright, "What You Need to Know about the United Nations," [VS], 1 June 1993, pp. 486ff; Madeleine K. Albright, "The Future of the US-UN relationship," [DSD], 25 July 1994, pp. 493ff;

and Robert Gibson, "Global Problems, Government Limits," [ALT], November–December 1993, p. 1. • *"In a society where . . . "*: Vicky Hutchings, "Whose Common Future?" [NSS], 7 May 1993, p. 93. • *"As our global consciousness . . . "*: Boutros Boutros-Ghali, "Empowering the United Nations," [FA], Winter 1992, pp. 89ff; and "The United Nations," [TE], 26 December 1992, pp. 57ff. • *"It sought to cajole . . . "*: Paraphrased from Marrack Goulding of the UN, per ibid.

The Third Try: *"It is likely . . . "*: Llewellyn D. Howell, "The Time Has Come for an International Police Force," [USA], September 1993, p. 49; and Madeleine K. Albright, "What You Need to Know about the United Nations," [VS], 1 June 1993, pp. 486ff. • *"Laws require enforcement . . . "*: Boutros Boutros-Ghali, "Empowering the United Nations," [FA], Winter 1992, pp. 89ff; Tom Fox, "United Nations, 50, Is Ill," [NCR], 11 November 1994, pp. 8ff; Charles Krauthammer, "The UN Obsession," [TM], 9 May 1994, p. 86; and Jeff Trimble et al., "Into the Valleys of Death," [USN], 21 June 1993, pp. 45ff. • *"Perhaps what is . . . "*: "The United Nations," [TE], 12 June 1993, pp. 21ff; Tom Fox, "United Nations, 50, Is Ill," [NCR], 11 November 1994, pp. 8ff; and Boutros Boutros-Ghali, "Empowering the United Nations," [FA], Winter 1992, pp. 89ff. • *"Peacekeepers have to be . . . "*: Madeleine K. Albright, "The Future of the US-UN Relationship," [DSD], 25 July 1994, pp. 493ff. • *"Because all of this . . . "*: John Isaacs, "Just Put It on Our Tab," [BAS], October 1993, pp. 7ff; "Knock-Out," [TE], 28 January 1995, p. 41; and "The United Nations," [TE], 12 June 1993, pp. 21ff. • *"Global taxes will . . . "*: Jakob von Uexkull, "It's Time for a Peoples' Council for Global Sustainability," [ALT], November–December 1993, pp. 47ff; Harlan Cleveland, "Rethinking International Governance," [TF], May–June 1991, pp. 20ff; and William E. Halal, "Birth of a New World," [TF], September–October 1993, pp. 43ff. • *"A billion people live . . . "*: Boutros Boutros-Ghali, "Empowering the United Nations," [FA], Winter 1992, pp. 89ff.

The Unresolved Challenges: *"The global government of the twenty-first . . . "*: Tom Fox, "United Nations, 50, Is Ill," [NCR], 11 November 1994, pp. 8ff. • *"It is more likely to be . . . "*: Harlan Cleveland, "Rethinking International Governance," [TF], May–June 1991, pp. 20ff; William E. Halal, "Birth of a New World," [TF], September–October 1993, pp. 43ff; Harlan Cleveland, "Rethinking International Governance," [TF], May–June 1991, pp. 20ff; and Cynthia G. Wagner, "Challenges for Governance," [TF]," September–October 1991, pp. 33ff. • *"In the past, the . . . "*: "The United Nations," [TE], 12 June 1993, pp. 21ff; Boutros Boutros-Ghali, "Empowering the United Nations," [FA], Winter 1992, pp. 89ff; and Harlan Cleveland, "Rethinking International Governance," [TF], May–June 1991, pp. 20ff. • *"A successful global governance . . . "*: Ibid. • *In 'big science' . . . "*: Robert Wright, "One World, Max," [TNR], 6 November 1989, pp. 68ff. • *"We know that global . . . "*: "New Ways to Run the World," [TE], 9 November 1991, pp. 11ff. • *"A French diplomat . . . "*: Paraphrased from Secretary-General Boutros Boutros-Ghali, as quoted in Ina Ginsburg, "United Notions?" [TCM], March 1993, pp. 50ff; and Robert Wright, "One World, Max," [TNR], 6 November 1989, pp. 68ff. • *"Winston Churchill . . . "*: Rhoda Thomas Tripp,

The International Thesaurus of Quotations (New York: Thomas Y. Crowell Company, 1970), pp. 146–147.

CHAPTER 14: THE PLACELESS FAMILY

Introduction: *"The reordering of society . . . ":* Richard John Beuhaus, "A Voice in the Relativistic Wilderness," [CT], 7 February 1994, pp. 33ff; and James Q. Wilson, "What Is Moral," [CM], June 1993, pp. 37ff.

The Millennium Generation: *"It is here that . . . ":* Michael Wolff, *Where We Stand* (New York: Bantam Books, 1992), pp. 229–239, 288–297. • *"But for all its . . . ":* Shervert H. Frazier, "Psychotrends," [PT], January–February 1994, pp. 32ff; and Claudia Wallis, "The Nuclear Family Goes Boom!" [TM], Fall 1992, pp. 42ff. • *"As we enter the . . . ":* Suzanne Fields, "Moral Deprivation Breeds Youngsters with Attitude," [ISN], 21 February 1994, p. 40; and John D. Long, "Common Courtesy," [BH], January–February 1990, pp. 133ff. • *"The sexual revolution . . . ":* "Something Happened," [TE], 26 October 1991, pp. SA-6ff; Shervert H. Frazier, "Psychotrends," [PT], January–February 1994, pp. 32ff; Claudia Wallis, "The Nuclear Family Goes Boom!" [TM], Fall 1992, pp. 42ff; and William J. Doherty, "Private Lives, Public Values," [PT], May–June 1992, pp. 32ff. • *"The income equality . . . ":* Claudia Wallis, "The Nuclear Family Goes Boom!" [TM], Fall 1992, pp. 42ff; Lillian M. Beard et al., "Family Life in the '90s," [GH], September 1993, pp. 156ff; and David A. Hamburg, "The American Family Transformed," [SY], January–February 1993, pp. 60ff.

Lost in Place: *"Many children from . . . ":* Janice Castro, "Watching a Generation Waste Away," [TM], 26 August 1991, pp. 10ff; "Something Happened," [TE], 26 October 1991, pp. SA-6ff; Karen Levine, "The Witching Hour," [PRM], May 1992, pp. 71ff; and David A. Hamburg, "The American Family Transformed," [SY], January–February 1993, pp. 60ff. • *"Does placelessness account . . . ":* [WA], p. 942; and William J. Doherty, "Private Lives, Public Values," [PT], May–June 1992, pp. 32ff.

The New Instructors: *"The family unit has been . . . ":* James Q. Wilson, "The Family Values Debate," [CM], April 1993, pp. 24ff. • *"We already witness . . . ":* George Howe Colt et al., "For the Foreseeable Future," [LF], December 1991, pp. 76ff; and Claudia Wallis, "The Nuclear Family Goes Boom!" [TM], Fall 1992, pp. 42ff. • *"More than any other . . . ":* Myron Magnet, "The American Family," [FR], 10 August 1992, p. 42ff; William J. Doherty, "Private Lives, Public Values," [PT], May–June 1992, pp. 32ff; and Charles Colson, "Society Must Cultivate Man's Innate Moral Sense," [ISN], 22 November 1993, pp. 24ff. • *"Traditions are formed . . . ":* Digby Anderson, "What Killed Regional Differences?" [NR], 21 November 1994, pp. 61ff; James Q. Wilson, "The Family Values Debate," [CM], April 1993, pp. 24ff. • *"Lost for the Millennium Generation . . . ":* Michael Posner, "The Canadian Dad," [CHT], June 1994, pp. 31ff; "The Daddyless Society?" [TF], November–December 1992, p. 55; and Myron Magnet, "The American Family," [FR], 10 August 1992, pp. 42ff. • *"That might be fine . . . ":* American

Psychological Association, per Mary Mohler, "Unplugged!" [LHJ], March 1994, pp. 94ff; Charles Colson, "Society Must Cultivate Man's Innate Moral Sense, [ISN], 22 November 1993, pp. 24ff. • *"The dumb repetition . . . ":* Peter Uhlenberg of the University of North Carolina, per William R. Mattox, Jr., "America's Family Time Famine," [CTD], November–December 1990, pp. 9ff; and Kathleen M. Heide, "Why Kids Kill Parents," [PT], September–October 1992, pp. 62ff.

"Family" Redefined: *"In the Fourth Dimension, association . . . ":* William J. Doherty, "Private Lives, Public Values," [PT], May–June 1992, pp. 32ff; James Q. Wilson, "The Family Values Debate," [CM], April 1993, pp. 24ff; Shervert H. Frazier, "Psychotrends," [PT], January–February 1994, pp. 32ff; "New Families, Old Values?" [TF], January–February 1993, p. 45; "The Revolution in Family Life," [TF], September–October 1990, p. 53; David A. Hamburg, "The American Family Transformed," [SY], January–February 1993, pp. 60ff; Myron Magnet, "The American Family," [FR], 10 August 1992, pp. 42ff; John D. Long, "Common Courtesy," [BH], January–February 1990, pp. 133ff; James Q. Wilson, "What Is Moral," [CM], June 1993, pp. 37ff; Bernard J. Reilly et al., "Ethical Business and the Ethical Person," [BH], November–December 1990, pp. 23ff; Han Suyin, "The Family of Tomorrow," [WH], November–December 1993, p. 16; Amanda Spake, "The Good News about the American Family," [RB], June 1994, p. 71; Richard Louv, "How Religion Reaches Out to Parents," [PRM], May 1993, pp. 161ff; Claudia Wallis, "The Nuclear Family Goes Boom!" [TM], Fall 1992, pp. 42ff. • *"The United States is not alone . . . ":* Constance Sorrentino, "The Changing Family in International Perspective," [MLR], March 1990, pp. 41ff. • *"It is as if . . . ":* James Q. Wilson, "The Family Values Debate," [CM], April 1993, pp. 24ff. • *"In the United States . . . ":* Rushworth M. Kidder, "Ethics," [TF], March–April 1992, pp. 10ff.

The Price of Madness: *"The Chernobyl 'accident' . . . ":* Paraphrased from Rushworth M. Kidder, "Ethics," [TF], March–April 1992, pp. 10ff. • *"Bertrand Russell . . . ":* Rhoda Thomas Tripp, *The International Thesaurus of Quotations* (New York: Thomas Y. Crowell Company, 1970), p. 414. • *"Thus, cultures devoid . . . ":* Peter F. Drucker, "How Schools Must Change," [PSY], May 1989, pp. 18ff.

Challenging Faith: *"With the advance of . . . ":* Leo D. Lefebure, "Global Encounter," [TCC], 22 September 1993, pp. 886ff. • *"The problem is that . . . ":* John R. Coyne, "Ultimate Reality in Chicago," [NR], 4 October 1993, pp. 26ff; and Leo D. Lefebure, "Global Encounter," [TCC], 22 September 1993, pp. 886ff. • *"The polycentric culture . . . ":* Dawn Gibeau, "Religious Belief Remains Vital Around the World," [NCR], 28 May 1993, pp. 4ff; Carol Tavris, "Don't Tell Me What God Thinks," [RB], June 1993, p. 35; and "The Good Fight against Ecumenism," [TE], 3 September 1988, p. 18. • *"Even if this abyss . . . ":* Rodney Stark, "American Religion Remains Robust," [ISN], 11 July 1994, pp. 20ff; and Henry Gurnwald, "The Year 2000," [TM], 30 March 1992, pp. 73ff. • *"In the Placeless Society, many . . . ":* Jeffery L. Sheler et al., "Spiritual America," [USN], 4 April 1994, pp. 48ff.

The Coming Renaissance: *"These new churches . . . ":* Charles Colson et al., "Welcome to McChurch," [CT], 23 November 1992, pp. 28ff. • *"Religion will not die . . . ":* John D. Long, "Common Courtesy," [BH], January–February 1990, pp. 133ff; Rodney Stark, "American Religion Remains Robust," [ISN], 11 July 1994, pp. 20ff; and Jeffery L. Sheler et al., "Spiritual America," [USN], 4 April 1994, pp. 48ff. • *"In the rich First . . . ":* Nathan Gardels, "The Magnanimous Soul," [NPQ], Spring 1994, pp. 2ff. • *"The polycentric culture of . . . ":* Ibid. • *"Much of the adaptation . . . ":* Eleanor Smith, "The New Moral Classroom," [PSY], May 1989, pp. 32ff. • *"But schools in the . . . ":* Linda Burton, "Let's Fix It!" [FC], 7 June 1994, p. 168. • *"Many argue that . . . ":* George Leonard, "The End of School," [TA], May 1992, pp. 24ff; and Peter F. Drucker, "How Schools Must Change," [PSY], May 1989, p. 18.

CHAPTER 15: PILOTS OF THE TWENTY-FIRST CENTURY

Introduction: *"Those who know how . . . ":* Peter F. Drucker, "How Schools Must Change," [PSY], May 1989, p. 18. • *"In such a world . . . ":* George Leonard, "The End of School," [TA], May 1992, pp. 24ff; and "When School Comes to You," [TE], 11 September 1993, pp. F-43ff.

Schoolrooms Without Walls: *"To adapt to the Fourth . . . ":* George Leonard, "The End of School," [TA], May 1992, pp. 24ff; "Tribes Go High Tech," [TF], January–February 1994, pp. 48ff; and "When School Comes to You," [TE], 11 September 1993, pp. F-43ff. • *"Especially for children . . . ":* Peter F. Drucker, "How Schools Must Change," [PSY], May 1989, pp. 18ff. • *"Even something as seemingly . . . ":* Ibid.; and Loren J. Anderson, "New Methods for a New World," [USA], September 1993, pp. 32ff. • *"Perhaps even more important . . . ":* George Leonard, "The End of School," [TA], May 1992, pp. 24ff. • *"In the midst of these . . . ":* "When School Comes to You," [TE], 11 September 1993, pp. F-43ff. • *"Classroom teachers will . . . ":* Michael D. Lemonick, "Tomorrow's Lesson," [TM], Fall 1992, pp. 59ff. • *"In the twenty-first century . . . ":* David A. Hamburg, "The American Family Transformed," [SY], January–February 1993, pp. 60ff; and William E. Halal, "Telelearning," [TF], November–December 1994, pp. 21ff.

What Do I Do With Alex?: *"Parents of the Millennium Generation . . . ":* Emily Sachar, "Will Your Child Be Ready for the 21st Century?" [LHJ], September 1991, pp. 124ff. • *"For many, the . . . ":* Mary Mohler, "Unplugged!" [LH], March 1994, pp. 94ff. • *"Most important, parents . . . ":* Lillian M. Beard et al., "Family Life in the '90s," [GH], September 1993, pp. 156ff.

INDEX

ABOUT THE AUTHOR

WILLIAM KNOKE IS the founder and president of the Harvard Capital Group, an investment banking firm that specializes in adapting global corporations to the challenges of technological change. He is also vice president for corporate finance of Spectrum Securities.

In the course of his work, Mr. Knoke has been exposed to a wide range of industries, such as computers, electronics, aerospace, defense, banking, health care, and insurance. A seasoned guest lecturer, he has delivered keynote addresses at annual shareholder meetings and sales conferences.

Mr. Knoke holds an M.B.A. from Harvard Business School, and a B.A. in Economics from Stanford University. He has worked or traveled in sixty-four countries and speaks several languages. He lives in Southern California with his wife and two children.